No One Is Unemployable:

Creative Solutions for Overcoming
Barriers to Employment

DEBRA L. ANGEL

ELISABETH E. HARNEY

WorkNet
Publications

No One Is Unemployable:
Creative Solutions for Overcoming Barriers to Employment

Debra L. Angel
Elisabeth E. Harney

Manufactured in the United States of America
Library of Congress Catalog Card Number: 94-012045
ISBN: 9-9657057-0-6

Design: Daniel Woolley
Project Editor: Patricia Harney
Publisher: WorkNet Publications
Printer: BookCrafters

WorkNet Training Services
P.O. Box 5582
Hacienda Heights, CA   91745-0082

Toll Free: (888) 9-WORKNET
Phone: (818) 810-4447
Fax: (818) 810-4117
E-mail: worknetts@aol.com

This book is dedicated to the past and present staff of the WorkNet programs who have worked so creatively and diligently to give people a second chance, to our employers who care about their employees as well as their companies, and to God for His wonderful plan for our lives.

About WorkNet

The WorkNet Model

O ver the last decade, the WorkNet Model has evolved into a successful tool for populations with significant employment barriers. The first step in Career Development is job placement; the final result is individuals who enjoy their work, are focused, promotable and economically independent.

Via the WorkNet Model, thousands have been placed in employment. In 1994, during the height of Southern California's company closures and lay-offs, a team of five WorkNet Career Developers placed 284 people in full-time career-related positions with a one-year retention rate of over 65%. Welfare dependents became self-sufficient, parents became better role models, and the down-and-out became upwardly mobile. These workers earned almost $3.5 million in wages, and paid, along with their employers, over $500,000 in taxes. If they had remained on unemployment, welfare or other public assistance, they would have cost the American tax payer almost $1.5 million, making a total difference of nearly $2 million in the tax base during that year alone. Overcoming barriers has been at the heart and is the hallmark of WorkNet's incredible success.

WorkNet Training Services (WNTS)

W orkNet Training Services is committed to assisting organizations establish effective Career Development (CD) programs based on the WorkNet Model, as well as to providing education and developing materials to promote CD among populations with significant barriers. To fulfill this mission, we are involved in:

◇ analyzing existing programs for the purpose of designing a CD component to meet their needs
◇ implementing CD components based on the WorkNet Model
◇ staff training for existing or newly established job placement and CD programs
◇ equipping service providers through 1 or 2-day seminars
◇ educating through the development of training materials, classroom curriculum and books

WorkNet Services (WNS)

A gencies around the country which use the complete WorkNet Model are given the right to use the WorkNet name and logo. The WorkNet Model is tailored to meet the special needs of the agency and clientele, and each agency is provided with an individualized program design, classroom curriculum, tools to conduct Career Development and job placement with candidates, on-site staff training for 6 to 24 months and on-going consultation. A WNTS trainer acts as their mentor.

WorkNet Charities

WorkNet Charities is a non-profit organization dedicated to promoting Career Development by empowering national and community-based organizations to provide CD services and by educating employment program staff and volunteers about CD among difficult-to-place populations. A portion of the proceeds from this book will be donated to WorkNet Charities to assist in the establishment of non-profit CD programs across the nation and the training of their staff.

About The Authors

Debra L. Angel

D ebra is a woman of amazing vision. She has been developing innovative programs to address poverty and homeless issues for over fifteen years. She has developed numerous employment, shelter, emergency service and youth programs. Debra also spearheaded the writing and lobbying of the first Homeless Assistance Bill which was funded in the state of Nevada. She has been recognized nationally and locally for her work on behalf of the homeless and poor, including *Outstanding Young Woman*, presented by the United Nations' National Council of Women, United States; *Ten Outstanding Young Americans,* presented by the National Jaycees; *Woman Of The Year,* presented by The Salvation Army and *Women Helping Women*, presented by Soroptomist International.

Debra has been an employer or assisting with employment issues for over seventeen years. Under her leadership, the WorkNet model was developed and demonstrated to be effective among stabilized homeless and urban poor populations. Most recently, Debra has devoted her time to assisting organizations throughout the United States to design and implement Career Development programs which meet the needs of their specific clientele. Through her training company, WorkNet Training Services, she provides one-on-one consultation and staff training and conducts workshops at national conferences. She also designs corporate training programs for new franchises.

Debra holds Bachelor's degrees in Communications and Biblical Studies, with a minor in Psychology from Azusa Pacific University in California.

Elisabeth E. Harney

E lisabeth is a dynamic trainer. She has over four years experience in Career Development among difficult populations, and three years experience in staff training and program development. She managed a Career Development program for formerly homeless, welfare dependent single mothers in Los Angeles for nearly three years. She has devoted the past two years to training staff and developing Career Development programs in communities across the country.

A sought after public speaker, Elisabeth's speaking engagements include:
Career Development Among Formerly Homeless Families, Beyond Shelter, Washington DC, '93
Aid to Scholarship: A New Approach for the Urban Poor & Welfare Dependent, World Vision, '94
Overcoming Barriers to Employment, International Union of Gospel Missions (IUGM), National, '95
Steps Toward Self-Sufficiency: Employing the Homeless, LAHSA/Shelter Partnership in LA, '95
Employing The Homeless: Steps Toward Economic Self-Sufficiency,
   IUGM National Super Seminar, '96

Elisabeth holds Bachelor's degrees in International Studies and English, with a minor in Spanish from Azusa Pacific University in California.

Acknowledgments

We wish to thank the many people who have helped us write this book. Daniel Woolley designed the cover and layout, and stayed up many late nights to see it through completion. Patricia Harney edited the book under a very tight schedule. Our wonderful readers—Gretchen Maswadeh, Paula Johnson, Joan Angel, Elaine Fudenna, Becky Newby, Tanis Harber, Kevin and Kay Marie Brennfleck, Angela Scoggins, Leroy Jiles, Cam Gittler, Ann Benzel, Sanford Sacks, Barth Medina, Francisco Martinez, Kathleen Berk and Reggie Salazar—took time out of their busy schedules to read our first draft and offer their critiques, praises and ideas. Sherina Raja did whatever was needed to get the job done. William Phelps has shown continuous faith in the WorkNet model and came up with a great book title. Stephen Derrivan has always shown continuous love and support, and always provided Debra with a quiet hide-a-way so she could write. Thank you all.

We would also like to thank Gary Bolles for mentoring Debra in the concepts and practices of Career Development and to his father, Richard Bolles, for the training which opened her mind to many new possibilities for helping our candidates.

We would both like to thank our parents for their contributions to this project, for their love and support over the years, and for teaching us to be "challengers" who never give up.

And to our Heavenly Father who has designed a wonderful plan for our lives and who constantly provides us with direction and a sense of purpose.

For I know the plans I have made for you, says the Lord,
plans for your welfare and not for evil,
to give you a future and a hope.

Jeremiah 29:11

Table of Contents

INTRODUCTION

The process, insights and sample solutions contained in this book were born out of a desire to help our candidates to find and keep good jobs. We have had a lot of help in developing these ideas from the WorkNet Services staff, colleagues, employers and candidates across the country. Many of the ideas are not original, and none of them are the last word on the topic. Our hope is that in this book these ideas are organized and expounded upon in a way that will allow you to grab hold of them and use them to improve the lives of your candidates—whether urban poor, displaced professionals, homeless, recovering addicts, limited English speakers, older workers, inner-city youth, ex-felons or welfare recipients. Even if you are merely a mother helping your children, a neighbor or church member helping friends, or a concerned community member who wants to help others, this book is for you. Once you learn the process, you will never again look at employment barriers in the same way.

Learning how to identify and overcome the barriers which stand between our candidates and a good job has been an ongoing process. Our hope is that what we have learned will help you to see that your candidates are employable. Often, a candidate believes that no one will hire him, and unfortunately, we become overwhelmed by his barriers and agree. At WorkNet, we have found that all barriers, even those which seem insurmountable—a felony, homelessness, no high school education—can be overcome creatively and honestly. After nearly ten years of success, we can give you real examples of people who have done it and are working in good jobs. If our candidates can do it, so can yours! Along the way, we have learned that a candidate's success depends more on our ability to teach them how to be their own Career Developer, than on our ability to do it for them. As a result of applying THE TEN STEP PROCESS with your candidates, we believe that you, too, will see changed attitudes, higher placement rates and longer job retention. Your candidates will come to the happy realization that they are truly employable!

After you have read THE TEN STEP PROCESS and JOB SEARCHING FROM THE EMPLOYER'S PERSPECTIVE, and reviewed the ENCYCLOPEDIA OF BARRIERS, we encourage you to send us your comments, suggestions, success stories and ideas. We would like this book to become a collaborative reference tool, where those who are on the front line share their expertise… so that together we can make a difference.

When you know,
and you know you know,
confidence replaces fear.

HOW TO USE THIS BOOK

No One Is Unemployable is divided into five key sections: first, the ESSENTIAL VOCABULARY which provides an explanation of terms and concepts used in this book; second, THE TEN STEP PROCESS by which you can learn to identify and overcome any barrier to employment; third, JOB SEARCHING FROM THE EMPLOYER'S PERSPECTIVE which outlines how to market your candidate, given his barriers, his strengths and the employer's needs; fourth, the ENCYCLOPEDIA OF BARRIERS which discusses specific concerns and sample solutions for numerous common barriers; and fifth, the CROSS-REFERENCED INDEX in which you can easily find where in the ENCYCLOPEDIA OF BARRIERS a specific barrier is addressed. Throughout the book, we have included true stories of how we and others have used THE TEN STEP PROCESS to overcome barriers. *Please remember that there is no magic wand, only great ideas which, when mixed with your creativity and hard work, can produce miracles.*

Below, we have provided a brief introduction to each of the five key sections and some brief instructions and disclaimers. Please read on.

Essential Vocabulary

In developing the WorkNet Model we have adapted some terms which may differ from their traditional definitions. ESSENTIAL VOCABULARY will explain how we use various terms. It is arranged by related topics, rather than alphabetically, so that the subtle differences and progression in definition are pronounced. If you are new to the field of career development or social services, this section will be particularly helpful because it includes brief explanations of various terms and concepts which are common to these fields.

The Ten Step Process

THE TEN STEP PROCESS is the most important part of this book, because it shows you how to resolve any barrier your candidate may have, not only the ones listed in the encyclopedia. It is divided into ten short chapters, each dealing with a different step. We have included true stories entitled "In The Real World" and information tables which illustrate the steps. Learning how to assist your candidates in overcoming their barriers will develop new confidence in you and your candidate. In fact, this point is probably best made by sharing a story told by our colleague Dean Curtis: *One day an older woman returned from an interview, confident that she would get the job but disappointed that she was not asked the hard question—"How old are you?" You see, throughout her job search, the fear of being asked about her age had haunted her. She knew it was not legal for an interviewer to ask, but she felt sure they would discover that she was 69 years old and not want to hire her. As a result of her fear, interviewers would sense that she was hiding something and eliminate her from consideration. When her employment counselor realized the problem, he immediately helped her Develop a Good Answer in case the question was asked. Together they decided she would say, "I am young enough to learn and old enough not to get pregnant." She thought the answer was so clever, she could hardly wait for someone to ask. Unfortunately, the next employer did not ask, but he did hire her.* The confidence she gained from having a good answer eliminated the employer's concern about her. Such is the case for many of our candidates, and so it will be for yours—when you learn to use this process consistently, honestly and creatively.

Don't Read This!

I knew that would catch your attention! It is very important when using THE TEN STEP PROCESS that you never encourage your candidates to lie. ***Good answers should NOT DECEIVE the employer; rather they should truthfully market the candidate and explain why he is the best candidate for the job.*** If you lie, you may severely hinder the candidate's opportunity to advance in his career because employers often conduct a thorough background check after they have decided to keep or promote an employee. Unfortunately, we have seen many candidates who chose to lie on their application or resume to get hired, get fired months later when the company discovered the lie. Often, the candidate's supervisor did not want to let him go because he was doing excellent work, but was forced to adhere to company policies regarding falsification of information. Excellent marketing and a few good references could have gotten him hired without the lie.

Job Searching from the Employer's Perspective

A primary barrier faced by most candidates is a lack of effective job search skills. Often the candidate is unaware of how the employer views the hiring process, what to expect during the job search and which techniques and tools best market him to the employer. We have also learned over the years, that whether the candidate is a college graduate or a high school drop-out, his natural tendency is to talk about what he likes to do or does well, rather than explain how he meets the employer's needs. Addressing the employer's needs is essential to good marketing. Consequently, the information in this section is given as if the employer, rather than the candidate, is the most important person in the job search process. In this section we discuss seven keys to marketing the candidate successfully and provide "power tips" on how to help those who are unable to get an interview or get interviews but are never hired.

Encyclopedia of Barriers

The largest section of this book is the ENCYCLOPEDIA OF BARRIERS. The barriers are listed alphabetically under major headings. For example, EDUCATION includes four barrier issues: Lack of Computer Literacy, Lack of English Literacy, Lack of a GED and Lack of Vocational Training or a College Degree. Related barriers are grouped together under a major heading because they share similar **employer concerns**, **candidate concerns** and **general information**. Each major heading first explores the employer and candidate concerns surrounding the barrier(s), then offers general information about the barrier(s) before moving on to **specific barrier issues.** For a total understanding of each barrier and our suggested solutions, it is important that you read these three sections before advancing to the specific barrier of interest. As you develop new solutions or discover additional barriers which you would like to see addressed, please write to us... we love to get mail.

Cross-Referenced Index

Located at the back of this book is an easy to use CROSS-REFERENCED INDEX. In this index, barriers are listed alphabetically according to the operative word. For example, "Lack of Identification" and "Poor Work History" are listed as "Identification, Lack of" and "Work History, Poor" respectively. In addition, because barriers can be viewed from various angles or referred to in various terms we have cross-referenced them. Simply identify the idea behind the barrier in the most basic terms possible and look it up. You will be referred to the section(s) in the ENCYCLOPEDIA OF BARRIERS where the barrier is addressed. For example:

Basic Idea	Look up	Referred to
Has been arrested twice	Arrests	See Criminal Record
Is always late	Punctuality	See Dependability
Is a minority	Ethnicity	See Employer Bias
		See Candidate Bias

Gender Usage

We want this book to be comfortable to read, so we decided to eliminate the "she/he," "him/her" dilemma and the confusion of making both the candidate and employer the same gender. Consequently, at the beginning of each barrier entry, we have noted the gender of these two major players so you can tell them apart. In this section and Job Searching from the Employer's Perspective, the candidate, the main focus of the book, is male and the employer is female. In an effort to be sensitive to gender issues, in the Encyclopedia of Barriers we have divided the roles equally so the candidate is male half of the time and female the other half. We are sure that our decision makes for easier reading, and hope that you are not uncomfortable with it.

Icons Denoting Solution Approaches

In Step 4 of The Ten Step Process, we introduce the approaches we have developed to resolve barriers. To easily reference which of the five approaches we suggest, we have placed one or more icons in the margin next to either the "In general" or the specific barrier. However, remember that these are "creative solutions," so if you determine that a different approach would work better, use it (...and then share the information with us so we can share it with your colleagues nationwide!). Below are the five approaches we have developed with a brief explanation of when they are to be used and a sample of the icon which represents them throughout the Encyclopedia of Barriers.

Develop a Good Answer is needed for any barrier which the employer might bring up in an interview, such as a felony, gaps in work history, being fired and addiction. The candidate must be able to confidently address the employer's concern, then move on to his qualifications and why he is an excellent candidate for the job.

Provide a Resource is directed toward barriers for which services, physical items or information are needed, such as when a candidate needs psychological counseling, credit repair, a phone, a message service, child care, housing or identification. In these cases, the employer should never become aware of the "now former" barrier issue.

Change Where You Look is used only when the barrier is specific to the company, industry or position in which the candidate wants to work. For example, a candidate who wants to sell high-end clothing will find that dread-locks are a barrier at Niemann Marcus, but could easily change where he looks and pursue trendy designer shops where his hair style would be a plus. Matching is especially important with these types of barriers.

Adjust the Candidate's Outlook is recommended when overcoming the barrier has to begin inside the candidate's head. Your job is to assist him in understanding how his present thinking impacts him negatively, identifying other ways of looking at his situation and determining which new options will bring about his desired results. This is easier to do when you realize that most of the habits and beliefs we hold come from our up-bringing. For example, if the candidate was raised in an environment in which he did not learn basic business protocol or employer expectations, he probably does not know and value them. You must help him determine why he should learn basic business protocol and "what's in it for him."

Teach a New Skill is required when a barrier will resurface if the candidate does not gain a certain job search-related skill, i.e., finding resources, approaching employers on the telephone, quantifying his selling points or answering difficult interview questions. This book, and other resources referenced in this book, will assist you in teaching these skills. Understand when you see this icon that we are not suggesting that you teach new vocational skills. If new vocational skills are needed, we will recommend that you *Provide a Resource* for training, if funds and time permit. If immediate employment is needed or no funding is available to provide training, we will suggest that you look for paid an on-the-job training position and *Adjust the Candidate's Outlook*. This will allow him to begin in a position for which he is qualified and work for advancement so that the employer will agree to train him in the skills needed for the desired position.

Icons Denoting Special Features

In an effort to make this book "user-friendly" and easy-to-understand, we have included ideas and stories which might have been shared over a cup of coffee, if you were here.

The stories shared **"In The Real World"** are true. They come from WorkNet Services staff, the staff of WorkNet Model programs across the country and colleagues who have shared their successes throughout the years. The names have been changed to protect candidates' anonymity and literary license has been taken where minor facts were unknown.

Throughout the Encyclopedia of Barriers and Job Searching from the Employer's Perspective, we share "**Sample Solutions**." These sample solutions are not the only answers; they are merely ideas which have worked for us or a colleague. Results will vary for each candidate, because each solution MUST BE TRUE for your specific candidate. Each sample solution exemplifies one of the five approaches presented in The Ten Step Process. The approach used in the sample solution is listed next to each sample solution icon.

At the end of most chapters and major sub-headings in the The Ten Step Process you will see a **Key Point** icon. Here you will find the key ideas for that section. Our intent is to capture the heart of the information for easy reference as you review the steps after your initial read-through. We have purposely limited the number of key points to those we feel are especially important so you will read them all.

Power Tips are found in Job Searching from the Employer's Perspective. They are similar to sample solutions in that they offer suggestions on how to deal with common problems encountered during the job search. They differ in that they do not deal with specific barriers, but rather with job search issues, such as candidates who easily get interviews but are not hired.

The final icon is used as a **Note of Caution** to warn you of problems we have seen when addressing a specific barrier. Many of these cautions have been learned the hard way as we have operated programs and assisted individuals with overcoming barriers during the last decade. We have carefully chosen only the most important issues and hope you learn from our experiences.

Legal Issues

We are **not** experts in the law. We have done our best to ensure that the information in this book is accurate; however, we may have been misinformed or may be unaware that a specific regulation differs from state to state. If you have questions about the accuracy of a statement or specific regulations for your state, call your state Labor Commission or the Federal

Department of Labor. Additional information which you may want to secure includes:

◇ The Americans with Disabilities Act (ADA)
◇ Your state's pre-employment inquiry guidelines
◇ Federal and local legislation governing Welfare to Work programs
◇ Eligibility information for the Department of Vocational Rehabilitation

Related Topics

As an easy reference tool, at the end of each major heading in the Encyclopedia of Barriers, we have listed related barrier topics. This is particularly helpful because many issues cause multiple or related barriers, and because we have focused each entry and endeavored to avoid duplicating information from entry to entry. We believe that referring the related topics will give you the information and sample solutions you need.

WNTS' Resource Materials

In order to keep our explanations in the Encyclopedia of Barriers to a reasonable length, we have referenced other WorkNet Training Services' manuals in which additional information or classroom curriculum can be found. References to these materials are italicized. WNTS' materials include:

Career Development Workshop Series in English, Teacher's and Student's Editions:
    Introduction to Life/work Planning Workshop
    Creating a Winning Application & Resumé Workshop
    Job Searching from the Employer's Perspective Workshop
    Finding a Job on The Phone Workshop
    Interviewing For Success
    Career Path Strategies Workshop
    Career Advancement & Business Acculturation Workshops
    Motivating Your Candidates Workshop

Career Development Workshop Series in Spanish, Teacher's and Student's Editions:
    Creando Una Buena Aplicacion
    Fuentes de Empleo Y El Uso Del Telefono
    Cultura Del Mundo de Los Negocios
    Las Entrevistas
    La Guia Profesional

Career Developer's Manual
Employer Cultivation Manual
Professional Correspondence for Employment Programs
Career Development from a Biblical Perspective

If you have access to these manuals, you should review the material referenced. If you do not have access to the materials and would like information on how to purchase them, please contact WorkNet Training Services by writing or calling:

WorkNet Training Services
P.O. Box 5582
Hacienda Heights, CA 91745-0082

Toll free: (888) 9-WORKNET
Voice mail: 818-810-4447
Fax: 818-810-4117
E-mail: worknetts@aol.com

Using WNTS' Worksheets

To help you apply the information in the book with your candidates, we have included two worksheets designed and copyrighted by WorkNet Training Services—the *Overcoming Barriers Worksheet* and the *Quantified Selling Points Worksheet*. As a purchaser of this book, you are granted permission by WNTS to duplicate and use these forms at your site with your candidates. However, you may not sell it, give it away or reproduce it for commercial gain without specific written permission from WorkNet Training Services.

"All words are pegs
to hang ideas on"

—HW Bucher

Essential Vocabulary

This section is not organized alphabetically. Instead, the terms are organized into groups of related ideas. This arrangement will allow you to compare related terms more easily, and see the subtle differences and progression in definition. We also realize that we have taken some traditional terms and used them in a non-traditional manner. This glossary will explain our non-traditional usage of various terms. To find a specific term, either look it up by main idea or just scan the next few pages.

Concepts

Job Placement is the process by which an employment specialist briefly reviews what the candidate has done in the past and locates current job openings in which the candidate can continue to use those skills. The focus is limited to gaining employment without consideration of the candidate's interests, dislikes, long-term goals or dreams.

Life/work Planning is the process by which the *candidate investigates* what skills he loves to use, what fields fascinate him and what personal goals motivate him in order to identify or create a job which will meet his needs in all three areas. The purpose of Life/work Planning is that the candidate find enjoyment in his work. The result is a "dream job."

Career Development is the process by which the *candidate pursues* his long-term career goal or dream job. The first step in Career Development is securing an entry-level career job; the final result is an individual who is focused, promotable and economically independent. The candidate must first identify a career goal or dream job, determine the path necessary to attain that goal or job, and research what he must do to successfully travel that path. Next, he must secure an entry-level position on his career path. Once he has mastered his current job, he must pursue transition jobs that move him closer to his career goal and dream job. Important factors which will assist him in advancing include getting a professional mentor, building a network, furthering his education, performing with excellence in each job he holds and regularly evaluating his career path to ensure that he is going in the right direction. It is not uncommon, during a regular evaluation, for the candidate to determine that another position

within his career field better meets his long-term goal, and thus adjust his career path or change his dream job.

Business Acculturation is the process by which the candidate gains an understanding of and ability to successfully perform in the business world. The WorkNet Model is based on the idea that the U.S. business world has its own culture, including language, customs, protocol and dress and that to succeed within the business culture, the candidate must become bi-cultural.

Mythology is the term we use to reflect an unfair prejudice which stems from beliefs, often learned in childhood, which have never been re-evaluated. The main difference between our "myth" and the more common "prejudice," is that myths are not malicious, although they can be damaging. Also, myths can be more easily changed when challenged by facts, such as numerous "exceptions to the rule." For example, the myth that minorities could not compete athletically against Caucasians has been shattered as exceptions proved it untrue. People who hold onto a belief in spite of the overwhelming proof to the opposite are prejudiced.

An Exception to the Rule is a person who does not match the stereotype of his given group. We encourage candidates to avoid the impossible task of trying to change the employer's entire belief system during the job search, but instead to focus on challenging the belief that the myth is *always* true. If the candidate can become the "exception to the rule," he can gradually introduce the employer to other exceptions until the rule no longer applies.

Challengers are individuals who realize that people hold myths, and who are committed to constructively re-educating and challenging people to recognize and adjust their myths. Challengers do not allow themselves to become victims who give up, or become rebels who succeed only in destroying themselves and those around them. Rather, challengers become the "exception to the rule" and seek to educate others. If they are unable to change someone's mythology, they simply find other constructive ways of reaching their goals and hope the person will learn as they continue to meet other challengers.

Networking is the process of building professional friendships with co-workers, supervisors, customers, vendors, competitors and those in related fields which result in access to information, people of influence and career opportunities.

The Open Job Market refers to jobs which are publicly advertised. More than 80% of job seekers use these sources as they seek employment. Open market sources include the classified ads, job boards and hotlines, help wanted signs, placement agencies and job fairs. Open market tools include completing applications, sending general resumés and scheduling employment interviews. In general, less than 20% of all jobs available are ever advertised through the open market, yet more than 80% of job seekers use these sources. The result is tremendous competition for fewer jobs. The open market has proven to be a less effective arena for our candidates because competition can be fierce, and because our candidates often do not look good on an application or traditional resumé.

The Hidden Job Market refers to lesser used, more effective sources and tools used to secure employment. Hidden market sources and tools include networking, watching the market for new trends or businesses, Investigative Interviewing, developing employment proposals and volunteering. More than 80% of jobs available are accessed only through the hidden market, and less than 20% of all jobs seekers use these sources. Although job searching in the hidden market requires additional research and effort at the front-end, it has proven to be very effective for our candidates because it offers more jobs and less competition.

Work Credits are the unwritten "points" acquired by an employee for doing "the extra." Work credits are earned *only* when the employee does what is important to the employer, and when the employer is aware that the employee did "the extra." Work credits can be cashed in for benefits such as personal praise, public recognition, raises, promotions, special work assignments and preferential vacation days. In order for the employee to get the benefit he desires, he must carefully and subtly make the employer aware of "the extra" and let the employer know what he wants in exchange. To be effective, "the extra" must be perceived by the employer to be a part of the *employee's work ethic, not an attempt to gain favoritism.*

Government Programs

CDBG stands for Community Development Block Grants which are federal grants given to local governments to disburse among local social service providers. They often fund employment programs. For more information, contact your city counselperson or county commissioner.

JTPA stands for Job Training Partnership Act. JTPA programs are federally funded programs administered by the state or local government to provide job training and placement for low-income and at-risk populations. For more information about local programs, contact your state JTPA office at your state capital.

Welfare to Work Programs are federally mandated programs which are designed to move people off welfare and into the workplace. Stipulations and services offered vary from state to state. For more information about programs offered in your state, contact your county Department of Social Services.

Housing Options

Residential Recovery Programs are drug or alcohol treatment programs which require that participants live on-site. Programs range in length from thirty days to two years. Most cities have free programs such as a local rescue mission or a Salvation Army Adult Rehabilitation Center. For-profit programs can be very expensive and are used most often when the candidate has insurance or his employer pays.

Shelters/Emergency Shelters are programs which offer overnight or short-term housing for the homeless, usually one to thirty days. In general, shelters offer only basic services to address emergency needs.

Transitional Housing is a longer-term residential program designed to assist the homeless in addressing the problems which precipitated or developed as a result of their homelessness, and to assist them in making a transition into permanent housing. They usually charge minimal rent or a small program fee, and candidates can stay ninety days to two years.

Permanent Housing is an apartment or house for which the candidate pays rent which does not limit the amount of time the candidate can live there.

Section-8 Housing is permanent housing subsidized by the federal government. Rent is based on the tenant's income and generally does not exceed thirty percent of the monthly income.

Interview Styles

Investigative Interviews occur between the candidate and *a person who DOES the job the candidate is pursuing or considering*. The purpose of the investigative interview is for the candidate to learn more about the job, decide whether he would enjoy doing the job, gain an understanding of the employer's needs and prepare for the employment interview. The candidate should also begin building his professional network by asking for the names of others in the industry and ask about other related jobs which may better fit his dreams. For the person being interviewed, the benefit is a free cup of coffee, the compliment that she possesses a degree of expertise and the feeling that she is helping someone. Be sure that she does not feel that her position is threatened, that she is obligated to refer the candidate to her employer or that she must disclose the names of colleagues, unless she chooses.

Mock Interviews occur between the candidate and *an employer in the field who IS NOT HIRING currently*. The purpose is for the candidate to practice interviewing skills and identify interviewing weaknesses so he can improve.

Mock interviews are only helpful if you contact the employer afterward to get honest feedback. For the employer, the benefit is the feeling that by giving an hour of her time, she has helped the candidate succeed. Do not make her feel obligated to hire the candidate or directly refer him to colleagues.

Employment Interviews occur between the candidate and *the person who IS HIRING for the job the candidate is pursuing*. The purpose of the employment interview is for the candidate to get the job. For the employer, the purpose is to determine whether the candidate has the right attitude, projects the company image, is able to apply the experience and knowledge he brings, and matches the personality of the company. NOTE: In general, the employer only interviews candidates whom she believes possess the basic qualifications to do the job, so the employment interview is often about whether she wants to work with the candidate and resolving any concerns.

Job Categories

We classify jobs into four major categories. The category into which a job falls is determined not by the type or level of position, but by how the candidate views the job in relation to his career path. For example, a food server position is a *survival job* for a medical student in college, an *entry-level career job* for a food service management student, a *transition job* for a restaurant host moving toward his dream job of restaurant manager and a *dream job* for a mother who wants a part-time job with flexible hours so she can be home when her children are out of school.

Survival Jobs are positions which offer only a means to survive with little or no job satisfaction or opportunity for advancement. They are NOT in the candidate's field of interest (career field). Survival Jobs are useful while in school or for immediate short-term employment. The candidate should not stay in a survival job for more than one year, and should avoid moving from survival job to survival job.

Entry-Level Career Jobs are positions which allow the candidate to begin a career path within his career field. The level of entry will vary based on the candidate's experience, education and current network, as well as what is available in the industry and local job market. Every industry offers entry-level positions through support departments such as the mailroom, food service, security, groundskeeping, building maintenance, general office and telemarketing. These jobs are fairly easy to secure, due to high turn-over, and also allow for career advancement. The candidate should use an entry-level career job to begin building a professional network, find a mentor and prove that he is the type of employee the company needs so he can advance.

Transition Jobs are positions which the candidate holds as he moves from his entry-level career job to his dream job. Transition jobs are always in the candidate's career field. They are always a step beyond the last position he held, or they teach a new skill needed to pursue his dream job. Moving into a transition job is generally the result of planning, hard work and networking. It seldom just happens.

Dream Jobs are positions which match the candidate's interests, utilize the skills he loves to use and help him attain his ***personal goals***. They are jobs which are fun for him. Somewhere along the way, many of our candidates traded their dreams for something less. Often the jobs that will allow them to live their dreams are still achievable. Helping the candidate create a plan to pursue a dream job will restore his hope and allow him to advance with each step. Also, it is true that if he loves his work he will work harder, learn faster and be more promotable. The candidate's dream job helps determine his choice for entry-level career job and transition jobs.

People/Groups

An Employment Specialist is the generic term we use to identify someone who works in the employment field.

Employment Counselor is an employment expert whose focus is on job placement. In general, she focuses on the candidate's past experience, education and immediate needs, and the needs of the local job market. Usually, limited follow-up is provided to ensure that the candidate settles into the job.

A Career Developer is an employment expert who is committed to facilitating Career Development in each candidate. Much of her time is spent identifying and overcoming barriers so the candidate can succeed in the long-term. She also thoroughly assesses the candidate's interests and skills so she can help him choose a dream job, design a career path and select appropriate employers. Her goal is always an entry-level career job with opportunity for advancement. A Career Developer provides ongoing career advancement support (we suggest at least one year), including assistance with on-the-job challenges, moving successfully into at least one transition job and determining the role of education. Her hope is that at the end of one year, the candidate becomes his own Career Developer.

A Job Developer is an employment expert whose focus is on cultivating relationships with employers for the purpose of placement. They usually work with an Employment Counselor or Career Developer.

Stabilized Homeless are people who are living in shelters, residential recovery programs, transitional housing or with friends or family. Their temporary housing provides them with a place they can shower, eat regular meals, be assured of a warm bed, receive messages, receive basic care and have at least 30 days to job search. If they have been addicted in the past, they must have been clean and sober for at least four months. If they have a mental illness, they must have been on their medication for at least one year.

A Professional Mentor is someone who works in the candidate's field of interest who regularly spends time with the candidate to help him excel on the job and advance in his career. The mentor may teach the candidate the latest industry vocabulary and trends, help him troubleshoot for problems on the job, assist him in adjusting his career path, introduce him to professional acquaintances and help him advance by identifying job leads or using his own network.

Skills

Job Search Skills are the skills required to conduct a successful job search. The job search process is a distinct game with unspoken rules and expectations. Job search skills include researching industries and companies, identifying the employer's needs and concerns, marketing to the employer, using the telephone, resumé writing, selling yourself in the interview and closing the sale.

Killer Skills are skills the candidate possesses but dislikes using. It is not uncommon that the candidate continually finds himself in jobs which rely heavily on his killer skills because he is good at them and it is easy to remain in jobs which he can do well. To avoid getting trapped in a job that he hates, the candidate must identify both his killer skills and the skills he enjoys. To do this, use a field/skills card sort, interview the candidate about past jobs and the skills he liked and disliked using, or use Richard Bolles' "fun accomplishment" stories and Transferable Skills Chart from his book *What Color is your Parachute.*

Transferable Skills are skills the candidate presently possesses which are needed in the field into which he is transferring. Traditionally, skills and transferable skills have been identified by reviewing the candidate's paid work experience and formal education. Today, other sources are being used to prove that a candidate is qualified for a particular position including life experience, natural abilities, hobbies, regular reading of industry magazines, having a professional mentor and volunteer experience. We strongly encourage using these sources to prove your candidates' abilities, especially when they lack the traditional proof. You will note that we also encourage using skills which candidates have gained as a result of barriers (usually without mentioning the context in which they were gained), such as work experience and education gained in prison, a residential recovery program or programs for welfare dependents.

Vocational Skills are the skills required to do a specific job, such as the ability to type at a certain speed, fly an airplane, apply standard accounting principles, cook a specific type of cuisine, etc. Vocational skills can be identified by reviewing the sources listed above in transferable skills.

Work Experience

On-The-Job Training (OJT) occurs when the candidate is paid by the employer to work while he is in training. JTPA often arranges OJT work experience.

An Internship (paid or non-paid) is work experience which occurs on-the-job but is tied to formal education. We often have the candidate take a single class at the city college so he can request that the employer provide him with an internship in his field of interest. These types of internships are arranged by the candidate or you, rather than by the school. This will allow the candidate to begin building a professional network, gain work experience in his field of interest and investigate his options so he can determine what position he will pursue next.

An Apprenticeship is a long-term paid training program usually associated with a trade such as carpentry, plumbing, electrical or printing. Upon successful completion of an apprenticeship, the candidate becomes a journeyman.

Volunteer Experience is non-paid work experience which can be used to gain skills and knowledge, offer evidence of vocational skills and gain professional references. Volunteer experience can be listed on resumés and applications to prove the candidate's qualifications, especially when the candidate enters a new field which utilizes skills he gained as a volunteer. This is most powerful when the volunteer situation included a "supervisor" who can verify the high quality of the candidate's work performance.

Paid Employment, traditionally called "work experience," is a situation in which the candidate is employed by a company and paid for performing specific tasks.

Decisions are based not on what is true, but on what is perceived to be true.

The Ten Step Process for Overcoming Barriers to Employment

Overcoming barriers to employment is a challenging yet central part of helping candidates secure and maintain employment. Whether your candidates are those coming out of homelessness, upwardly mobile executives, inner-city youths seeking their first job or others, they will experience barriers which could hinder them from securing, maintaining and advancing in employment. The following section presents THE TEN STEP PROCESS for overcoming employment barriers which has proven to be effective with even the most complex issues. In Section V, you will find the ENCYCLOPEDIA OF BARRIERS which contains more than eighty barriers with sample solutions which were developed according to THE TEN STEP PROCESS.

Luck is a crossroad where preparation and opportunity meet!

However, this book is not just about the solutions; more importantly, it is about the process by which those solutions were developed and how you can use it to develop solutions for your candidates' barriers.

We strongly encourage you to read the entire TEN STEP PROCESS. However, for those who wish to go straight to the ENCYCLOPEDIA OF BARRIERS, we have provided a brief summary of THE TEN STEP PROCESS to expose you to how the solutions in the ENCYCLOPEDIA OF BARRIERS were developed. After reviewing the summary, if you have any additional questions about a step, read the corresponding chapter in THE TEN STEP PROCESS.

The Ten Step Process

1. Identify the Barrier

2. Identify the Candidate's Perception of the Barrier

3. Identify the Employer's Perception of the Barrier

4. Determine Which Approach to Use in addressing the Barrier

5. Eliminate the Employer's Concerns

6. Identify the Candidate's Selling Points Which Meet the Employer's Needs

7. Turn the Candidate's Barriers into Selling Points

8. Put it All Together in the Candidate's Words

9. Practice the Answer Until it is a Natural Response

10. Carefully Match the Candidate to Appropriate Employers

Step ① Identify the Barrier

C orrectly identifying the candidate's barriers is the first step in making him employable. Identifying barriers is an on-going process, and as you work with the candidate you will continually become aware of new issues. In chapter one, we have provided a list of questions which will help you identify barriers by considering the employer's needs and concerns. Your assessment of the candidate must be done from the employer's perspective, since the employer is the one who determines whether an issue is a barrier or not. Many barriers can be removed before the candidate begins job searching, while others will require a good answer in the interview.

Step ② Identify the Candidate's Perception of the Barrier

O nce you have identified a barrier, you must determine how the candidate views the "problem" in order to determine how best to help him resolve it. We have identified four common responses: 1) the candidate is unaware of the barrier, 2) he feels it cannot be solved, 3) he thinks it is the employer's problem not his, or 4) he is aware of the problem but needs your help to solve it. This chapter will offer ideas on how best to deal with each perception. It is important to complete this step, because the candidate, not the employment specialist, must take "ownership" of his job search and future.

Step ③ Identify the Employer's Perception of the Barrier

U nderstanding the employer's needs and concerns is the key to correctly identifying barriers and developing effective solutions. It is important to remember that what is a barrier to one employer may not be a barrier to another. For this reason, identifying the employer's perception of various barriers occurs throughout the job search as the candidate approaches new employers. This chapter will provide you with ideas on how to anticipate the employer's perception by understanding her needs and concerns.

Step Determine Which Approach to Use in Addressing the Barrier

This chapter deals with the core information of The Ten Step Process. Some barriers are easy to identify and resolve, while others require a great deal of creativity and resourcefulness. We have identified five basic "approaches" for overcoming barriers. They are: *Provide a Resource, Change Where You Look, Adjust the Candidate's Outlook, Teach a New Skill* and *Develop a Good Answer.*

How you approach each barrier will depend on many factors, including whether the barrier can be resolved before the job search begins or whether it must be addressed during the job search. For Barriers which can be resolved before the job search begins, you may:

> *Provide a Resource*
> *Change Where You Look*
> *Adjust the Candidate's Outlook*
> *Teach a New Skill*

Using any one of these four approaches will require you to use Steps 1-7 and Step 10 of The Ten Step Process. As a result, the employer may never become aware that the issues was a barrier. For barriers which must be addressed during the job search, you may:

> *Adjust the Candidate's Outlook*
> *Develop A Good Answer*

To Develop A Good Answer, you must use Steps 1-10 of The Ten Step Process.

In this chapter we teach you to choose the approach(es) you will use to address various barriers. We also provide examples and detailed explanations of how to implement each approach. We have found that all the barriers in this book can be addressed by using one or a combination of these five approaches. However, we encourage you to be creative in overcoming your candidate's barriers.

Step Eliminate the Employer's Concerns

As an employment specialist, it is important to remember that you have two clients—the candidate and the employer. If you lose credibility with the employer, you hurt yourself and future candidates. For this reason, it is important that you never encourage your candidates to lie. In fact, you must actively discourage it. There are honest solutions to every barrier. These solutions begin with addressing the employer's concern or need, not merely her stated requirements or questions. This chapter will show you how to do that by building on Step 4.

Step ⑥ Identify the Candidate's Selling Points which Meet the Employer's Needs

You must market your candidate as the best applicant for the job, not merely as someone without barriers. It is not enough just to remove the negative barriers; you must also identify positive selling points. In this chapter we will teach you how not only to identify selling points, but also to *quantify* them so that the candidate stands out from the others. For example, "I'm dependable," becomes "On my last job I was regularly to work 5 to 15 minutes early," or "I only missed two days of work in a year on my last job."

Step ⑦ Turn the Candidate's Barriers into Selling Points

Often the very issues which you identify as barriers can be turned into selling points if you match the candidate to the right employer, or if the solution to the barrier demonstrates a skill that the employer needs. We call this turning lemons into lemonade. Chapter 7 will discuss how this is done.

Step ⑧ Put it All Together in the Candidate's Words

If you eliminate a barrier using *Provide a Resource, Change Where You Look* or *Teach a New Skill,* you can skip Steps 8 and 9 and proceed directly to Step 10. For barriers which require you to use *Develop a Good Answer,* or *Adjust the Candidate's Outlook,* you will need to complete steps 8, 9 and 10. For either of these approaches, the candidate must demonstrate or explain in the interview why the employer's concerns are not valid *in his case*. To do this, the results of each previous step must be included in the candidate's response. This chapter will show you how to put it all together in the candidate's words and warn you of pitfalls. To assist you with putting it all together, we have provided an

Overcoming Barriers Worksheet at the end of each chapter, along with an explanation of how to apply each step by using the worksheet. A master form which you may copy and use is provided at the back of the book.

Step

Practice the Answer
Until it is a Natural Response

When using *Develop a Good Answer* or *Adjust the Candidate's Outlook*, the candidate's discussion with the employer regarding the barrier must sound honest and natural. If it sounds like a memorized script, the employer may assume it is a lie. This chapter gives ideas on how to help the candidate develop a natural sounding response.

Step

Carefully Match the Candidate to
Appropriate Employers

Matching the candidate to appropriate employers requires accurately assessing your candidate, carefully listening to the employer and a lot of practice. Our colleagues in Human Resources tell us that this skill, above all others, is what separates the real professionals in the field of job placement from those they want to avoid. This chapter examines various reasons candidates are considered a bad match and gives tips on how to make a good match.

These steps are designed to be used as a complete process. If you skip a step or do not thoroughly apply a step, the process will NOT work. If you find that you are having trouble developing creative solutions, read the entire Ten Step Process again completely and ask yourself if you are using the whole process correctly.

Step ①

IDENTIFY THE BARRIER

In this section the candidate is male and the employer female.

A barrier to employment is anything which makes the candidate "unemployable" or "unattractive to the employer." Barriers may stem from the candidate's physical, emotional or social traits; present, past, temporary or permanent life situation; ideologies, beliefs or attitudes; work-related or personal issues; skills, aptitudes or experience; or various other factors.

Barriers will differ from candidate to candidate and from employer to employer. What is viewed as a barrier by one employer may be a selling point to another. For example, one employer might like hiring young people because she believes they quickly learn "the way we do it," while another employer may avoid young people because she believes it is not cost effective to teach them.

To succeed, first imagine what the employer needs. ***This process requires you to think like an employer*** in the industry or company in which the candidate is applying. Then get on the phone and confirm your assumptions. Remember, the employer is your customer too.

Also, realize that whether the barrier actually hinders the candidate from getting or doing the job is not the issue. What matters is whether the candidate PERCEIVES that it stops him, or whether the employer PERCEIVES that it will hinder him from doing the job. Decisions are based not on what is true, but what is PERCEIVED to be true. As an employment specialist, your job is to create the honest PERCEPTION that your candidate is the best applicant for the job.

Not All "Barriers" Are Barriers

An employer who owned a large bike shop hired one of our candidates for the position of Warehouseman. When asked why this particular candidate was selected, the employer replied, "Because he was nice and laid-back." It was the first time I had ever heard an employer say he wanted someone "laid-back" in a warehouse. Obviously, the employer was concerned that all his employees match the company's easy-going, laid-back attitude.

Tips On Identifying Barriers

Barriers arise when the employer perceives that a situation causes concern or leads her to believe that the candidate cannot meet her needs. To identify barriers, ask the following five questions, which represent the five major areas of employer needs:

1. **Does my candidate appear dependable and trustworthy?** Dependability is consistently rated one of the top two qualities sought in new employees. The employer assesses dependability and trustworthiness through reference checking, consistency of work history, length of residence, length and type of extra-curricular activities and by observing emotional stability, Steps 6 and 7, and JOB SEARCHING FROM THE EMPLOYER'S PERSPECTIVE will help you address these issues.

2. **Does my candidate match the company's attitude?** Attitude is also consistently rated one of the top two qualities sought in new employees. Employee interaction with customers and staff greatly determines a company's success or failure. It can affect the company's repeat customer base, word-of-mouth marketing, sales and teamwork. Be sure the candidate has a good attitude in general and the right attitude for the particular company and job he is pursuing. Step 3 and 10 will help you approach these types of barriers.

3. **Can my candidate do the job?** In proving the candidate's ability to do a job, do not limit yourself to paid work experience. Use transferable skills, volunteer experience, school experience, natural abilities, life experience and hobbies, as well as work experience from prison, a recovery program or a shelter. Step 6 will assist you in doing this.

4. **Does my candidate appear motivated and eager to learn?** As we continue to move from the Industrial Age into the Information Age, ability and willingness to learn are increasingly important. See Steps 6 and 7 for additional help.

5. **Does my candidate match the company's image for this particular position?** To determine company image, consider the company's target customers, marketing strategies and the appearance of their current employees. Do this by conducting a site-visit, talking with present employees, talking with a contact in the Human Resource Department and reviewing the company's marketing materials. Step 3 will help you do this.

If the candidate is not getting interviews, look at his application, resumé and appearance when dropping off the application to identify issues which could create a negative perception.

If the candidate is getting interviews but not getting hired, look for "red flags" raised through his interview answers, presentation, references or attitude. For more ideas on how to address these issues, see the Power Tips in Job Searching from the Employer's Perspective.

Some barriers are more difficult to identify than others, namely, those dealing with fear and dishonesty. Fear—of success, failure, responsibility, having a paycheck or almost anything else—is often concealed in other distracting behaviors. You may observe absenteeism, defensiveness, hopelessness or anger, and think they are the barriers when they are actually the result of fear. Careful reference checking, dual case management, observation and time will reveal these hidden issues. Be sure to consistently look for new barriers and to reassess barriers which persist after you have applied The Ten Step Process.

Prioritizing Barriers

If you attempt to deal with all the barriers at once, you may overwhelm the candidate and make it difficult to progress in resolving any of the barriers. For that reason, we recommend dividing the barriers into the four categories listed below in the Priority Key.

Priority Key:

A. Barriers which must be resolved before even discussing the job search, such as active drug use.

B. Barriers which may be resolved while preparing for the job search, such as the need for a mailing address.

C. Barriers which may be resolved while job searching, such as having to discuss a felony conviction.

D. Barriers which may be resolved after the candidate is employed, such as the need for additional education.

These general categories will help you to determine which barriers to address first, and how much time, energy and resources will be required to get the candidate job-ready.

OVERCOMING BARRIERS WORKSHEET: Below is a sample of the Overcoming Barriers Worksheet designed to assist you in applying The Ten Step Process. As soon as you identify barriers, write them in Step 1a: Barriers. Then, immediately determine when each should be addressed. Using the Priority Key, place a letter A-D in Step 1b: Priority, so you can easily see which to address first.

Overcoming Barriers Worksheet

✗	Step 1a: Barriers	Step 1b: Priority	Step 2: Candidate's Perception	Step 3: Employer's Needs and Concerns	Step 4: Approach	Step 5: Solution	Step 7a Lemons into Lemonade	Step 7b: Company or Position
	No phone number	B						
	Felony conviction for armed robbery	C						

KEY	**Barrier:**	**Priority:**	**Candidate's Perception**	**Approaches:**
	List barriers as they are identified ✗ each barrier as it has been resolved	A: resolve before even discussing job search B: resolve while preparing to job search C: resolve while job searching D: resolve after employed	1. unaware of the barrier 2. feels the barrier cannot be solved 3. thinks the barrier is the employer's problem 4. needs your help solving it	1. develop a good answer 2. provide a resource 3. change where you look 4. adjust the candidate's outlook 5. teach a new skill

© WNTS 1996

 ② **IDENTIFY THE CANDIDATE'S PERCEPTION OF THE BARRIER**

Once you have identified a barrier, you must understand how it is perceived by the candidate. The candidate may be completely unaware of certain barriers and overwhelmingly focused on others. How the candidate perceives the issue will significantly affect which approach you choose and the length of time required to resolve it. To identify the candidate's perception, you need only to steer your conversation toward the barrier. If the candidate is aware of the barrier, be direct. If not, listen for clues so that you can determine when best to begin addressing it. We have grouped possible candidate perceptions into four basic categories, as listed below.

The Candidate Is Unaware Of The Barrier

As an employment specialist, you will see barrier issues and solutions which the candidate does not realize exist. These barriers often include poor hygiene, destructive attitudes, inappropriate behavior and unprofessional appearance. During your first meeting with the candidate, inform him that an important part of your job is teaching him the employer's perspective. This means that you may have to say things which, although they are difficult to hear, are necessary if he wants to be hired and promoted. Ask his permission to speak honestly with him so when these difficult issues arise you have permission to address them.

 *You do the candidate a disservice by not making him aware of "embarrassing" issues, i.e., that he has a body odor problem, that his clothing is inappropriate for the chosen industry, or that he talks too much. Chances are these barriers have caused problems in the past and will continue to do so if not addressed. With your kind honesty he can overcome them and begin moving toward his career goals.*

The Candidate Feels the Barrier Cannot be Solved

Often candidates are fully aware of barriers, but do not believe they can be resolved to an extent that will allow them to get the job they want and move up.

This attitude, if left to fester, can be devastating to the job search process and the candidate's career. Your ability to bring the candidate to a place where he believes each barrier can be resolved and is willing to invest in the process is essential to his success. If you fail to do this, he may feel compelled to lie so the employer will not discover the barrier, or sabotage both his efforts and yours during the job search.

We have not come across a barrier yet which cannot be honestly neutralized, and in many cases turned into a selling point, when the candidate is willing to deal with it and the employment counselor has the time, resources and creativity to address it. Solutions come as a result of many things—changing the candidate's view of the situation, helping him to create new habits and attitudes, educating the employer, locating needed community resources, or selecting a different field, company or job title.

To help you bring your candidates to the realization that the barrier can be overcome, we have included many stories and examples throughout this book which you may want to share with the candidate. Step 4 and a lot of practice will help you become good at this. Practice will perfect your skill.

Don't Hire Me!

I once had a candidate who started each interview with a hand shake and the statement, "You probably do not want to hire me because I'm illiterate, huh?"

He was a very capable janitor and well matched to the positions for which he applied. However, I did not realize how afraid he was that he would have to talk about the illiteracy or be expected to read on the job. I had not asked enough questions. Once I found out what he was saying, we discussed what aspects of being a janitor he feared he could not do because he could not read. He replied, "the ordering of supplies." I helped him to think of options. We determined that he could order supplies with a phone call to the main office or the supplier, rather than in writing. When he received a written note, his wife would read it or he would call the main office to "check in and see how things are going" at which time they could give him verbal instruction.

Helping him change his attitude about how debilitating his "barrier" actually was gave him the confidence to focus on the things he did well and the courage to begin a literacy program.

Your candidate may not directly say something like this, but if he is thinking or worrying about a barrier, the employer may perceive "a problem" in his attitudes and reactions and choose to hire someone else.

Key Point

In general, you will see more solutions to barriers than the candidate. Do not assume that the candidate is aware of his options—it is likely he was never taught to see them. Educate yourself so you can always present several different options or approaches to a barrier. The information in this book, your experience with candidates and your inquiries to employers regarding their areas of concern will help.

The Candidate Thinks the Barrier is the Employer's Problem, Not His

There are two situations in which the candidate might believe the barrier is the employer's problem, rather than his own: 1) when the candidate is unwilling to acknowledge or deal with a barrier which precludes him from working in a certain position or company, or 2) when the candidate is dealing with an issue that has traditionally prohibited people from working in the type of position he wants, i.e., gender, age, race, religion, education level or socio-economic background. However, simply proclaiming a certain barrier to be the employer's problem alone, (i.e., "If he won't hire you because you are a woman, that's his loss!") without taking additional action is dangerous and will set the candidate up to fail. If the candidate believes a certain barrier is the employer's problem, determine which of the two above explanations best fits. This determination will help you choose an approach, although both require action on the part of the candidate.

It is difficult to work with a candidate who will not acknowledge a barrier which precludes him from working in the position which he is pursuing. Persuading him to change his opinion about an issue he has consciously determined not to be his problem is difficult—but try. The candidate who can be persuaded to change his view will most often do so because you have shown him "what's in it for him," or have given him new options which he did not realize existed. Help the candidate see how he benefits by acknowledging the barrier and changing his attitude.

The candidate who is still unwilling to adjust to the mandates of the company, industry or job should seek other positions which better match his attitudes, lifestyle and personality. This may mean searching in a different field, approaching companies with specific images or looking in a non-traditional area. If you do not know of a field or company in which the issue is acceptable, have the candidate do the research, rather than doing it yourself, not only because he will learn but because the process is a result of his personal choices or

An Exception to the Rule

Linda enjoyed working with her hands and was interested in going into some aspect of construction. To assist her, we called the Equal Opportunities Office at our local city hall and asked for the name and number for a female contractor. To our surprise, there was an entire book of female contractors. We found a couple of contractors who were willing to meet with her. As a result she learned about different job opportunities, began to ascertain which direction would be best for her, began building her professional network and was recommended for a plumber's apprentice program.

unwillingness to conform, so he must take responsibility for it. When he returns with new ideas and information, continue to work with him. *Changing Where You Look* and *Adjusting the Candidate's Outlook* are discussed in more detail in Step 4.

When dealing with a candidate who faces an issue he cannot change (such as age, race or gender) which could prohibit him from being hired in the type of position he wants, he must either consider whether he wants to endure the stress of challenging the mythology that he cannot do the job or change where he looks. Ask the candidate, yourself and colleagues in the field, whether the candidate has the fortitude to be a pioneer in this area and whether he can prove and market himself as "the exception to the rule." This is a big undertaking, as most rules are changed only when there are enough exceptions that the rule no longer applies. This may take years, but it is possible. For example, in the 1950's it was generally thought that women would not make good sales

Barriers in One Situation but Not Another

Issue	Barrier	Not a Barrier
Hair in dread locks	Nordstrom	Many trendy retailers
Foul language or stories	Most traditional businesses	Construction, or refineries
Does not want to work with others	Working for someone else	Indep. contractor artist, long haul driver or software developer

associates for large-ticket items such as real estate, stocks and bonds and cars because they had "no money sense." Today, women are top producers in these areas. Also, in the 1980's there were very few minority television shows because it was believed that they were not profitable. Pioneers in the field fought for recognition of their skill and the potential profitability of the market. Today, there are minority shows every week night on every major channel.

If the candidate wants to be a pioneer, he must learn the rules so he can market himself to the employer as the "exception." Also, encourage him to find a mentor, build a strong network and help others become "exceptions" so the rule will eventually change.

Prejudice or Mythology ?

We have chosen to use the word "mythology" rather than prejudice because we think that often much of what is termed "prejudice" are beliefs which have been handed down for generations and which have not been challenged. We think that these beliefs are based on ignorance rather than malice. Once evaluated, many of these beliefs prove themselves to be myths.

Key Point

This is the candidate's life and job search. Allow him to take responsibility for the direction he wants to go, whether it is to implement the changes you recommend, to redirect his job search because he is unwilling to make the changes or to be a pioneer in a new area by becoming the "exception to the rule."

The Candidate Is Aware Of The Barrier, But Needs Your Help To Solve It

Barriers & Answers

No Permanent Address	Use the address of the shelter, a family member or local friend
No Interview Clothing	Take the candidate to a thrift store to get two outfits or begin a clothing closet for interview and work clothes
No ID	Write to the county in which he was born for a birth certificate, go to the DMV for state ID or driver's license, go to the SSI office to get a Social Security card and number
No Car	Focus on jobs within walking distance or those with carpool programs, or provide bus tokens and teach him how to use public transportation
Anger	Refer the candidate to anger management classes, discuss new ways of dealing with his anger on the job, and create an agreement that before he acts on his anger he will call you.

Often, the candidate is completely aware of his employment barriers but is not equipped to overcome them on his own. He may need advocacy, resources or an expert opinion. At other times, he may need the support and encouragement provided by working with someone else on the problem. Your willingness to take on some of the tasks will lift his burden enough to allow him to move forward. Through the assistance of your agency, referrals to partnering organizations and your ingenuity, help can be secured. If the candidate becomes discouraged, remind him that you will work with him through THE TEN STEP PROCESS. Also, as you use the process you will see many successes and will be able to assure him that the barrier can be overcome.

To help you, each entry in the ENCYCLOPEDIA OF BARRIERS begins by identifying possible candidate concerns. We do not state the surface concern—the fear that no employer will hire him because of the barrier—but rather, the deeper reason(s) why the candidate is concerned that no employer will hire him.

Key Point

Consistently make the candidate take part in the process. Do not do for him what he can do for himself, but always offer the support and assistance needed to move ahead. Empowerment starts with your belief in his ability to help himself—and is accomplished when he gains the tools for success and you come alongside only when he is unable to do it alone.

OVERCOMING BARRIERS WORKSHEET: After listing and prioritizing the barriers, select one of the four options from Candidate's Perception which best matches your candidate. This will allow you to assess, at a glance, the amount of counseling needed to begin addressing the barriers.

Overcoming Barriers Worksheet

✗	Step 1a: Barriers	Step 1b: Priority	Step 2: Candidate's Perception	Step 3: Employer's Needs and Concerns	Step 4: Approach	Step 5: Solution	Step 7a: Lemons into Lemonade	Step 7b: Company or Position
	No phone number	B	4. needs help					
	Felony conviction for armed robbery	C	2. Feels barrier can't be solved					

Barrier:	**Priority:**	**Candidate's Perception**	**Approaches:**
List barriers as they are identified ✗ each barrier as it has been resolved	A: resolve before even discussing job search B: resolve while preparing to job search C: resolve while job searching D: resolve after employed	1. unaware of the barrier 2. feels the barrier cannot be solved 3. thinks the barrier is the employer's problem 4. needs your help solving it	1. develop a good answer 2. provide a resource 3. change where you look 4. adjust the candidate's outlook 5. teach a new skill

KEY

© WNTS 1996

Step ③   IDENTIFY THE EMPLOYER'S PERCEPTION

One of the most important steps in creating solutions to employment barriers is understanding how the barrier is perceived by the employer. This includes understanding the employer's **needs** and how she might perceive the barrier to negatively impact those needs, as well as any additional concerns raised by the barrier.

To identify the employer's needs and concerns, you must put yourself in her place, learn to think like her and allow yourself to see the issues she faces every day. This is a good exercise to do with the candidate so he can learn how the employer thinks too. Next, listen closely to the questions the employer asks and the qualifications she requires for the job. Employers usually ask questions because they have had problems in the area before (i.e., *Have you ever used drugs?....What does being dependable mean to you?*) or because a specific skill is deemed necessary for getting the job done (i.e., *How many words per minute can you type?* or *How many hours have you operated a floor buffer?*). The skills they emphasize are usually those which are most important to them or have been most difficult to find. If you are unfamiliar with the types of problems which plague a specific industry, call and ask. If you are unfamiliar with the employer's top six needs for a specific position, call and ask. In addition, you can arrange for the candidate to do an investigative interview, or you can ask current employees about the problems the employer is most concerned about, what types of behavior she rewards and what skills the job uses most. The largest and most universal employer concern is profit. Most employer concerns are related to increasing income through sales, customer retention, marketing, product value and profit margin, or decreasing costs through limiting liability, decreasing sick time, eliminating theft and

Examples of Employer's Concern and Needs if the Candidate is a FELON

Concern	Needs
Steal or cheat company	Honest, trustworthy employees
Bring criminals onto the business site	Positive environment for customers and staff
Use or sell drugs on site	Drug-free workplace
Threaten or intimidate the boss or staff	Employees who want to learn and are willing to follow instructions
Always take shortcuts	Hard workers who do more than is required

ensuring efficient spending. Once you have an understanding of the employer's needs and concerns, you can begin to formulate a solution.

Many barrier issues can be resolved BEFORE the candidate begins to job search, which means the employer need never know about them. If a barrier does not effect the candidate's ability to do the job or is resolved before he interacts with employers, it should NOT be discussed with the employer unless a direct question is asked. In most cases, it is unlikely that the employer will bring up a barrier unless the candidate gives her a reason to. For example, the employer will not ask about living arrangements unless the candidate leads her to believe it is out of the ordinary. Nor will the employer ask about public assistance, domestic violence, depression or the extent of the candidate's wardrobe unless she is given cause to be concerned.

One of the biggest mistakes the candidate can make is to tell on himself by accidentally initiating discussion about a barrier issue. This is done by *alluding to problems* ("My case worker suggested I…" or "My counselor said…") or *introducing a negative topic* ("I'm on public assistance so I can't afford to…" or "I don't have a car so I can't…"), rather than *neutralizing the situation* ("I'm a little tight financially; is it possible to get an advance to cover the cost of the uniform?") or *presenting the issue a positive way* ("I hear you have a ride share program. I would love to participate!").

Once a barrier issue has been brought up, however, the candidate must address the employer's concerns and needs in a straight-forward and honest manner. Help prepare the candidate to address barriers which are routinely discussed (i.e., criminal convictions, being fired, major illnesses, and limited language skills), as well as unique employer concerns and needs which might come up due to the candidate's resumé, application, appearance or other unavoidable "red flags." Each barrier entry in the ENCYCLOPEDIA OF BARRIERS presents several concerns the employer may have and states how the barrier may be perceived to negatively impact her needs.

Don't Let Them Tell on Themselves!

I worked with a candidate who was a recovering drug addict, but was well qualified for the positions for which he was interviewing. He interviewed several times, without success. Finally, I called one of the employers who had interviewed him and found out that he had introduced himself by saying, "Hi, I'm Matt, a grateful recovering addict."

The employer did not need this information. She told me that she might have been interested in him, except that after the introduction the interview was very awkward and she felt uncomfortable with him.

***

To help my candidates understand, I often ask them something like:

"Would you ever approach an attractive man or woman you wanted to date and saying, 'Hi. I would really like to go out with you, but before you agree I want you to know that my feet really stink.'? When they laugh, I reply, 'Of course not. The prospective date does not need this information, and at the point that it becomes important, she'll find out. The same principle applies to candidates and employers. Do not give them negative information which does not apply to the situation.'"

Key Point

The employer will make her hiring decision based on HER needs, HER concerns and HER perceptions, not the candidate's.

OVERCOMING BARRIERS WORKSHEET: Once you have identified why the barrier may be a concern to the employer or be perceived as hindering the candidate from meeting the employer's need, briefly list this information in Step 3: Employer's Needs and Concerns. This will remind you to develop a solution which resolves these specific issues.

Overcoming Barriers Worksheet

✗	Step 1a: **Barriers**	Step 1b: **Priority**	Step 2: **Candidate's Perception**	Step 3: **Employer's Needs and Concerns**	Step 4: **Approach**	Step 5: **Solution**	Step 7a: **Lemons into Lemonade**	Step 7b: **Company or Position**
	No phone number	B	4. needs help	Needs easy contact with candidate. Concerned about candidate stability				
	Felony conviction for armed robbery	C	2. Feels barrier can't be solved	Needs someone who works hard & doesn't take short cuts. Concern about trustworthiness, safety & attitude.				

KEY

Barrier:	**Priority:**	**Candidate's Perception**	**Approaches:**
List barriers as they are identified ✗ each barrier as it has been resolved	A: resolve before even discussing job search B: resolve while preparing to job search C: resolve while job searching D: resolve after employed	1. unaware of the barrier 2. feels the barrier cannot be solved 3. thinks the barrier is the employer's problem 4. needs your help solving it	1. develop a good answer 2. provide a resource 3. change where you look 4. adjust the candidate's outlook 5. teach a new skill

© WNTS 1996

 ## Step ④ DETERMINE WHICH APPROACH TO USE IN ADDRESSING THE BARRIER

After you have ascertained how the candidate *perceives* the barrier and how the employer *may perceive* the barrier, you are ready to select an approach to address it. Creating a plan to address the barrier will minimize the candidate's fear and give him self-confidence. It will allow him to appear prepared, thoughtful and competent.

We have found that solutions to barriers generally fall into one of five categories. As a result, we have developed five approaches to use in overcoming them (you may find additional approaches which work for your candidates—be creative). Below is an explanation of the five approaches and the icons which represent them in the Encyclopedia of Barriers. Next to each encyclopedia entry, we denote the approach(es) we recommend by placing the icon in the margin, and provide sample solutions using the suggested approach(es).

Approach 1: Develop a Good Answer

A good answer is required for barriers which cannot be entirely eliminated before the job search process and which may come up in an interview. To develop a good answer, determine why the barrier should no longer concern the employer. Ask the candidate leading questions to get all the details needed for developing a solution. We suggest you ask the following questions:

◆ What caused the barrier?
◆ How long was it a problem?
◆ When did it last occur?
◆ Has it recurred more than once? What was the length of time between recurrences? Is there a pattern?
◆ Why did you stop? What has changed in your life to make me believe it is no longer an issue?
◆ What steps are you taking, or have you taken, to ensure that it does not recur?
◆ Why will it not be an issue again, especially on the job?

Include any additional questions which his answers create in your mind. The employer will probably have the same questions and, although she may not ask

Develop a Good Answer

I assisted a woman who had been convicted of felony manslaughter. Through careful questioning, I discovered that she had killed her abusive husband. An employer might be concerned that the candidate would view violence as an acceptable means of dealing with problems, show anger toward all men, find a new abusive man resulting in her coming to work battered, call in sick often or that her new abuser would pose a threat to employee safety if he came to her workplace.

I learned about the history of her abuse. She thought if she loved him enough, she could change him. Once she realized she could not change him and that she and her daughters would always have to endure the abuse, she became obsessed with escaping. She knew she could not go on living like that. He told her if she ever tried to leave him, he would kill them. Afraid for herself and her daughters, she knew she had to act first or he would keep his word. She said, "I paid a high price—but I thought it was him or us." Today she recognizes the signs of abuse and knows of other actions she should have taken.

Her greatest fear is that her daughters will follow her bad example—so they are all in group counseling. With this information, we developed a good answer regarding the felony. Presented calmly with good eye contact, it sounded like this:

"I was young and naive when I got married. I ended up in a very abusive situation. I thought if I loved him enough, I could change him—but it only got worse. I was afraid for myself and my daughters and I knew I couldn't keep living that way. When I tried to leave, he made it clear that we would never get away alive. He said he would find me and kill me—I believed him. I felt I had only one option—to act first. Through counseling I have learned about other actions I could have taken. Most importantly, I have discovered the value of freedom. I enjoy being with my daughters and have developed new friendships through a social group I belong to—we watch each other's children, help each other and have fun. I look forward to simple things like eating out, wearing business suits, getting back to work and expanding my computer skills. I presently know WP5.1, MS Word…

the questions, she may screen him out based on her imagined answers. The truth is seldom worse than what the employer can imagine. It may feel intrusive to ask such personal questions, but you cannot create an HONEST good answer without this information.

Once you are convinced that the barrier issue has been resolved or that steps are being taken to minimized its negative effects, use the information the candidate has given you to create an HONEST answer. Read "In The Real World: Develop A Good Answer" about the woman who had been convicted of manslaughter before proceeding. Use this information and the process described below to learn how to develop a good answer. A good answer should:

1) **Briefly explain why the barrier developed.** Have the candidate take responsibility, but offer an explanation which includes how she is different today (i.e., "was young and naive"). Also, avoid harsh terms or images (i.e., "I murdered him" is replaced by "I had to act first").

2) **Briefly explain how she has changed, what she has learned, and why things are different today.** Be specific, but brief, in showing what is different (i.e., "learned about other actions…," "through counseling…").

Be sure the changes you list are valued by or significant to the employer. This may mean illustrating an ability, an attitude or basic work habits like dependability, stability and the desire to learn.

3) **Briefly introduce why the barrier will not recur.** Implying that the barrier will not recur, rather than directly stating it, will sound more honest and less like a "sales job" (i.e., relationship with daughters, discovery of the value of freedom, support from new friends).

4) **Quickly lead the employer back into why the candidate would be great for this job!** Always end a good answer by redirecting the conversation away from the candidate's weakness and toward her selling points (i.e., " presently know WP5.1 and MS WORD...").

Steps 5 through 9 will help you develop this skill and will explain how to go beyond simply minimizing or neutralizing the barrier to actually making it a selling point.

Approach 2: Provide a Resource

Often barriers can be resolved before the job search process begins. In these cases, the employer need not become aware of the barrier. The next four approaches are often used to address these types of barriers. Many barriers can be resolved by accessing resources offered by your agency or by a partnering organization. As you become aware of your candidate's barriers, begin asking who in the community provides or could provide for those needs. For example:

◇ ask large corporations to sponsor business clothing drives to help you create a clothing closet.
◇ ask local service clubs to sponsor tuition costs or buy tools for one candidate per quarter.
◇ ask a temporary placement agency to test candidates' computer skills and allow candidates to use their computer tutoring programs.
◇ ask a community college or adult education program to waive tuition and book costs for your candidates.
◇ ask the public transportation department for free or discounted tokens and bus passes.
◇ ask local Marriage, Family and Child Counselors to volunteer once a week to help candidates who want to put their lives back together.
◇ ask a retired judge to voluntarily assist candidates in resolving pending legal issues.
◇ ask a local phone company to provide free voice mail boxes so job candidates can easily receive calls from interested employers.
◇ write a joint grant with a non-profit child care center for a certain number of spaces for children of newly employed parents.

These are only a few of the partnerships which we have seen work across the country. As you identify various needs, make a list of where the needed resources could be found. You may attend community meetings, visit other programs, contact colleagues to see who they know, read a local social service directory or use the yellow pages. As you pursue these relationships, realize that the worst thing they can say is "no." It is like job searching: one "yes" in ten attempts is average. If the candidates can do it, so can we!

Approach 3: Change Where You Look

When an issue precludes the candidate from working in a specific field, company or position, it becomes necessary to change where you look. However, it is important when selecting your new direction that you choose only fields or titles which match the candidate's interests; otherwise he will be unhappy and perform poorly, impeding his ability to keep the job and be promoted. When looking for a new field or title, do away with the traditional way of assisting candidates and get creative. The following are the three main reasons you would change where you look for a position.

Out Of His League: If you determine that the candidate is not qualified for the position he wants, recommend that he look in the same field for a lower-level position for which he is currently qualified. For example, if the candidate dreams of being a chef in a top restaurant but has cooking experience only from the Army, he obviously knows how to cook but has not yet proven himself to be a chef. Assisting him to start as a prep-cook in a top restaurant would provide him the opportunity to discover the difference between being a cook and being a chef, gain new skills, add a top-name restaurant to his resumé, learn what top restaurants look for in a chef, and begin building a network.

If the candidate disagrees with your assessment of his skill level, honestly express the barriers you see, but remember that this is his life and his job search. If he persists, agree to support him in his job search only if he agrees that if he is still unemployed in a month he will try it your way. This allows

Changing Where You Look

A colleague shared how she assisted a candidate with a facial deformity due to severe burns. The candidate was an excellent tailor, but was unable to find work because most tailors work in high-end clothing stores or tailor shops where customers would feel uncomfortable with his appearance. The solution to this barrier was to find a field which needed a tailor, but would not be offended by facial burns. The answer was easy—emergency and medical personnel who wear uniforms, such as firemen, police officers, nurses and doctors. She went to a local hospital and proposed that they hire an on-site tailor for altering the staff's uniforms. She explained that it would save them money, since they had been contracting the services out at a higher price. They agreed. In fact, his deformity may have been a selling point, because he became a daily example to staff and patients how one could overcome physical adversity—plus they acquired an excellent tailor!

him to maintain responsibility for himself and allows you to act as a mentor. Explain that while he pursues the position for which you do not think he is suitable, you will support him in any manner you can, short of setting up interviews for positions, because the employer is also your customer and relies upon you to do good matching. Help him tailor his resumé, give him job leads for employers who are not "your customers," and meet with him to discuss his progress. We have learned the hard way to respect the candidate's belief in himself. More than once we have had a candidate prove us wrong by landing a job we did not think he could get. You may be pleasantly surprised to see the same things. However, if after a month he is still unemployed, suggest he try it your way. Reinforce that your way will also move him toward his dream job, but that it might take a little more time. His ultimate goal is still the focus.

Key Point

Never rob the candidate of his dreams. Dreams are what keep us motivated. Instead, help him to design a realistic path to achieve his dream. This almost always starts with matching his present skills to a position in his dream field.

Unacceptable Barrier: If the candidate has issues which pose a barrier for a particular position and is either unwilling or unable to change them, you must get creative. Do not decide that you cannot help him; just redirect.

For example, imagine that you have a male candidate with long hair who does not want to cut his hair, but wants to work in an office. You know that most corporate offices want a clean-cut look, so what do you do? First, remind yourself that this is the candidate's life and that he has the right to keep his hair and have a job using the skills he loves to use. Next, begin brainstorming with the candidate, colleagues and friends about offices in which they have seen men with long hair working, or companies which will not see his hairstyle as a barrier. In this case, turn your attention away from "most offices" and begin looking at offices in industries where long hair on men is acceptable, even hip, such as the entertainment industry, fashion industry, some areas of the advertising industry, fine art industry or places where people from those industries congregate. The key to this approach is to open your mind to all of the possibilities and ask many questions.

> *"The will to win, the desire to succeed, the urge to reach your full potential... these are the keys that will unlock the door to personal excellence."*
>
> Eddie Robinson, Football Coach
> Grambling University

If the unacceptable issue is one on which the candidate could compromise (ie. hair), have him do a lot of the research. If it is something over which he has no control (ie. facial deformity), he may need more of your input and assistance.

Industry Trends: As we continue our move into the Information Age, markets are shifting and companies are changing rapidly. It may seem like there are no positions in the candidate's field of interest. However, even in our changing world, there are openings in every industry because people constantly retire, move, quit, get promoted, and die. If the candidate really wants to work in a specific, more competitive industry, he must be ready to clearly articulate why he is the best candidate for the job, and build a network so that he can learn about openings immediately.

Old Position	Transferable Skills	New Position
Aero-Space Engineer	Computer programming	Software developer, Computer consultant
Assembler	Works well with hands	Computer repair, Finishing carpenter
Drug Dealer	Built repeat customer base without advertising	Sales
Mother	24 hour child care	Teacher's aid, Home daycare

Therefore, the question is never "Are there jobs?," but rather "Is securing and maintaining employment in this industry worth the extra work it requires?" If the answer is "yes," the candidate should start building a network. If the answer is "no," you must begin identifying transferable skills and researching industries in which he could use them. Most candidates will need a lot of assistance in identifying transferable skills. As you look for them, be sure to include hobbies, daily activities and volunteerism, as well as skills for which he has been paid to use. To help you identify transferable skills you may use a card sort system, career testing, Richard Bolles' approach of graphing accomplishments or have the candidate tell you stories and examples of things he does well. For more information, see WORK RELATED SKILLS in the ENCYCLOPEDIA OF BARRIERS.

Using Transferable Skills

A colleague of mine worked with a man who had spent most of his life as a laborer and had recently found himself unemployed, homeless and starting over. When she mentioned to him that he had an impressive speaking voice, he remarked that he had always wanted to be a sports radio announcer. She helped him find steady employment as a painter and handyman, but also wanted to help him pursue his dream. With a little creativity, she convinced her director to let him do the agency's radio commercials. She also contacted the local sports radio station and arranged for him to do volunteer work there. The station manager said if he hung around awhile and proved that he really knew his stuff when it came to sports, he would give him a shot on the radio.

As employment specialists, we are often more aware than our candidates of how the transition into the Information Age will impact specific industries. You may encourage one candidate to transfer his current skills into a new industry and begin building a new career immediately. For another you may advise that he use his current knowledge to continue working in his present industry while pursuing additional education and volunteer experience in a new industry rather than changing fields immediately. This will lead to a smoother transition. Remind candidates, especially older workers who expected to work for the same company their entire career, that changing fields and starting a new career is normal in today's job market. Experts estimate today that the average adult will have 5-8 different careers before retiring. It is key when changing fields that the candidate consider what he truly loves to do. Then help research fields and jobs which incorporate those skills and interests. Be sure you consider non-traditional jobs as well. Change is inevitable—but it can be fun and profitable if the candidate is prepared.

The Dictionary of Occupational Titles lists over 12,000 jobs titles. The Enhanced Guide for Occupational Exploration says that 95% of all employees work in only 2,800 different jobs. This means there are more than 9,000 jobs for people who want something different. A few out-of-the-ordinary jobs include tutors for child actors, underwater construction workers, designers of restaurant menus, tailors of airline curtains, food testers for large manufacturers, repair technicians for nuclear medicine machinery, and virus designers for the protection of software copyrights. Be creative. Learn about unusual jobs by regularly asking people what they do and how they got started. When conversing with employers, ask them about the more unusual jobs in their industry.

Approach 4: Adjust the Candidate's Outlook

Adjust Candidate's Outlook

In most employment surveys, ATTITUDE is listed as a top concern by employers. Repeatedly, employers have told me that they would rather hire someone with a good attitude and teach him the skills needed, than hire someone who has the skills but has a bad attitude, because it is easier to teach a skill than to change an attitude. As employment specialists, we are often more successful in this area than employers, because we can deal honestly with issues without fear of legal repercussions. We also have more influence because we are trusted as friends or mentors, rather than seen as an adversary. We may also have control over services the candidate wants such as housing, child care and job leads. A few attitudes which commonly must be taught are a willingness to learn, respect, the value of simply saying "okay" without a long justification, politeness, friendliness, honesty, openmindedness, willingness to ask questions, understanding the value of time, and knowing how one's actions impact the company as a whole. Adjusting the candidate's attitude is often a slow process. It is most successful when you can work in conjunction with other people in his support network, i.e. Case managers, a sponsor, professional mentors and friends. It ia also helpful when each little success along the way is "celebrated."

In adjusting the candidate's outlook, your job is two-fold. First, you will need to help the the candidate see how his specific attitude is perceived by the employer, explain the results of holding that attitude and then teach him an alternative attitude and reaction. In most instances you will find that the candidate does not understand how his attitude is perceived, nor is he aware of other options. The second part of your job is to help the candidate to understand the rules of the American business culture and how management generally thinks. As the candidate learns to anticipate the employer's needs and to correctly interpret her actions, he will become significantly more employable and promotable.

Adjusting the Candidate's Outlook

I once assisted a friend who was starting a new food franchise in a local mall. He needed someone to help him open his first store, design operating procedures and train staff. I agreed to help for the first month.

Most of the teenagers hired did not understand the importance of pleasing the customer or their responsibility to make customers want to return. Nor did they understand the relationship between the customer's return and their job security.

As I trained them I repeatedly asked "Would you rush back if someone treated you that way?" In the end, those who were willing to learn the art of being a friendly, helpful, clean and fast worker were kept. Those who were not willing to learn were let go.

Understanding Attitudes: Attitudes and reactions are based upon our beliefs, whether conscious or unconscious. You will be unable to change the candidate's attitude or reactions without first changing his beliefs. The A-B-C Theory can help show the candidate the impact of his belief system on his attitude and reactions, by showing how an everyday **A**ction combined with his particular **B**elief system results in a unique **C**onsequence. To illustrate: **A**ction—A friend of mine and I see a blue racer snake in a pet store window; **B**elief—I believe that snakes make great pets, because as a kid growing up in rural Idaho I had a pet blue racer. My friend, who grew up in the city, believes snakes are dangerous; **C**onsequence—I would happily buy the snake for my adolescent child, while my "city-slicker" friend would definitely not allow her child to have a pet snake. The same **A**ction resulted in different **C**onsequences, based on different **B**eliefs.

Encourage the candidate to evaluate his belief system—not to determine whether it is right or wrong, true or false, but to identify whether it is CONSTRUCTIVE or DESTRUCTIVE. Once he has assessed which beliefs are constructive and which are destructive, you can help challenge his beliefs and CHOOSE new ones which give him the greatest opportunity to succeed.

For example, if a female candidate believes that no one will hire her because she is a woman, she places herself in a no-win situation because she cannot change her gender. It is true that certain employers may not hire her because she is a woman. However, by choosing to attribute her lack of success to something she cannot change, she has rendered herself powerless. At the very least, this destructive belief will cause her to market herself poorly, show anger or take a job she dislikes. Other more-extreme consequences include giving up and living on welfare, staying

The longer I live, the more deeply I am convinced that the difference between the successful person and the failure, the strong and the weak, is a decision.

— Willie E. Gary

in an abusive relationship for financial support, numbing the pain by using drugs, or becoming so hopeless and angry that she considers suicide. This may sound extreme but people with destructive belief systems do destructive things.

If you can help her identify and change this destructive belief by helping her to see that in most cases, being a woman has nothing to do with her ability to meet the employer's needs, she can then begin to market herself as the "exception to the rule." Now when she is not hired, she can take constructive action by determining how she failed to prove to the employer that she is an exception to the rule.

> *I learned early that excellence is the greatest defense against racism and sexism.*
>
> —Oprah Winfrey, Talk show Host

She may determine that she was not persuasive enough in explaining why she is the best candidate for the job, did not express clearly enough how she could make or save the company money, lacked certain skills the employer needed or did not develop an extensive enough network. Now she is in control. She can improve with each experience, examine how to market herself better, choose jobs which better match her current skills and build a stronger network to promote her candidacy. With this attitude she will find an employer who will recognize her value.

The ABC Theory does not deny that prejudice exists. The candidate may come across employers who will not hire her because of prejudice or false mythology about a certain race, age group, gender, socio-economic group, etc. However, people who succeed in life do it in spite of prejudice, in spite of circumstances and in spite of rejection, because they CHOOSE to let these things make them stronger rather than defeat them. CHOOSING a constructive attitude does not mean that you are unaware of prejudice and potential barriers, just that you are not going to be stopped by them.

It is important to note that employers may discriminate based on factors which seem trivial. The employer may lose interest because a candidate's golf score is too low, she graduated from the wrong university, she is too short or too skinny, she is from the wrong part of the country or she mentioned having enjoyed a book the interviewer did not like. Without extensive research into the employer's personal prejudice and preferences, there is little the candidate can do to guard against these biases. However, developing a constructive belief system,

A Great Attitude!

An acquaintance of mine was the first Hispanic hired in the advertising department of a large Los Angeles-based company. He believes that his constructive approach to being a minority and his ability to use it to meet the employer's needs are what got him hired. In his interview he first educated the firm's partners about how much money the Hispanic market spends annually in the LA area and demonstrated its amazing growth rate. Next, he explained that he understood what the market will buy because he was part of the community and could make the company a lot of money. He was hired.

Note Of Interest: The #1 radio station in Southern California is a Spanish-speaking station, because English-speaking listeners are divided among many stations and there are fewer choices for the large Hispanic population.

as in the example of the woman above, will benefit the candidate regardless of the intentions of the employer. Regardless of whether the employer meant her harm or not, the candidate will learn, improve and keep moving forward. Although some employers will discriminate unfairly based on various issues, *many will not*.

The most practical way to assist the candidate in overcoming this obstacle is to find other people with the same barrier who have succeeded and find out how they did it. Encourage the candidate to find a mentor who identifies with her and works in her field of interest to guide her through the process.

If the candidate proves that she can make the company money, most employers will ignore everything else.

Understanding the American Business Culture: The American business world has a culture all its own. If you go to Japan you would not expect the Japanese to start speaking English, abandon their customs for yours or adopt your values. Neither can the candidate expect the business culture to change its language, customs or values because he has arrived. Therefore, in order to be accepted and succeed in the American business culture, the candidate must become familiar with it. Part of your job is to teach him a new culture so he can become BI-CULTURAL. The candidate does not need to abandon his own culture to succeed, but he must function differently when in the business culture.

Do not assume that the candidate understands the American business culture. We often take for granted the things we already know and forget that at some point we had to learn them too. When we meet someone for the first time we shake hands and introduce ourselves. We know better than to talk about personal problems with an employer. We understand the importance of always delivering what we promise. Whether we learned from our parents, from college professors, by watching successful people or through trial and error, these basics have now become second nature. Yet, millions of Americans do not understand how employers think, nor is basic business protocol second nature. When working with a candidate, start with a basic premise that there is no reason why he should know...anything in particular! Strive never to make him feel stupid for not knowing something, realizing that we do not like to be made to feel stupid when we don't know something. We too have had to learn much, and we are aware that there is much we still do not know. So, do not assume, ask!

Remember, the need to learn about the culture of the business world does not apply only to the candidate who has been unemployed for a long period of time, has never worked or is immigrating from another culture, but also to the candidate who has been isolated in a single industry or distinct "company culture" for a period of time. He too must understand how to succeed in today's business culture, how to conduct a successful job search and what current employers are looking for.

When teaching new concepts, we often state the obvious in a humorous way and then follow-up with specific examples which also explain to the candidate how this new information will benefit him. We explain how to apply concept and the potential consequence of choosing not to apply it. Realize that your job is to persuade the candidate to develop a new behavior, but understand that he will not do it if it is too hard or unclear. These concepts can be introduced by using WNTS' *Career Advancement & Business Acculturation* workshops. These lessons can also be learned through continual counseling during the job search process and after the candidate is working.

One of the greatest barriers facing the candidate today is lack of understanding of the business culture. Not only is he entering a foreign culture, but a culture that is constantly changing. You must NEVER assume he already knows what is appropriate and how his attitudes or behaviors are interpreted.

Approach 5: Teach a New Skill

Often, what the candidate needs in order to succeed is a specific skill which can be learned. By this we are referring to skills which pertain to finding and maintaining employment, rather than specific vocational skills needed to perform the job. If vocational skills (i.e., the ability to use a certain computer program, to drive a forklift, to take a patient's vital signs) are needed to secure an immediate position, you may choose to find an employer who is willing to provide on-the-job training, consider the suggestion given in approach 3 to *Change Where You Look,* or find resources in your area where these skills can be acquired in a reasonable amount of time. Skills for finding and maintaining employment which candidates often need to learn include:

◇ choosing positions that match the candidate's skills and interests
◇ identifying transferable skills
◇ writing and using a resumé as a marketing tool
◇ completing an application that "sells" so they can get an interview
◇ locating job openings in the hidden market
◇ using the yellow pages to locate employers
◇ marketing to employers over the phone
◇ asking good questions
◇ following up after a phone call or interview
◇ dressing for success (including make-up and hygiene)
◇ marketing their abilities using Quantified Selling Points
◇ interviewing successfully
◇ dealing with difficult situations on the job
◇ being promotable once on the job
◇ understanding employee rights and obligations
◇ adopting a lifestyle of learning
◇ advancing along a career path

Steps to Teaching a New Skill

1. Tell
2. Show
3. Watch
4. Praise
5. Correct
6. Repeat

We suggest an interactive teaching style which accommodates different learning styles and uses various means of communication (i.e., verbal explanation, visual illustrations, examples and stories, practical hands-on experience and discussion). We recommend that you use the following six-step process as you teach new skills.

Teach a New Skill

I assisted a welfare mother with five children in re-entering the work force. She had an expired certification as an Emergency Medical Technician (EMT) which she had never used, a brief experience as a cashier, and very little self-confidence. She knew she needed to recertify before she could become an EMT so we decided to look for a cashier position in a hospital cafeteria or gift shop.

To job search, she needed to market herself to employers over the phone, but was very nervous. I explained how the process works, basic phone etiquette and together we created a script for her to use. We practiced as if I were the employer. I then made an example phone call to a local hospital and marketed myself using her script so she could listen. We practiced again, then she was ready to try it on her own. Her voice was a bit shaky, but she relied on her script and her first telephone call went very well—they were not currently hiring but said she sounded "very qualified" and gave her the name and number of another local employer who was hiring. She was ecstatic! As we debriefed, I pointed out how well she presented her selling points and the good follow-up questions she asked. I also reminded her to speak more clearly and put a "smile" in her voice. As we continued the process of calling and debriefing, she improved greatly.

Had I merely told her how to do it, she would not have done as well. Her first phone call would not have resulted in a referral. Surely she would have decided the new way was "too hard and didn't work anyway" and returned to her old way, or given up altogether.

First: **TELL** the candidate what you want him to know. Introduce the new concept by explaining why it is important and when to use it. Use verbal discussion, written materials read by the candidate and entertaining exercises to explain how to apply the concept. This will be of significant help to *auditory learners*.

Second: **SHOW** him how to apply the concept by actually doing it yourself as he observes. This provides him with a clear idea of how it looks and sounds, and it will provide him with practical tools. This will be very helpful to *visual learners*.

Third: **WATCH** the candidate as he applies the concept. If he feels uncomfortable with you watching, you may choose to let him do it alone, then debrief afterward. This will be of significant help to *experiential learners*.

Fourth: **PRAISE** what he did well, so he will feel good about the process. This will be of significant help to all learners.

Fifth: **CORRECT** anything he did not understand or which needs to improve by telling him what he did wrong (auditory learner), showing him how to do it right (visual learner) and observing him as he tries to apply it again (experiential learner).

Sixth: **REPEAT** steps 3 and 5 until he does it well consistently and feels comfortable enough to use t on his own.

Learning new skills often takes time. Depending upon the skill you are teaching, this may occur within a single meeting (i.e., shaking hands) or may occur over a period of weeks (i.e., maintaining eye contact or answering common interview questions). In either case, it is important that the candidate understands the value of the lesson and knows that it is common to "fail" the first couple of tries. To remind them that failing is a part of succeeding, share examples like Babe Ruth who holds the record for the most home runs but also for the most strike outs. Realistic expectations will keep him from becoming discouraged and reverting to what he has always done.

Also, if your goal goes beyond merely placing the candidate in a job and you want to promote retention and career advancement, you will continue to use this process of teaching long after he is working. We encourage employment specialists to maintain contact for at least one year after placement to assist the candidate in learning and applying new skills and advancing in his career.

Always be truthful when developing solutions to barriers. When honestly and creatively dealt with, any barrier can be neutralized, and perhaps even turned into a selling point. If you are not honest, you will not gain the respect of the employer and will set the candidate up to fail. The candidate is your "product;" the employer is your "customer." Your long-term success depends on a reputation of honesty and consistency. Never be dishonest or encourage the candidate to be so.

OVERCOMING BARRIERS WORKSHEET: Once you have identified which of the five approaches listed above will best resolve the specific candidate's barrier, list it in Step 4: Approach.

Overcoming Barriers Worksheet

✗ Step 1a: Barriers	Step 1b: Priority	Step 2: Candidate's Perception	Step 3: Employer's Needs and Concerns	Step 4: Approach	Step 5: Solution	Step 7a: Lemons into Lemonade	Step 7b: Company or Position
No phone number	B	4. needs help	Needs easy contact with candidate. Concerned about candidate stability	2. Provide a resource			
Felony conviction for armed robbery	C	2. Feels barrier can't be solved	Needs someone who works hard & doesn't take short cuts. Concern about trustworthiness, safety & attitude.	1. Good answer			

KEY

Barrier:
List barriers as they are identified
✗ each barrier as it has been resolved

Priority:
A: resolve before even discussing job search
B: resolve while preparing to job search
C: resolve while job searching
D: resolve after employed

Candidate's Perception
1. unaware of the barrier
2. feels the barrier cannot be solved
3. thinks the barrier is the employer's problem
4. needs your help solving it

Approaches:
1. develop a good answer
2. provide a resource
3. change where you look
4. adjust the candidate's outlook
5. teach a new skill

© WNTS 1996

 **Step ⑤**

ELIMINATE THE EMPLOYER'S CONCERNS

Employers have many concerns—most having to do with profit, public image, company growth, safety and legal issues. The employer often has valid reasons for her concerns, because a particular issue has cost the company money in the past, has had a negative impact on a colleague's business or has been the recent topic on the evening news. Other concerns may be based on false mythology which still stands because it has never been challenged. However, changing the employer's mythology is far more difficult than changing the candidate's, because you have less influence with the employer, and the employer has less to gain. Additionally, the employer tends to believe that what a person has done in the past, he will do again. If the candidate "punched-out" his last boss and stole from the company, he will do it again; if the candidate made the company a million dollars, he will do it again. These factors demand that you identify and eliminate any employer concerns raised by the candidates' barriers. If you do not eliminate these concerns, the candidate will not be hired—regardless of how qualified he is.

To deal with the employer's concern you must first determine whether: 1) the barrier has been or can be resolved to the extent that the employer will not know about it, so it will not be of concern to her, 2) the barrier has been or can be resolved but will still be apparent to the employer and may be of concern to her or 3) the barrier has not been resolved or the candidate does not intend to resolve it.

If the barrier has been resolved and is no longer a concern (i.e., the candidate has no car but uses the public transportation system, buys a monthly bus pass and only seeks employers located along the bus route), the candidate *should not mention*

Two Examples of Eliminating Concern

To eliminate the concern that an ex-offender will cause problems on the job, the candidate may say, "I was young and stupid, and running with the wrong crowd when I committed the crime. I have new friends now. In fact, I am involved with (a respected community organization). I used my time in jail (never say prison!) to gain expertise as a printer. I also learned to be punctual and work hard. I am married now, and would never put my wife and child through what my parents went through."

***

To eliminate the perception that all youth have short attention spans, are irresponsible, do not care about the quality of their work and are always late, a young candidate may say, "I know I am young, but being on the school basketball team has taught me the importance of being on time, working hard, functioning as a team member and always giving my best."

the barrier to the employer. If it is mentioned, the candidate can present the solution you have developed together.

Matching the "Image"

A friend of mine who is a headhunter told me a story about a man he recommended to be the president of a large corporation. The candidate had all the skills the board sought, but thought the board might not be comfortable with his youthful appearance. To help the candidate overcome the barrier of "appearing too young," my friend had him put silver hair dye at his temples. His candidate got the job.

If the barrier has been resolved but may still cause concern (i.e., the candidate was once fired from a job but has since changed his behavior and made amends with the employer, and now receives a neutral reference from the company), *the candidate must be prepared to address the barrier*. Often this will mean developing a good answer or demonstrating an adjustment in attitude. Return to Step 4 to determine which approach you will use.

If the barrier has not been resolved (i.e., the candidate is a single parent with no child care) or the candidate does not intend to resolve it (i.e., the candidate is actively using drugs), *DO NOT help him find employment until the barrier is resolved.* You may choose to assist him access resources to deal with the barrier. To do this, return to Step 4, approach 2 *Provide A Resource.*

Key Point

DO NOT avoid or hide an unresolved barrier. Doing so will come back to haunt you. You may lose a valuable employer and could set the candidate up to fail.

Can You Believe It?

Several years ago at the end of an important business negotiation, a successful businessman with whom I was dealing leaned back in his chair and said, "You're pretty smart for a blond." I am sure the look on my face conveyed my shock at being subject to the long-standing myth that "blondes are dumb." He immediately apologized. I looked him in the eyes with a smile and said, "I guess you haven't met many blondes." My challenging response to his mythology pointed out the ignorance of his statement. I became the exception to the rule. Perhaps he reconsidered his myth at that point, or maybe as he meets more intelligent blondes his myth will change. In reality, the businessman's mythology may have given me the advantage during our negotiations because he did not anticipate needing to be alert and savvy.

The art of persuasion is a slow and tedious process, because beliefs are intertwined. Often to change a single belief, a person must reconsider many beliefs. The longer a person has held a belief, the more intertwined and difficult it becomes to change. However, it is less difficult to convince an employer that your candidate is the "exception to the rule." This is because it does not require a change in belief system, only the acknowledge-ment that every rule has "exceptions." Your goal, therefore, is not to change the employer's entire belief system—about the homeless, youth, women, non-English speakers, displaced engineers, etc.—but to help the candidate become the "exception to the rule." To assist the candidate in becoming the "exception to the rule," you must know the "rule." Use the information uncovered in Step 3 to do this.

Once you understand what the employer needs and why she is concerned that the candidate may not meet that need, you can work on eliminating the concerns. Using information gathered from the series of questions listed under Step 4: Develop a Good Answer, figure out why the employer should believe that her concern will not become a reality. The candidate will not be hired until you have developed answers which acknowledge the employer's concerns and offer a persuasive explanation as to why the candidate will not cause concern. Once the candidate has been hired, he can subtly challenge the employer's mythology through his success and pave the way for other "exceptions." When there are enough exceptions, the rule will change.

Promoting the candidate as the "exception to the rule" is not a sell-out; it is the first step on the road to the candidate's success and to changing the rule.

OVERCOMING BARRIERS WORKSHEET: Once you have identified which approach you will use to resolve the barrier, list it in Step 5: Solution. Refer to the Step 3: Employer's Needs and Concerns to be sure each item listed is addressed.

If the barrier requires that you develop a good answer, briefly list the heart of the information you will use directly on the worksheet. Use Step 5: Solution to record details as you interview the candidate and he expresses how he is different today and what steps he has taken which would prove it.

Overcoming Barriers Worksheet

✗	Step 1a: Barriers	Step 1b: Priority	Step 2: Candidate's Perception	Step 3: Employer's Needs and Concerns	Step 4: Approach	Step 5: Solution	Step 7a: Lemons into Lemonade	Step 7b: Company or Position
	No phone number	B	4. needs help	Needs easy contact with candidate. Concerned about candidate stability	2. Provide a resource	Provide a voice mail box		
	Felony conviction for armed robbery	C	2. Feels barrier can't be solved	Needs someone who works hard & doesn't take short cuts. Concern about trustworthiness, safety & attitude.	1. Good answer	Change: Got GED, new friends, new attitude, in college, has goals		

Barrier:	Priority:		Candidate's Perception	Approaches:
List barriers as they are identified ✗ each barrier as it has been resolved	A: resolve before even discussing job search B: resolve while preparing to job search C: resolve while job searching D: resolve after employed		1. unaware of the barrier 2. feels the barrier cannot be solved 3. thinks the barrier is the employer's problem 4. needs your help solving it	1. develop a good answer 2. provide a resource 3. change where you look 4. adjust the candidate's outlook 5. teach a new skill

© WNTS 1996

 **Step ⑥** **IDENTIFY THE CANDIDATE'S SELLING POINTS**

Once the employer's concern has been eliminated, the candidate MUST direct the conversation to why he is the best applicant for the job. If he does not, the focus will remain on his weaknesses rather than his strengths. To move from the candidate's barriers to his strengths, he should present selling points which clearly illustrate how he meets the employer's needs. To do this:

First, make a list of the employer's needs for the position for which the candidate intends to apply. Review Step 3 if you need help in identifying the employer's need.

Second, determine what in the candidate's past work history, education, volunteer experience, daily routine, hobbies or personality qualifies him to meet those needs. As you read your list of "employer's needs" for each position, ask the candidate the following questions:

- ◇ Why do you think you can…lift 100 pounds, build a house, clean a room, etc.?
- ◇ When have you done it in the past?
- ◇ Why were you good at it?

Do this for all the knowledge, experience and skills that the employer may want.

Third, once you have determined how he meets the needs, ask the question:

- ◇ Do you have proof that you were good at it?

Quantified Selling Points for a Woman Who Wants to Work in Child Care

Education	I have 10 credit hours of Early Childhood Development.
Past Work History	One year experience working in child care.
Story	I've spent the last 22 years raising six children who all graduated from high school, have never been to jail and are drug free.
Opinion of Others	The director of the child care center always bragged about my ability to handle even the most difficult children (she may present a rating or comment given on a performance evaluation).
Example using Numbers	15 new students were enrolled in my first year due to referrals from my students' satisfied parents.
Example using Percentages	Enrollment in my class increased 35% in one year, due to referrals from satisfied parents.
Example using Ratio	On my last job, I was able to increase the number of full price students in my class vs. sliding scale students 2 to 1, allowing us to hire additional staff.

Giving proof is important because many of the applicants whom the employer interviews will say, for example, that they are dependable, but the candidate who offers that he "only missed work twice in a year" proves that he is truly dependable. Evidence can be found in education, work history, accomplishment stories, the opinions of others or samples of the candidate's work.

CASE STUDY	SKILLS &	QUANTIFIED SELLING PTS
Mindy is a single mother of 3 who has been on welfare for the last 7 years. Her last job (which she held for 22 months) was as a waitress. She enjoyed the work because she was helping people, was physically active, worked on a team and averaged $70 a day in tips. Her dream job is nursing, but she needs a flexible job, which pays well and has weekend hours so she can attend school.	Friendly	Built a base of 45 weekly repeat customers
	Dependable	Called-in sick only 3 days in almost 2 years on last job
	Hardworking	Worked overtime or double shifts at least twice a week
	Good Memory	Memorized menu of 250 items and prices in four days
	Team Worker	Received "Excellent" rating on last 3 evaluations for "working well with others"
	Good Coordination	Carried five plates or four large glasses at one time

Converting each of the responses into Quantified Selling Points (QSPs) goes one step beyond simply telling the employer that the candidate meets her needs; it paints a picture and gives proof. Strong Quantified Selling Points are created by:

1) addressing a specific employer need (i.e., a motivated person to be a shift leader).

2) identifying a situation in which the candidate proved his ability to meet the need, whether on-the-job or in a non-employment situation.

   If the situation was job related, the QSP should include the phrase "on my last job…" or "on a previous job …" If the proof of the candidate's qualifications occurred in a non-employment situation (i.e., at church, with friends or family, in a recovery program or coaching a community baseball team), remove it from the specific situation. For example, "I coached a winning baseball team," becomes "I managed a team of 15 people, motivating them to advance from tenth place to first place in just one year." In a case like this, the candidate should be prepared to further discuss the transferable skills, mention the situation in which they were learned and explain how they benefit the employer.

3) giving a time frame, such as "daily…in the first 3 months…over 2 years…"

4) using percentages, numbers, ratios or specific examples to complete the illustration. For example, "…arrived 15 minutes before my shift …was late only 3 times …increased sales by 15% …had repeat customer base of 35."

5) checking the QSP for believability. If your candidate looks "too good to be true" it will raise a red flag, inviting the employer to wonder, *"If he's so wonderful, why is he unemployed—what is wrong with him?"* She may decide your candidate is lying, exaggerating or taking credit for more than is due

him. For example, "I increased sales by $80,000 in one year" or "I more than doubled sales in my first year" sounds more believable than "I increased sales by 600% in one year." Step 10 will help you match the candidate's QSPs to the employer's needs.

Whether the candidate faces difficult barriers or not, Step 6 and the use of QSPs are necessary as the candidate approaches the employer. They are used not only to re-direct the conversation after answering a difficult question, but in answering almost any question the employer may ask. The candidate should be able to give three to six Quantified Selling Points for each job title he is seeking.

Always have the candidate answer questions by giving proof that he can meet the employer's needs. Your candidate will be hired only if he can convince the employer that he is the best candidate for the job.

QUANTIFIED SELLING POINTS WORKSHEET: Information from Step 6 is recorded on the QSP Worksheet rather than on the Overcoming Barriers Worksheet. A master of the QSP Worksheet is proved at the back of the book. Please take a moment to review it.

Quantifying Selling Points Worksheet

Title and Field: Secretary in the Medical Field

EMPLOYER'S NEEDS	SELLING POINT	PROVE IT
Someone who is patient and compassionate with sick people	Enjoy helping people, especially those who are sick	Took care of my elderly grandmother for 4 years until she died. Took care of sick father for 9 months until he was released from doctor's care
Someone who is computer literate	I know how to use a computer	I have two years computer experience. I am proficient in MS Word, WP 5.1, Excel.
Someone who is organized	I am very organized	Managing a household of six people, while attending school and working part time, over the last two years has taught me to be very organized and a good time manager.
Someone who has knowledge of medical terminology	I took a class in medical terminology	I have three credit hours in Medical Terminology and learn quickly.
Someone who is dependable	I am very dependable	My last employer rated me as very dependable during my last review.
Someone who can maintain files and do prof. correspondence	I know how to do all basic secretarial tasks	I graduated with a 3.6 GPA from secretarial school.

Step ⑦

TURN THE CANDIDATE'S BARRIERS INTO SELLING POINTS

Barriers can often be used as selling points. In Step 5 you neutralized barriers to eliminate employer concerns. In Step 6 you developed Quantified Selling Points to demonstrate the candidate's strengths. Step 7 challenges you to consider whether any of the candidate's barriers can actually be used to further qualify him for a position. This is called turning lemons into lemonade, and it is done in two ways. First, by showing how the barrier and having overcome it has provided the candidate with special skills or knowledge the employer needs. A few examples include: a candidate of ethnic descent with an accent being able to help a company move into a new market, a woman being able to address issues facing working mothers so the company can function more smoothly or a recovering drug addict being able to spot on-the-job drug use and deal with it constructively.

Secondly, you can turn lemons into lemonade when overcoming a barrier demonstrates a skill or a quality the employer needs, such as resourcefulness, the ability to plan ahead or persistence.

As with any selling point, when you turn lemons into lemonade, be sure you are addressing valid employer needs. The fact that "no one can con a con" is not a selling point for the host of an upscale restaurant because the employer is not afraid of being conned. However, it is an excellent selling point for employees of a social service organization which works with people who make a living "working the system."

Barriers & Benefits

Recovering Addict
- I am proving my honesty by telling you I am in recovery. If you hire someone else, you don't know if they are "clean" or lying.

- I am serious about my recovery and can create a safe environment for non-users so peer pressure does not turn the whole shop "dirty."

- Because of my recovery, I am aware of my goals and priorities. I am motivated, focused and very dependable.

Older Worker
- Experience has taught me numerous ways of handling difficult situations.

- I have worked successfully under several different management styles.

- I am very responsible and mature.

Felon
- I am "street smart." I am extremely resourceful. I watch everything and can easily spot trouble, like shoplifters.

- I can tactfully handle confrontation.

- No one can con a con.

When helping the candidate determine what additional benefits, if any, the employer gains by hiring a person who has faced and overcome his particular barriers, be realistic and practical. If the benefit is significant enough, use the barrier and the fact that it has been overcome as a selling point—then quantify it. As you read the sample solutions in the ENCYCLOPEDIA OF BARRIERS, you will see many examples of turning lemons into lemonade.

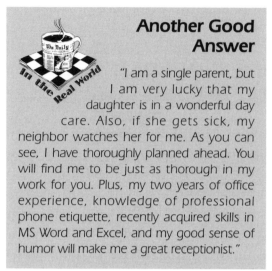

Another Good Answer

"I am a single parent, but I am very lucky that my daughter is in a wonderful day care. Also, if she gets sick, my neighbor watches her for me. As you can see, I have thoroughly planned ahead. You will find me to be just as thorough in my work for you. Plus, my two years of office experience, knowledge of professional phone etiquette, recently acquired skills in MS Word and Excel, and my good sense of humor will make me a great receptionist."

Key Point

What appears on the surface to be a problem, can actually be an asset if presented correctly to the right employer. Teaching the candidate how to turn his weaknesses into strengths is one of the best gifts you can give him. Not only does it give him another selling point, but it restores his self-respect.

OVERCOMING BARRIERS WORKSHEET: Once you have identified a solution, consider if the solution to the barrier provides any added benefit to the employer or whether there is a particular industry or position which might benefit from the candidate's success in overcoming the barrier. List the benefits in *Step 7a: Lemons into Lemonade* and the correlating company or position the candidate may pursue in *Step 7b: Company or Position*. Once a barrier is resolved, place an **✘** on the far left.

Overcoming Barriers Worksheet

✘	Step 1a: Barriers	Step 1b: Priority	Step 2: Candidate's Perception	Step 3: Employer's Needs and Concerns	Step 4: Approach	Step 5: Solution	Step 7a: Lemons into Lemonade	Step 7b: Company or Position
✘	No phone number	B	4. needs help	Needs easy contact with candidate. Concerned about candidate stability	2. Provide a resource	Provide a voice mail box	Will get messages 2x's/day (even from remote sites), return calls same day	All positions
✘	Felony conviction for armed robbery	C	2. Feels barrier can't be solved	Needs someone who works hard & doesn't take short cuts. Concern about trustworthiness, safety & attitude.	1. Good answer	Change: Got GED, new friends, new attitude, in college, has goals	Good role model for juvenile delinquents, youth in general or other ex-offenders	Counselor at a youth center, school boys ranch, mission. Recruiter at a school serving this population

KEY

Barrier:	Priority:	Candidate's Perception	Approaches:
List barriers as they are identified ✘ each barrier as it has been resolved	A: resolve before even discussing job search B: resolve while preparing to job search C: resolve while job searching D: resolve after employed	1. unaware of the barrier 2. feels the barrier cannot be solved 3. thinks the barrier is the employer's problem 4. needs your help solving it	1. develop a good answer 2. provide a resource 3. change where you look 4. adjust the candidate's outlook 5. teach a new skill

© WNTS 1996

 ## PUT IT ALL TOGETHER IN THE CANDIDATE'S WORDS

If the solution to your barrier **does not** require you to *Develop a Good Answer*, skip Steps 8–9 and go directly to Step 10. If your solution does require that you ***Develop a Good Answer*** **to a difficult question,** complete the next two steps before progressing to Step 10.

Develop the candidate's good answer by using the information on the Overcoming Barriers Worksheet. Always write out the answer first, making sure that all necessary considerations are addressed. Then have the candidate read through the whole answer to choose which words and phrases sound most like him. Be sure he does not delete needed information. Have him rewrite his good answer. Remember, a good answer is only good if the employer is satisfied with the responses. Remember the following:

◇ Be sure the answer is true and does not conflict with other information the candidate gives.

◇ The answer should sound natural—not like something someone else has written and the candidate has memorized. The language, tone and comfort level of the candidate should be consistent throughout the interview, not calling attention to "scripted" answers to difficult questions.

◇ The answer must become the candidate's natural response to any question which addresses the topic. Questions may be asked in many forms other than that which he practiced. Be sure the candidate digests the thought process and reasoning behind the answer so he can address it confidently and comfortably from many angles. REMEMBER: "Natural" is about half an hour in practice time beyond memorized.

◇ The candidate must look the employer in the eye when answering difficult questions, because in our culture eye contact is perceived to communicate honesty, confidence and sincerity.

The following is an example of how to put The Ten Step Process into a good answer in the candidate's words.

Step 1	**Identify the barrier**
	Poor English skills (English as a second language)
Step 2	**Identify the candidate's perception of the barrier**

I can only get low paying or manual labor jobs with no future because I don't speak English very well. No U.S. employer will give me a good job.

Step 3   **Identify the employer's perception of the barrier**
The employer might assume the candidate:
◇ is not legally eligible to work in the U.S., creating problems with the federal government
◇ is uneducated or unskilled
◇ is not able to communicate with the customers, staff or boss
◇ is unreliable or lazy

Step 4   **Determine which approach to use**
This case requires a combination of two approaches:
Develop a Good Answer (as below)
Change Where You Look (which compels us to seek employers with bi-lingual supervisors)

Step 5   **Eliminate the employer's concerns**
"Hello, my name is Jose. I am learning English, but am fluent in Spanish and Quichua (an Indian dialect). I have been working in the United States for two years and my past employers will tell you I'm a hard worker and always on time." He should say this in English even if the employer is willing to speak Spanish and even if it is the only English he knows—it shows determination.

Step 6   **Identify the candidate's selling points**
I have four years experience as a driver, a clean DMV record and can read a map.

Step 7   **Turn barriers into selling points**
Because I speak Spanish, maybe I can help bring in more Spanish-speaking customers —OR— I can make your Latino customers feel important.

Step 8   **Put it all together**
"Hello, my name is Jose. I am learning English, but am fluent in Spanish and Quichua. I have been working in the United States for 2 years and my past employers will tell you I'm a hard worker and always on time. I have 4 years experience as a driver, a clean driving record and I can read a city map. And because I speak Spanish, maybe I can help to bring in more Spanish-speaking customers. May I give you my resumé? "

Step 9   **Practice The Answer**
This script should be fairly easy to memorize and use. Have him practice it in front of several different people until he is not embarrassed. Do not be too particular about pronunciation as long as he is easily understood.

Step 10   **Carefully match the candidate to appropriate employers**
Match him to jobs which require only basic English skills, such as businesses to the Latino community, or those with Spanish-speaking supervisor. Also, encourage him to take an ESL class to learn more English so that he can advance.

Overcoming barriers is not about fooling the employer into believing a lie. Rather, it is about constructively dealing with each issue that hinders the candidate from confidently marketing himself as the best candidate for appropriate positions and assisting him to see himself, his situation or his options in a positive light.

Step ⑨ PRACTICE THE ANSWER UNTIL IT IS A NATURAL RESPONSE

If the candidate is still fearful of answering hard questions, be patient. Take small steps and allow him to see the successes along the way. Arrange mock interviews during which he can practice answering difficult questions and receive positive reactions from the interviewer. Remind him that job searching is a numbers game, much like sales—one "yes" in every ten attempts is the average. Therefore, he should think of his first nine interviews as dress rehearsals which will allow him to perfect his marketing skills. Thinking this way will allow him to relax and feel less disappointed if he is not hired. Rarely will he need more than ten interviews to get a job if he is well prepared and improves after each interview as a result of debriefing with you.

Practice Makes Perfect

My first mock interview with Tanya was comical. She was nervous, and it showed. Her answers to the hard questions were awkward and seemed staged. Twice she muttered, "That's not how you asked it before." When she did answer, her responses included terminology and phraseology which did not "sound like her." To help her become more comfortable with her answers, I first made sure that she agreed that all the answers were true—so she did not have to remember a lie and worry about making other information consistent with a lie. Next, we discussed how questions could be asked in various ways and also reviewed how each good answer could be used for different questions. I reminded her to address the employer's concern, not just answer the question.

Then, I had her replace any words or phrases which she would not use in regular conversation. As we practiced, I asked her the same question in several different ways until she was comfortable answering them and naturally used her Quantified Selling Points to address my various concerns. Then, after each employment interview we immediately discussed difficulties, and talked about how she would improve her responses the next time. When Tanya's employer called me to say she wanted to hire her, she thanked me for finding such an articulate, professional and charming candidate.

Key Point

For the employer to believe that the candidate's good answers and new outlook are legitimate, his good answers must come as a natural response to appropriate questions. Remember, a "natural" response will only occur if the candidate takes ownership when developing it, if the answer is true and if the candidate has practiced for at least 30 minutes.

CAREFULLY MATCH THE CANDIDATE TO APPROPRIATE EMPLOYERS

C orrectly matching the candidate to the right job is as important as all of the preceding steps. If you resolve the candidate's barriers, but refer him to a company which does not appreciate his unique selling points, you have assured his failure. The more you understand about the specific needs, personality, image and goals of the company and hiring manager, the more accurate your matching will be. For example, I worked with a hiring manager whose son had died at 22 years of age. He looked for young men who showed potential to whom he could mentor and give opportunities. It was his way of honoring his son's memory. He appreciated the ambitious young men I sent him, and I was able to refer men who were eager but had limited experience. Another employer with whom I worked had recently achieved her doctorate degree and only hired managers with at least a master's degree. Knowing this, I only sent candidates who had master's degrees or above— demonstrating that I understood her needs.

The Importance of Good Matching

The Human Resource Director of a large hospital once told me that she selects placement agencies and employment specialists based on their ability to match the right candidate to her needs.

She explained that she uses these professionals to save her (and her staff) time and money. If they do not take the time to understand the needs of her company, they cannot match those needs and are simply recruiting bodies for her to screen and match. For this reason, she remains loyal to a handful of employment specialists who have proven their ability to match candidates to her needs, and does not bother with the rest.

Matching consists of considering the needs of specific company and hiring manager, as well as general industry needs, such as job skills, vocabulary, networking ability and stability. If you are unsure what types of industries, companies and positions are best for a candidate, call employers in the industry and ask. Once you have determined the industry and positions the candidate will pursue, call and ask employers to describe an ideal candidate for the position. Have the candidate do investigative interviews or arrange a mock interview for the candidate with an employer in the industry who will give you feedback, so you can determine whether he is a good match for the position.

When a candidate interviews with one of your employers, always ask the employer why the candidate was or was not selected. Inform the employer that her feedback will allow you to better match future referrals and will also help you to identify and address barriers for the candidate. When a candidate interviews with employers you do not know, debrief the candidate afterward by reviewing which difficult questions were asked, the responses given, and at what point the employer gained or lost interest. Debriefing can help him improve for future interviews.

Matching requires that the candidate presents only the information which relates to the position he is pursued. For example, we would not include selling points about cooking on a candidate's resumé for an office position, unless the office position was in the culinary industry. We would not include a candidate's master's degree if he is applying for an entry-level position. We have found that a highly educated candidate with no related work experience is one of the most difficult to place because employers may wonder what is wrong with him, or be leery of paying a master's level salary when the candidate has not yet proven his ability to effectively apply what he learned in school. (There are some fields in which this is less true, primarily in the sciences). Learning what to build up, what to play down and what to leave out is important in matching.

In Career Development, the goal of good matching is not just to get the candidate a job, but to help him get one he loves and in which he can be promoted. If the candidate loves what he does and feels like he belongs, he will automatically work harder and learn more, thus distinguishing himself as someone who is promotable. When you do successful matching, everyone wins! The employer gains a great employee, the candidate gets a job he loves and you get a great reputation and repeat business. You also have an employee on the inside who is loyal to you because you helped him get his job; as he is promoted, he can help you get job leads and special consideration for other candidates. For more information on matching and cultivating employer relationships, see *WNTS' Employer Cultivation Manual.*

The Key Questions to Ask when Making a Good Match

1) **Job Skill:** Does the candidate have the ability to do the work required?

2) **Personality:** Does the candidate's personality fit the company culture; does he share interests with the interviewer?

3) **Stability:** Will the employer believe the candidate is trustworthy, dependable and going to stay with the company for a reasonable length of time?

4) **Presentation:** Does the candidate match the company image in dress, hygiene, speaking voice, language, etc.?

5) **Goals:** Does the candidate share similar goals or motivation with the company?

NOTE: In matching, "company" can also apply to the hiring manager since he has the final say.

Key Point

Do not become too intimidated by matching; rather, make it a skill you are always improving. Do not be afraid of the employer. Let her teach you and share her expertise as you assist her in finding well matched candidates. Matching is what makes the difference between an excellent placement agency which receives consistent repeat business and a mediocre program which is always searching for new employers.

Quantified Selling Point	Not A Match and Why	Good Match
Master's in Business Management… but no business experience	**Underqualified**: Management position, because he has not yet learned how to practically apply his knowledge gained in school within the industry.	Entry-level management training program where he can gain work experience and basic managing experience, while building a relationship with the company.
15 years experience as an accountant… but out of field for last five years	**Overqualified**: Assistant Bookkeeper position at a mid-size company, because the employer may fear he won't stay, won't be satisfied with the salary or will vie with the bookkeeper for control.	Accountant for a large or small firm with multiple accountants so he is among peers and can ask questions if needed.
20 years experience as head cook supervising a staff of 20…but in a prison setting	**Wrong "Pedigree"**: Chef position at a four star restaurant, because he does not come from the "right circles" or possess the "right" credentials, and has not been trained in the "right" schools.	Cook at a boys' ranch or school for problem students. If he can manage 20 inmates, he will have no problem managing youth. He may also share his experience as a deterrent and act as a role model.
Saved last employer over $10K by reducing repair costs via prevention plan… had freedom & authority	**Wrong Environment:** Maint. position where his boss wants him to "just do as he's told," do it "their way" and not change anything.	Maintenance Supervisor for a growing company which is always looking to improve and save money and appreciates an employee who can help do that.
Increased ad sales by 50% in less 6 months while working for an farming magazine… prefers that culture	**Wrong Field of Interest**: Sales position requiring an image with which the candidate is not comfortable, i.e. fashion, fine arts or academia. A good salesman can sell anything, but he must fit the company culture and image.	Sales position for any company in the farming industry whether selling tractors or ad space. Also, sales positions in related industries or industries which share a similar personality and image.

CONCLUSION

"**Luck is a crossroad where preparation and opportunity meet.**" In other words, luck is rarely mere luck, it is the result of being prepared and finding opportunities to apply yourself.

These ten steps may seem tedious and time consuming, but preparing the candidate to overcome employment barriers and market himself as the best candidate for the job is the fastest way to help him get a great job and establish a career. To make a long-term impact, you must become proficient in walking the candidate through this process. Skills that the candidate learns, the improved attitudes he gains and the answers he develops as you go through THE TEN STEP PROCESS will help him secure his next job, and every other job he may need for the rest of his life.

Address the employer's concern,

not merely the question

Job Searching from the Employer's Perspective

In this section the candidate is male and the employer is female.

We have often heard employers complain that they cannot find employees, while on their desk sits a stack of unreviewed applications from uninterviewed candidates. From the employer's perspective, the problem is not that no one is applying for the job, but that no one she wants to hire is applying for the job. Being able to job search successfully is a skill which most of us have never been taught. Even most college graduates lack job search skills. In our line of work, this is an advantage because with a little effort a candidate with serious barriers can appear more qualified than other applicants. However, you must teach him to deliver more than he promises once on the job so the employer sees him as promotable and his career begins.

> *"The person who gets hired is not necessarily the one who can do the job best, but the one who knows the most about how to get hired!"*
>
> Richard Bolles, Author, "What Color is your Parachute"

Job Searching from the Employer's Perspective is a compilation of excerpts from the WNTS' *Career Development Workshop Series.* Our hope is that this information will help market each candidate successfully for a job in his field of interest, which utilizes his current skills and provides an opportunity to advance toward his long-term goals and dream job.

As the title implies, this section is written from the employer's perspective, since she is the "customer" to whom the candidate must market himself. When seeking an employee, the employer does not have time to waste reading resumés and interviewing candidates who are

The Seven Keys to Marketing your Candidate

1) Determining the Candidate's Target Market
2) Understanding the Employer's Needs and How the Candidate Meets Them
3) Developing a Clear, Concise, Compelling and Friendly Presentation
4) Getting an Appointment with the Employer
5) Making the Presentation to the Employer
6) Closing the Sale
7) Delivering on His Promises

not qualified to fill the positions. She will not read between the lines to determine if a candidate has the skills and knowledge to do the job. She expects the candidate to clearly state why he believes he is the best applicant for the job. She is assessing not only job skills, but also whether his personality, image, goals and dependability match the company's needs.

Often the candidate fails to take the time to investigate what the employer needs and why. Instead, his focus is on his need to quickly find a good job within his field of interest, which pays the salary he needs to maintain a comfortable lifestyle. Often, he does not even understand the hiring or **The Screen Out Process**, which leaves him little power in determining their outcome and adds to his anxiety. Below is a chart which describes The Screen Out Process. The boxes across the top show the general employer concern, the boxes along the left hand side show various stages in the job search process and the dotted lines denote in which stage(s) the concerns are most closely assessed. Understanding this process and using the information contained in the following pages will return some control to your candidate.

The Screen Out Process	Interest & Availability	Ability & Quantified Edu., Exper.	Attitude & Motivation	Dependability	Presentation	Honesty	Cost
Answering the Advertisement	■						
Written Presentation	■	■	■				
Employment Interview	■	■	■	■	■	■	
Reference Checks	■	■	■	■	■	■	
Salary Negotiations	■		■				■

1   Determining The Candidate's Target Market

To determine the candidate's target market, identify the candidate's fields of interest. There are many aptitude assessments, skills inventories, interest inventory tests, field discovery games and interview techniques you can use to do this. For more information, see *WNTS' Job Searching from the Employer's Perspective Workshop, Teacher's Edition*, contact a local community college career testing office, visit your library or book store, or request a JIST Product Catalog by calling (800) 648-5478. Once you have identified the skills the candidate wants to use and the field in which he wants to work, brainstorm to determine which industries within that field need his skills. For example, if a candidate is interested in the hospitality field and is skilled as a cook, the industries he may approach include hotel, resort, cruise ships and airlines. If he is interested in the medical field and skilled as a cook, possible industries include hospitals, nursing homes, hospice, board and care homes, nutritional education programs and in-home care services. If he is interested in working with youth and is skilled as a cook, he may approach schools, camps, orphanages, youth centers, juvenile detention centers and restaurants at amusement parks. If you are unsure what industries exist in a field, call employers or college professors within the field and ask.

Need a Job Now?

PowerTip

Job searching is a process which has a normal course. There is little you can do to rush an employer in her decision, other than meeting all her needs. The length of the "hiring process," the period between the first interview and when the candidate starts work, varies with the level of employment being sought. Traditionally, for unskilled labor it is one week; for skilled labor and entry-level professional positions it is one week to one month; for management level positions it is one month to six months; for upper-level management it is six months to one year; and for executive-level it is more than a year.

For candidates who cannot wait the traditional amount of time, we suggest finding work assignments through a temporary placement agency or day-labor company, taking a position one level lower and working back up, seeking a job in a field which hires quickly (i.e., construction, fast food service, telemarketing), responding to "help wanted" signs or using your personal network to find immediate openings. It is also important to remember that smaller companies are able to make decisions faster than large corporations, since often the person who will make the final decision will also conduct the interviews.

Sample Solution

TEACH A NEW SKILL

The yellow pages of your local phone book is an excellent tool for identifying potential employers within a given field or industry. Once the candidate knows what position he would like to hold, have him read through the index found at the front of the yellow pages. If your yellow pages does not contain an index, have him scan through the book, looking at the categories listed across the tops of the pages. These index entries and categories represent various fields and industries. As he reads the categories, have him make a list of all those which could use his skills and in which he would enjoy working. Once he has identified the fields or industries, have him choose one to approach first, then help him tailor his one minute telephone script to the field and position. His script, which contains his top three Quantified Selling Points for the position, should market him to the employer. Now have him turn to the chosen section and begin making cold calls to local employers presenting his qualifications and asking if they, have a need for someone with his skills.

2 Understanding The Employer's Needs & How The Candidate Meets Them

We have found that the employer's needs are divided into five major areas—ability, attitude, motivation, image and dependability. All five of these needs must be met in order for the candidate to be employable. But, depending upon the industry, position and personal preference, employers prioritize the five areas differently. Your job is to ensure that the candidate can articulate how he meets the employer's needs in each of these areas. Below is a brief explanation about why each area is important to the employer, and a few ideas on how the candidate can demonstrate that he meets her needs.

Adopting Your Employer's Priorities

A friend of mine worked in the accounting office of a large HMO. Her supervisor's priority was to get the work done. He did not care if she came in an hour late as long as her reports were on time, which often meant staying two or three hours longer, working weekends or taking work home. He was very pleased with her performance. When the department got a new supervisor, the priorities changed. The new supervisor's main concern was regulating each person's hours so the office ran on a strict 8 a.m. to 5 p.m. schedule. She believed a bad example was being set by some of her most productive, senior staff members, giving permission to lower-level and lazy workers to produce even less. My friend was no longer allowed to be late or to make-up her time in the evenings or weekends. She had to be at her desk by 8 a.m. every morning. If she wanted to keep her job.

Ability (Job Skills)

Employees who bring needed skills, education or experience are able to produce results more quickly and require less training. This makes the company money sooner and saves them money on training. Therefore, a candidate's basic ability or experience using specific job skills plays an important role in who the employer will hire. However, most employers also agree that it is easier to teach a new employee job skills than to teach him to be dependable, have a good attitude or become motivated to work in the best interests of the company. Ability is weighed against these other factors.

To determine whether the candidate has the basic ability or specific skills the employer needs, ask the question, "Can you do the job?" If the answer is "yes," help the candidate prove it by a combination of the following:

Demonstrate the Skill the Employer Needs

Marcus' Work Motivation Inventory showed that his highest priority was having control over how much income he earned. We discovered that commission sales or having his own business would give him the type of control he wanted and agreed that he should start with commission sales because he did not have the capital required to start his own business. After reviewing his areas of interest and specialized knowledge, he choose car sales as his target job. He investigated which local dealership was the best and decide he wanted to work there, although I encouraged him to start with a less competitive position (he proved me wrong!). He went to the dealership early in the morning and spoke with the manager, explaining why he would be a great salesman for the dealership. Five minutes into the conversation, the manager asked what dealership he was presently working for. When Marcus said he was not working, the manager informed him that they found their salesmen by hiring away the top performers of other dealerships. Marcus would not be dissuaded. He stayed at the lot the entire day and evening refusing to leave until the manager gave him a chance to prove himself. Before leaving, the manager finally agreed to hire him on a two-week trial basis, saying, "If you show as much determination with the customers as you have with me, you will be our best salesman." Demonstrating the skills the employer needs is a great way to get the job.

- ◇ Detailing related work history
- ◇ Noting related education, whether vocational training, internships, seminars, apprenticeships, mentor relationships or formal education
- ◇ Creating a Skills Resumé which highlights all related skills, including transferable skills from hobbies, daily life, volunteerism, and possibly prison and recovery program work assignments
- ◇ Developing Quantified Selling Points which include examples, percentages, ratios or numbers
- ◇ Demonstrating the skills the employer needs
- ◇ Listing awards received for outstanding job skills
- ◇ Scoring well on a skills test given by the employer
- ◇ Volunteering for a project which could demonstrate that he possesses the needed skills
- ◇ Suggesting the employer hire him temporarily while they continue their search

Attitude (Personality)

Employees with good attitudes create a better work environment, are easier to supervise and are often more willing to learn and go the extra mile. This allows for healthy staff relations and increased productivity. Employees with good attitudes also give better customer service by making customers feel pampered, welcome and special, so they will return and bring friends. This creates higher profits. Attitude is often the deciding factor in a hiring decision.

To determine whether the candidate has the appropriate attitude, ask the question, "Do others want to work with you?" If the answer is "yes," help the candidate prove it by a combination of the following:

◇ Holding himself in a comfortable, approachable manner, smiling naturally and looking the employer pleasantly in the eye

◇ Speaking in a pleasant and confident tone

◇ Demonstrating a sense of humor, with a sense of appropriateness

◇ Never speaking negatively about past employers, co-workers or companies, although he may mention positive preferences

◇ Showing a willingness to learn and asking good questions while interacting with the employer

◇ Offering good personal references (now is the time to share his professional network)

◇ Sharing positive remarks given during a review or evaluation on a past job that praised his attitude, ability to get the job done without complaining or impact as a great team player

◇ Having been promoted, made a team leader or elected to represent others on a committee or project

◇ Having been elected to a post by a group of people, such as the treasurer of the PTA, volunteer of the year or "team mom" for a child's sports team

◇ Having received awards for attitude, such as "Most Inspirational" or "Best Customer Service"

◇ Demonstrating care for the community and a willingness to get involved through community volunteerism

◇ Finding things he has in common with the interviewer by "reading" her office. For example, if it is a no-nonsense business setting, he should talk only about the job and his qualifications. If it is decorated with pictures of family, vacation trips and hobbies, talk about areas of common interest before moving into conversation about the job and company.

Image (Presentation and Appearance)

Employers realize that their profit comes through sales, that sales come through marketing, and that marketing depends on the public's perception of the company, which is based largely on customer service given by company employees. In fact, employees determine a company's public image as much as, if not more than, the media or the company spokespersons. Therefore, because a company's profit is directly related to employee presentation, it is important that the candidate reflect the company image. Most companies have a carefully cultivated target market and image. Employees who do not project the company image, in both presentation and physical appearance, may dissuade targeted customers from patronizing the business, which negatively affect profits and reputation. Presentation includes his verbal and non-verbal communication, as well as the car he drives, the lifestyle he leads, the schools he attended, etc. Appearance includes his wardrobe, hairstyle, personal. hygiene, etc.

To determine whether the candidate has the image necessary to succeed in the company and serve their customers, ask the question, "Do you represent their company?" If the answer is "yes," help the candidate prove it by a combination of the following:

Examples of Corporate Images

Conservative Corporate (IBM)

Yuppie (Starbuck's Coffee)

Healthy (The Good Earth)

Casual (Northwest Airlines)

Economical (KIA Car)

Grunge or Trendy (Urban Outfitters)

Youthful & Daring (Mountain Dew)

International (AT&T)

Environmentally or Socially Conscious (Ben & Jerry's)

Family-oriented (McDonald's)

◇ Knowing and sharing the company's goals and attitudes
◇ Researching the company so he is familiar with their products/services, locations, accolades, reputation, plans for expansion, market share, corporate structure and history
◇ Demonstrating that his use of industry vocabulary, speaking and writing style and knowledge of the industry matches or exceeds that of other good employees within the company
◇ Demonstrating that his style of clothing, hairstyle, jewelry, body language, etc. match that of other good employees within the company at his level
◇ Demonstrating that where he was raised, where he went to school, what his hobbies and interests are, what he drives, where he lives, etc. match that of other good employees within the company at his level
◇ Demonstrating that who he knows, who knows him and who he has chosen as his mentors matches or exceeds that of other good employees within the company at his level
◇ Demonstrating that he understands the importance of loyalty to the company as an employee, but also as a customer by using the company products/services and encouraging family and friends to do so
◇ Showing interest in company activities, such as a United Way Campaign, training seminars, 4th of July picnics and office parties

Motivation (Goals)

Employees whose motivation and goals match those of the company will work harder, produce better results and be more promotable—all of which produce a better public image and generate profits. To remain competitive, employers need this type of employee. Employees whose motivation and goals do not match the company's often do not work in the best interests of the company. They have a higher turnover rate and are less willing to learn and go the extra mile. This results in more personnel problems, lower productivity and the need to hire and train new employees more often.

To determine whether the candidate's motivation and goals match or will be of benefit to employer, ask the question, "Will your goals benefit the company?" If the answer is "yes," help the candidate prove it by a combination of the following:

◇ Understanding that PROFIT is the company's number one goal, knowing how he affects profit and being able to give examples of how he can maintain costs and make or save company money

◇ Demonstrating his ability to learn the supervisor's priorities and do them first

◇ Researching the company's goals and values and showing that his are similar

◇ Understanding how his professional growth benefits the company

◇ Understanding how the company's growth and success affect him

◇ Showing a strong desire to work in the particular company or position

◇ Taking a course to improve his skills

◇ Being willing to commit for at least three years

◇ Showing a willingness to teach others (managers must be able to do this)

◇ Maintaining a positive and productive professional network

◇ Asking perceptive questions during the interview

◇ Sharing examples which demonstrate that he is a self-starter, takes initiative, will go the extra mile and deliver more than is promised (i.e., an accounting clerk who produces reports with graphics, a waitress who memorizes customer's names, a warehouseman who sweeps up after moving boxes and a secretary who stays until the project is completed)

Dependability (Trustworthiness)

Almost all employers list dependability and attitude as the two most important qualities in an employee. Most employers resent having to shift their focus from running the company to ensuring that employees are dependable and trustworthy. Employees who are regularly absent or late produce less, cause personnel problems and are often let go, resulting in the need to hire and train new employees. Employees who steal, sell information to competitors or make deals not in the best interests of the company cost American businesses billions of dollars each year. It does not matter how good a worker the candidate is if the employer cannot depend on him. Generally, dependability is the top priority for jobs which require one person to complete work before the next person can complete his/her work, i.e., assembly line, accounting, waitressing. Trustworthiness is particularly important if the candidate has access to money, merchandise or valuable information.

To determine how the candidate can demonstrate dependability, ask the questions, "Are you stable?" and "Are you trustworthy?" If the answers are "yes," help the candidate prove it by a combination of the following:

◇ Showing a consistent work history

◇ Never speaking negatively about past employers or co-workers

◇ Actively participating in a local church, a service organization or a respected social group

◇ Demonstrating a desire to work for the particular company by knowing the company's goals and advancement opportunities

◇ Sharing examples of loyalty, such as cultivating customers through friends and family, speaking positively about past employers and co-workers or having given a two-week notice to a past employer

◇ Demonstrating trustworthiness by explaining why stealing company time, money, merchandise or information is not a part of his value system

◇ Always delivering more than promised and more than expected, such as assuming "on time" means 5-15 minutes early, being willing to work through some lunch hours and regularly staying 5-15 minutes late to get the job done

◇ Having a reliable method of transportation, i.e., a car, a bike, a knowledge and use of public transportation and schedule, a residence within walking distance ora willingness to join the company car pool

◇ Having taken a low number of sick days in a previous job

◇ Having a reliable phone message service where professional phone messages can be taken

◇ Calling early to reschedule when running late

◇ Showing emotional stability, by not being easily angered, depressed, anxious or worried

◇ Not discussing personal problems, such as marital, financial, single parenthood, alcohol or drug addiction or children

◇ Residing in the same location or area for a considerable time span

◇ Demonstrating good physical health, such as the absence of chronic illness, exercising regularly, eating healthily or having a plan for dealing with stress

◇ Having good credit or a clean Department of Motor Vehicles record

◇ Having reliable child care and a plan for when his child is ill

◇ Demonstrating the ability to do multiple tasks simultaneously, i.e., working, going to school, raising a family and volunteering

◇ Showing that he is eager to return to work, not merely desperate for money

3 Developing A Clear, Concise, Compelling And Friendly Presentation

Every step in the hiring process and the interview—from the application to interview questions to reference checks—is geared toward assessing whether or not the candidate can meet the employer's need in the five categories mentioned above. Once you have identified the candidate's target market, determined the employer's needs and ascertained how the candidate can meet them, you must help the candidate to develop his presentation.

The first consideration in developing an excellent presentation is to become familiar with your options for presenting the candidate to the employer. Because the employer is the "customer" in the job search process, we must consider all of the ways she assesses whether the candidate meets her needs. When we do this, we find that the four main options for presentation are:

◇ the candidate's written presentation
◇ the candidate's verbal presentation
◇ the candidate's non-verbal presentation
◇ others' verbal presentation about the candidate

The employer uses tools from each of the four options to draw her conclusions. Therefore, the candidate must be prepared to present himself using all four. As you work with candidates you will find that each candidate is stronger in some areas and weaker in others. Your task, once you are familiar with the four areas and the approaches used to present the candidate in each is to determine which are his areas of strength, which specific approaches he will use and how he will minimize his weaknesses. The next section presents a brief explanation of the approaches used in each of the four areas.

Developing the Approach

The key to an excellent approach, is knowing how the employer assesses whether a candidate meets her **PowerTip** needs, familiarize yourself with the four options for presentation and understand the various tools in each option for presentation.

Written Presentation

Employment applications are designed to obtain basic information, reveal "red flags" and help employers find reasons NOT TO HIRE the candidate. To be hired, especially for an entry-level position which does not request a resumé, the candidate must have a good application. Have the candidate complete an application, then read it as if you were the employer. Look for "red flags, " such as inconsistencies, poor reasons for leaving a job, gaps in work history, lack of strong references or a criminal record. Address each area using the information contained in the The Ten Step Process and APPLICATION/RESUME entry of the Encyclopedia of Barriers. For more information, also see WNTS' *Creating A Winning Application & Resumé Workshop, Teacher's Edition* and WNTS' *Professional Correspondence for Employment Programs*. If the candidate's application is particularly weak, help him market himself with other tools such as a strong skills resumé, an employment proposal, the telephone, networking and the employment interview. These techniques will allow him to explain any obvious problems and give the employer a chance to decide that she likes him before seeing the application.

Resumés and cover letters are a great opportunity to present the candidate positively. However, a traditional chronological resumé may not work well with your candidates because it depends upon a strong work history and may highlight weaknesses rather than strengths. Fortunately, "skills resumés," which can easily be written to highlight transferable skills and selling points are increasingly common. This style of resumé minimizes the focus on work history and highlights the candidate's qualifications, regardless of where they are gained. Therefore, you can concentrate on the positive and pull qualifications from areas such as life experience, hobbies, volunteer work, recovery program activities and prison work assignments. Always include a brief work history at the bottom to validate the resumé and avoid suspicion, but realize that employers will have scanned the list of qualifications, experiences and skills before reviewing the chronology.

All resumés should be sent with a brief, personal cover letter which presents how the candidate learned of the opening, expresses the candidate's desire to interview for the position and focuses the reader on specific qualifications. The cover letter should always be addressed to the individual hiring, not merely to a department title or the Human Resources Department. The candidate should always follow-up after sending a resumé and cover letter by calling to schedule an interview.

When using the internet to post a resume, consider the requirements of preparing and submitting an effective Electronic Resume. This is outlined in *Using the Internet and the World Wide Web in Your Job Search* by Fred E. Jandt and Mary B. Nemnich, published and available through JIST at (800) 648-5478.

Proposal letters are similar to business proposals in that they offer a service and outline how the company will benefit from working with the candidate. They are particularly helpful in answering blind ads, submitting employment requests to several companies within the same industry or in assessing the employment climate within an industry when entering a new city. This type of proposal letter is most often used with professional-level positions.

Proposal letters can also be used to create new positions for all levels of candidates. To do this, identify the candidate's skills and interests, then determine which employers could benefit from his qualifications. Design a position which requires your candidate's qualifications and meets the employer's need. Now you are ready to market the candidate as the perfect (and only!) contender for the position. This is an excellent tool to use with candidates who have extreme barriers and cannot realistically compete for traditional positions, or candidates who are creative and want to do something new. There are several good books on this topic. For more information, see your local book store or the JIST catalog at (800) 648-5478.

Thank you notes are a simple way to make a profound and lasting impression on an employer. Rarely are employers extended this courtesy after a lengthy phone conversation or interview—especially for entry-level positions. After each interview, have the candidate send the interviewer a personal thank you note which includes the candidate's full name, the time and date of the interview, an appropriate thank you, a mention of something that happened during the interview (i.e., a common interest, inside joke, pleasant incident, tour of the facility or introduction to company employees), a reiteration of a major selling point, an expression of the candidate's desire to work with the company and a mention of the next step.

Creating your Own Job

A colleague worked with a single mother on welfare who lived in a local shelter. She planned to share a small house with another single mom, but needed more money than she had been able to save. She had never worked and did not have a high school education, but she was pleasant, motivated and had great presentation. Her skills included talking with people, handling money, driving, knowledge of the small town and a clean driving record.

Based on her skills, her desire to be self-employed and because she had recently bought her first car (a good used car donated to the shelter), and could purchase reasonable insurance, we determined that she could approach video stores located near pizza parlors and propose that they use her to deliver "Pizza & A Movie." The colleague suggested that whenever someone called the video store to ask if a certain movie was available, the attendant ask if they wanted the video delivered for an extra $2.00, and whether they would also like a medium pizza delivered for only $10.00 more. When customers called the pizza parlor they would be asked if they would like a movie delivered for only $4.00 more. They proposed that she work for $3.00 per delivery, plus tips. The first two video stores she approached were hesitant to try the new idea, but soon she found a video store and pizza parlor which saw the possibilities for increasing their customer base. She worked one day a week distributing flyers produced by the businesses and worked four nights a week. Most nights she made more than double minimum wage. Also, she could bring her baby to work.

Sample Solution

Teach A New Skill

Here is an example of an effective thank you note.

Dear John: I enjoyed interviewing with you on Friday, April 14 at 3:00 p.m. Thank you for your time and consideration. I especially enjoyed the tour of the Customer Service Department. It is obvious that we share a similar attitude about customers—make them feel special and they will return. Give my thanks to Larry for showing me around. I am excited about the possibility of working with Effertone and believe my sales experience and personality will be a great asset. I look forward to hearing from you by Wednesday to schedule a second interview. Thank you. Sincerely, Melinda N. Yardley.

The thank you note should be hand written, unless the candidate's handwriting is bad, and sent within 24 hours of the interview. If the employer plans to make a hiring decision before the note arrives, have the candidate dress appropriately and drop it off in person.

Work samples are often the best way to prove a candidate's ability to do the job. Samples may be introduced when the candidate initially meets the employer, presented during an employment interview or sent with a thank you note. A few examples of work samples used by our candidates include a young man who detailed and shined his car before interviewing with auto detailing shops, a woman who took a portfolio of flyers she had created for children's programs and activities when she interviewed with the city Parks & Recreation Department, a teenager who brought a portfolio of his drawings and the characters he had created when he applied as a sales clerk at an upscale comic book shop and an accounting clerk who brought a sample year-end report with complex graphics and charts when interviewing at accounting firms. One of our most unique uses of a work sample was an airplane mechanic who sent a photograph of himself fixing a 747 along with his thank you note.

Letters of reference and introduction. Employers listen to other employers, so the endorsement of another professional to consider a candidate can be a powerful tool in getting the job. Have the candidate consider who in his past or present network would be appropriate and willing to write a letter of recommendation. A former teacher, professor or trade school instructor, a professional mentor, a supervisor of a volunteer project or a business acquaintance would be appropriate. Letters of reference should also be secured from past employers who are difficult to contact, out of business or located out of state. Each letter of reference should include how the writer knows the candidate, general selling points about his attitude, work ethic, dependability and professionalism, and specific praise for certain skills he possesses, projects he was involved in, tasks he accomplished or awards he received. Remember that counselors, case managers and 12-step sponsors should be listed as friends so that no additional "red flags" are raised. When approaching people to write these letters, the candidate should be ready to provide them with a sample and basic guidelines so the letters are excellent. The candidate may also request that they send one letter specific to the position(s) he is presently seeking and a general letter to be used in the future. As his employment counselor, you may choose to write a letter of introduction presenting the candidate to employers. Whether the employer knows you or not, your observations and encouragement to consider the candidate (with good reason) can make a difference. Your letter should include the information listed above.

Verbal Presentation

Telephone contacts are a great way for the candidate to approach employers and schedule interviews. The telephone is the best tool for candidates who have a weaker presentation in person or on paper. It is also a great tool for those who are particularly good on the phone or those seeking positions which require extensive phone work. To be successful, the candidate must be familiar with basic phone etiquette, use a pleasant tone of voice and have a brief script which includes his top three Quantified Selling Points for the position. He should get the full name of the person who has the power to hire him and move past the receptionist to speak with that person directly. Once he gets the hiring manager's attention, he should present his script, inquire as to whether she needs someone with his qualifications and arrange a time to interview. For more information on how to create and use a phone script, see WNTS' *Finding A Job With The Telephone Workshop, Teacher's Edition.*

Answers to interview questions are crucial in the hiring process. The candidate must have good answers to commonly asked interview questions, as well as those which are particularly difficult or frightening for him. He must also be prepared to discuss salary and ask appropriate questions of the interviewer. To develop good answers to difficult interview questions and address other interview barriers, use THE TEN STEP PROCESS and the information in the ENCYCLOPEDIA OF BARRIERS. To learn more about the interview process, commonly asked questions, salary negotiations, and questions to ask the interviewer, see WNTS' *Interview For Success, Teacher's Manual.*

Sense of humor. It is important that the candidate display an appropriate sense of humor which demonstrates that he is both pleasant and mature. In general, the American business culture is uncomfortable with people who lack a sense of humor. If you perceive that the candidate lacks an appropriate sense of humor, observe him throughout your interaction, ask other staff members about their impressions and ask his personal references about these issues. If the candidate needs to improve these skills, ask his permission to call attention to specific incidences when his behavior is inappropriate. With each incident, articulate your impressions, what you assume about him as a result and how an employer might perceive it. Help him determine an alternative way to he can act or speak. If the candidate does not display an appropriate sense of humor, he needs to learn at least to laugh at others' jokes. Teach the candidate to become aware of smiling when people tell appropriate jokes. If necessary, teach the candidate that sexual, racial and religious jokes or comments are ALWAYS inappropriate when interacting with potential employers and co-workers and that it is best to err on the side of caution.

Language skills create perceptions about the candidate's level of education, maturity, professionalism and intelligence. They will be used to determine whether the candidate fits the company image, has the ability to do the job and is promotable. Language and communication skills cannot be learned overnight, so be sure candidates with weak language skills have an effective written presentation, strong references and are well matched to each position. Using the information contained in the COMMUNICATION SKILLS entry of the ENCYCLOPEDIA OF BARRIERS, help the candidate eliminate slang, minimize a speech impediment or accent and correct grave mistakes. Also, help him begin using the latest industry vocabulary, develop a brief script to use on the phone and practice approaching employers in person. He may also need to do several mock interviews to feel more comfortable and prepared for employment interviews. If his language skills are particularly bad and require extensive time to correct, match him to a position and company which will accept his present language skills. Then help him improve these skills and find a better job as his language skills improve.

Non-Verbal Behavior

In general, non-verbal behavior often speaks louder than words. Below we have explored a few non-verbal behaviors which are important in the interviewing process. As you identify additional non-verbal behaviors which keep your candidates from getting hired, use the information and the samples below, as well as THE TEN STEP PROCESS and the ENCYCLOPEDIA OF BARRIERS, to develop your own solutions.

Appearance is everything! Well, not everything, but it is very important in the hiring process. In addition to demonstrating whether the candidate matches the company image, appearance prompts the employer to make assumptions about the candidate's ability, motivation level and professionalism. Remember, the employer only has a few means by which to assess the candidate, so she will glean as much as she can from each. Therefore the candidate must have good basic hygiene, an appropriate wardrobe and an acceptable hair and make-up style. His appearance should also be tailored to the industry and company as much as possible. If necessary, have the candidate visit the business or call and ask about the dress code and image before interviewing. Use the information in the APPEARANCE entry of the Encyclopedia of Barriers to help address these issues.

Posture is often taken as an indicator of level of confidence, ability, interest, maturity, motivation and energy. Appropriate posture varies from industry to industry. However, in general, if the candidate slumps his shoulders, sits too casually, stands with one hip cocked to the side or walks in a way that communicates anything other than professionalism, he needs improvement before meeting employers in person. If a male candidate sits very casually— leaning way back with his legs sprawled apart and his arms hanging down or roped across his chest—have him envision professional men who hold positions into which he wants to be promoted. Ask him how they sit, walk and stand. Explain that to be successful and promotable, when in professional settings, he needs to take on the posture of these men. Have him sit upright and determine what to do with his arms and legs. We usually have him decide how closely he can keep his knees together and still be comfortable (10" to 15") and have him place his hands gently on his thighs or in his lap. Have him practice sitting this way during your meetings. The same techniques can be used to adjust how he stands and walks. If your female candidates are not used to wearing skirts, jackets or high heels, do the same. Suggest that candidates practice their new posture in public to see the difference in others' reactions. In our experience, candidates are shocked at the improved service, amount of positive attention and number of "hellos" and smiles they get.

Facial expressions and eye contact are key factors when approaching employers in person and during the interview. A pleasant smile, inviting expression and comfortable eye contact will allow employers to feel at ease with the candidate. If the candidate has distracting facial expressions—an overly big smile, a furrowed brow, a staring gaze or poor eye contact—it must be addressed. Have the candidate watch himself talk in a mirror, or videotape one of your meetings so he can observe the behavior. Then, help him adjust his behavior so it will be acceptable to the employer and comfortable for him. He should practice during your meetings and in other selected situations, such as informational interviews, telephone conversations, in church or at the market so he can get used to the new facial expressions.

Learn A New Skill

Sample Solution

Some non-verbal communication can be difficult to discuss, such as body odor, weight, make-up, hairstyle and bad breath, because the candidate may become embarrassed.

During your first meeting, explain that at times you will have to say difficult things, but that you only do it because you want the candidate to succeed. Ask permission to express your observations and talk honestly about potentially embarrassing issues. A trick we use to make this more comfortable for the Career Developer is to end each meeting by asking, "Let's see, is there anything difficult I wanted to address today?," thinking for a second, then replying, "No, not today," and closing the meeting by talking about how well the candidate is doing. Then when we needed to address a difficult issue, we could pose the same question, mention the problem and some solutions, then close the meeting with something positive. This allowed the candidate to feel successful, but also paved the way for us to mention difficult issues.

Handshake. A firm handshake communicates confidence and ability. If the candidate's handshake is limp, a bone-crusher, offers only the fingers or nearly pulls your arm out of the socket, it needs work. Spend a few minutes practicing how to appropriately shake an employer's hand. Shake hands with the candidate each time you begin and end a meeting so he becomes comfortable. Be sure a male candidate does not insist upon shaking a woman's hand by grabbing her fingers only—this may be appropriate in social settings but can be offensive in a professional situation. Also, be sure your female candidates do not offer only their fingers or feel the need to prove that they are "as good as a man" by gripping too hard.

Outside References

Good references from past employers, personal friends and professional acquaintances can make a powerful impression on an employer. The employer is trying to make an educated hiring decision, and the endorsement of other professionals can help her do that. To help the candidate cultivate good references:

1) have him list the names of everyone he knows who works in the field in which he would like to work. He should consider past co-workers, direct supervisors and other department supervisors, professors, church associates, 12-step associates, parents of childrens' friends, family members, school mates, etc.

2) then, have him narrow the names by placing an asterisk (*) next to those who live in the area, are respected in the field or have been in their current position for at least three years.

3) next, have him review the names with an asterisk next to them and circle those he has spoken with in the last year.

Treat Everyone Professionally

Alfred, the hiring manager for a major department store, gave his secretary a stack of sticky notes with strict instructions to write her impressions about each job candidate who came in. If she wrote anything negative, he immediately discarded the resume, realizing that any candidate who was rude to her did not have the attitude Alfred was looking for.

4)   reviewing the names he has circled, have him choose the most impressive to contact about acting as a reference for him.

When talking with those who agree to act as references, he should tell them about the specific position(s) and the types of industries he is pursuing, as well as specifically how he meets the employer's needs, so the references can "sell" him to the employer.

You can also act as a reference for the candidate by using your own professional network to provide direct referrals to employers with whom you have built a relationship. Another key aspect of making an excellent presentation using outside references is the candidate's interaction with the employer's receptionist or secretary. It is important that he ALWAYS make a positive impression on her by learning her name and being appropriately friendly, because she often has the power to screen him out.

4   Getting An Appointment With The Employer

Now that you are familiar with the four areas used to develop a presentation, you are ready to decide how the candidate will present himself to get an appointment with the employer. To determine whether to present him primarily on paper, in person, over the phone or by using his network, carefully review each of the four areas, considering the candidate's strengths and barriers, as well as the industry he is approaching. The candidate should conduct his job search as if he were working full-time, and schedule as many appointments to meet with employers as possible. The information below will help determine which approach is best for the candidate, and assist him in getting an appointment with an employer and help him prepare to make his presentation.

Who's the Boss?

The Human Resource Department does not decide who to hire—only who NOT to hire. Find out who will make the final decision, usually a department head or hiring manager, and address all correspondence to them.

PowerTip

Telephone

The telephone allows the candidate to contact a large number of hidden market employers in a short amount of time. It is more personal than mailing out resumés and often leads to an interview before the candidate has to complete an application. Using the telephone works best if the candidate develops a one minute telephone script which highlights his Quantified Selling Points. The telephone is a good approach for candidates who:

◇ speak English well, have a nice phone voice and have practiced their phone script.

◇ want to avoid completing an application until after the interview, due to "red flags" on the application (i.e., a prison record, gaps in work history or a change in field of work).

◇ do not make a good first impression in person.

◇ are very comfortable and professional over the phone.

◇ are applying for positions which require a lot of phone work.

Good Application

The application can be a good tool if the candidate takes the time to market himself on it, and if he does not have any "red flags" which are highlighted on the application. However, when used alone, the application is the least effective tool. To make it more effective, the candidate can deliver it directly to the hiring manager, introduce himself and schedule an interview, or follow it up with a phone call. It is a good approach for candidates who:

◇ do not have "red flags" which appear on the application.
◇ have good skills and Quantified Selling Points in the field or position for which they are applying.
◇ have a strong work history.
◇ have developed a model application and have extremely neat handwriting.
◇ are willing to dress for success, return the application in person and introduce themselves to a hiring manager.
◇ do not speak English well, but have a strong model application, nice handwriting and have a strong personal presentation.

Skills Resumé

Skills resumés are an excellent tool for building the candidate's self-esteem and for marketing him as a benefit to the employer. For these reasons, we believe that a skills resumé should be developed for each candidate, regardless of whether the employer will require it. A skills resumé is particularly helpful for candidates who:

◇ have low self-esteem.
◇ have "red flags" which appear on the application, but can be minimized or avoided on a skills resumé.
◇ have specific qualifications which come from a combination of non-employment and employment sources.
◇ have skills which qualify them for a job, but no formal work history or education related to these skills.
◇ have education and knowledge which qualifies them for a job, but no work history or practical experience in which they have applied the information.
◇ want to transfer their skills from one field or position into a new field or position.
◇ do not speak English well, but have other skills, experience and knowledge which qualify them for a job.

Chronological Resumé

The chronological resumé is seldom an effective tool for our candidates. It is an effective tool only for candidates who:

◇ have recently held a position in the field in which they are currently pursuing work and have a strong, consistent work history.
◇ have worked for respected companies in the industry in which they are currently pursuing work and have a strong, consistent work history.
◇ have long blocks of employment with the same company or in the same industry and are pursuing positions in an industry in which that is valued.

Walk-in

Walking in and introducing yourself to the manager is effective when approaching businesses in which the manager is readily accessible to customers, and when pursuing a position for which assertiveness is a desired skill. This is an excellent approach for candidates who:

◇ make a good first impression in person and who are articulate.
◇ want to avoid completing an application until after the interview due to "red flags" on the application.
◇ are limited English speakers, but have memorized a brief personal introduction. It will demonstrate personal fortitude, self-confidence and show the employer their "good presentation," desire to work and willingness to learn.

Introduction

Being introduced to the employer by someone she already knows or respects is the BEST means of getting an interview. When possible, the candidate should use this method along with a good resumé, proposal letter or proof of his ability, as described below. It is often used with candidates who:

◇ make a good first impression in-person and who are articulate.
◇ have good contacts within the industry in which they want to work.
◇ want to avoid completing an application until after the interview due to "red flags" on the application.

Proposal Letters

Proposal letters are a great way to gain an employer's interest and get an interview. Because the approach is non-traditional and the position is designed to meet the employer's needs, she may be more willing to listen to the candidate. Because the position is developed based on the candidate's qualifications, he is perfectly suited and the only contender for the job. Proposal letters is best used with candidates who:

◇ want to design their own job and name their own price.

◇ have disabilities and need specially-designed jobs or atmospheres.

◇ have special needs such as unusual hours or unique skills, want to work from their home or have specialized interests.

◇ face barriers which make it very difficult for them to complete against other candidates.

◇ want to avoid completing an application until after the interview due to "red flags" on the application.

Proof

In general, when the employer hires a candidate, she has never seen him perform the tasks needed to do the job. She relies on the four options for presentation approach. If the candidate can prove his ability to do the job, the employer will be more likely to hire him. Therefore, if the candidate has concrete, portable proof of his ability to meet the employer's needs, he should present it to the employer. Proof is a good approach for candidates who have appropriate, portable, concrete proof of their qualifications.

Unable to Secure an Interview

PowerTip

If the candidate is actively approaching employers, but is still unable to secure an interview, you may need to change where you look, change the candidate's presentation approach or correct a specific problem(s) which is hindering him from securing an interview: To identify your next step, do the following:

◇ assess the appropriateness of the employers he is approaching to see if he matches their needs in terms of image, ability and experience

◇ consider whether he is overqualified or underqualified for the position(s) he is seeking

◇ review his Quantified Selling Points and get feedback from employers within the industry

◇ review his application and resumé for "red flags", or ask an employer within the field to do so. If you find one, either adjust the resumé or use an approach which does not require a written presentation

◇ scrutinize his physical appearance and the company image

◇ observe him as he talks with employers over the telephone, including getting through to the person who can hire, voice tone, using industry vocabulary, presenting appropriate selling points and arranging a time to meet

◇ determine how many employers he is approaching each week. The job search is a numbers game—have him contact between 20 and 50 hidden market employers, or 5 to 10 open market employers per day, five days a week

◇ review the candidate's strengths and barriers, as well as the personality of the industry and companies he is pursuing. Reconsider which of the four presentation approaches would work best for him and, if necessary, change his approach and redevelop his presentation.

5   Making The Presentation To The Employer

The interview is a major step in the hiring process. The candidate's presentation must be smooth and natural and should be tailored to the employer's needs. As the employment specialist, you can control the candidate's final written presentation. But the candidate is solely responsible for his final verbal and non-verbal presentation to the employer. Therefore, the candidate must be heavily involved in developing his presentation. He must understand why each new action, answer or attitude is important so he can comfortably integrate it into his personality and style. Only then will it seem natural. Helping him to understand the importance of his verbal and non-verbal presentation and allowing him to develop his in-person presentation will allow him to succeed in his immediate job search, but also to maintain the changes and rely upon them to get promoted and develop his career in the future.

Remind the candidate that his goal in the interview is to market himself, to establish a professional acquaintance with the employer and to interview the interviewer to determine whether he wants

Unable to get Hired

PowerTip

If the candidate is securing interviews and following up with phone calls, but is unable to get hired, do the following:

◆ have the candidate "walk you through" his interview, detailing everything he and the interviewer said and did while you look for problem areas

◆ arrange a mock interview with an employer in the field where he is seeking employment and get detailed feedback from the interviewer

◆ assess his knowledge of the companies with which he is interviewing

◆ assess the appropriateness of the employers he is approaching to see if he matches their image and other needs

◆ reconsider whether he is overqualified or underqualified for the position(s) he is seeking.

◆ review his Quantified Selling Points and get feedback from employers within the industry

◆ scrutinize his physical appearance, considering basic hygiene, how he holds himself, and the company image

◆ review his interview follow-up presentation, i.e., thank you note, follow-up phone call, knowing the next step, sending any information promised.

to work with the company. Nervously sitting in the chair answering only the questions asked is a waste of time.

When meeting with an employer, the candidate must not merely answer her questions. He must address her concerns and demonstrate that he meets her needs. He can do this in many ways, such as demonstrating that his appearance and vocabulary match the company image, showing that he can make or save the company money, sharing his Quantified Selling Points for the position and projecting an attitude which mirrors the company attitude. This requires learning about the company before interviewing and asking good questions when interacting with the employer, then using this information in each progressive interview. For more information on how to developing Quantified Selling Points, see Step 6 in THE TEN STEP PROCESS and WNTS' *Creating A Winning Application & Resumé Workshop, Teacher's Edition.*

An Excellent Presentation

The best way to prepare candidates to make an excellent presentation to employers, **PowerTip** is to choose his approach very carefully. You must help the candidate determine whether his strongest presentation is on paper, in-person, over the telephone or using his network. Then help him utilize each tool to his best advantage. His success depends upon it.

When it comes to interviewing, practice makes perfect. Have the candidate practice his verbal and non-verbal presentation by conducting mock interviews during which he wears his interview outfit. The mock interview will allow you to observe and improve his presentation. As you begin to arrange interviews with employers, remind the candidate that the first six interviews are practice runs for the others. Prepare him beforehand and debrief immediately afterward so he can improve with each experience. Also, schedule interviews with employers who will give you feedback. As you get feedback, meet with the candidate to praise what he is doing well and address concerns. Be sure you wait until the candidate is very comfortable with his presentation to secure interviews with the companies with which he most wants to work, so he will be prepared.

DEVELOP A GOOD ANSWER

When answering an employer's questions, the candidate may either determine the concern behind various interview questions and respond directly to it, or he may ask a clarifying question to be sure he understands the concern and to get additional information.

Sample Solution

For example, if the employer asks if the candidate has a car and he does not, consider the CONCERN behind the question—that the candidate will not be dependable and punctual, or possibly that he is not stable or mature. Rather than merely responding, "No, I do not have a car," the candidate can address the CONCERN by saying, "I choose to use public transportation because I do not like fighting traffic every day. I know the bus system very well and by letting the driver deal with the traffic, I can review my 'to do' list for the day, read the paper and arrive refreshed and ready to work."

If the employer asks whether the candidate has had a drug or alcohol problem and he has had a problem, he can respond with a clarifying question to determine her CONCERN. He can inquire, "Why do you ask? Have you had a problem with that?" He can then listen as the employer reveals her CONCERN, "Yeah, it's been a big problem for us. It has cost us money in damaged merchandise, sick time, rehabilitation fees and employee theft." Once the candidate knows the employer's concern, he can address it directly in a way that makes him an asset. For example, "Well then, you need me because I have had a drug problem, but I have been clean for a year and I am very serious about my recovery. I will be a good example to the other workers. I am able to talk to the guys in a way that perhaps you can't. I will be able to offer those who don't use drugs an alternative group to hang with, and I might even be able to get some of the users to go with me to 12-Step Meetings since you are obviously cracking down and I'm sure they don't want to lose this great job. Additionally I have over two years experience…"

Closing The Sale

Once the candidate has effectively marketed himself using his written, verbal and non-verbal presentation, given strong references, demonstrated that his abilities, attitude, image and goals match the company's and proven that he is dependable, he is ready to close the sale. Most candidates, whether professionals or at an entry-level, fail to do this. The few who do usually get hired. To close the sale, the candidate must:

1) express his desire to work in this position with this company, especially now that he has interviewed and knows more about both.

2) clearly re-state how he meets employer's need, i.e., how he will save or make the company money, solve a problem or provide superior service.

3) avoid discussion money until after the employer is obviously interested in "buying" him. Only then will she consider the high end of the salary range for the position.

4) discover the next step, i.e., when the next interview will be conducted, when a final decision will be made, or when the first day of work is scheduled to be.

The Price Is Right!

PowerTip

If the candidate talks about money too soon he may either eliminate himself from consideration because he asked too much or be hired at a salary lower than would have been offered because he asked too little. When the employer brings up salary before being "sold" on the candidate, suggest the candidate put the ball back in the employer's court by asking, "What salary range did you have in mind for the position?" The employer may try again to get the candidate to mention the first number, but in general, "he who mentions the first number loses." The candidate may be able to get the industries salary range by from an industry publication, a professional acquaintance in the field or the local Chamber Of Commerce.

The employer has a salary range or wage in mind and will divulge it if the candidate puts the ball in her court. Once the candidate knows the salary range, if it seem reasonable, he should say, "That sounds fair," then return to market himself. If it is below the salary range he wanted give a non-committal "hum" and return to marketing how the candidate will make the company money or save the company money, proving he is worth the higher salary. Once the employer is excited about hiring the candidate, then he can begin the salary negotiations. It should take place at the last interview, which for most jobs is the second or third. For management position it may be the fourth or fifth.

Say Thank you!

A single mother who had been on welfare for over twelve years landed her first full-time position due to the professionalism she learned in the WorkNet workshops. The employer called her Career Developer to commend the Career Developer on the quality of her workshops. The employer was most impressed that the candidate had returned within twenty-four hours of her interview to hand-deliver a thank you note for the interviewer. The employer said he had never seen this type of professionalism at this level before, and that it became the deciding factor in offering her the job.

5) follow-up with a thank you note and any additional information he promised to send the employer within twenty-four hours.

6) call two to three days after the final interview to show his continued interest and to inquire as to the status of the hiring decision.

7) keep job searching until hired. A candidate who is pursued by other employers is more desirable than one who no one else wants.

Closing the sale requires the candidate to market himself well, take the lead in salary negotiations, follow up and set himself apart. It is a great way to impress the employer, get the information he needs and get hired. It may also be challenging and uncomfortable for the candidate, but if the candidate fails to close the sale, he may lose the opportunity. For more information on interviewing, closing the sale and salary negotiations, see *WNTS' Interviewing for Success Workshop, Teacher's Edition.*

7   Delivering on His Promises

A candidate should never promise more than he can deliver. In fact, he should make reasonable promises so that he always can go above and beyond what the employer expects. This is true both during the interview and once working. For example, it is better for an employee to call his employer to say that he will be an hour late and show up only 45 minutes late, than to say he will be a half hour late and show up 45 minutes late. The time frame is the same—he was 45 minutes late—but the perception is different. In the first situation he delivered more than promised, in the second he delivered less. Broken promises and unmet expectations in any of the five categories of employer need can devastate the candidate's chances of being hired as well as for performance raises, promotions or job offers from competitors once on the job. Continued involvement and support from you or a professional mentor will help the candidate set reasonable expectations and deliver on his promises.

One of the best ways to ensure that the candidate delivers all that he promised and more is to teach him to "work for advancement." This means that his goal is not merely to keep the job, but to move toward his personal and professional goals. This requires that he be in a job which is somehow connected to his long-term personal or career goals. The keys to working for advancement are:

◆ performing his current duties excellently
◆ representing the company image
◆ networking to find a strong professional mentor and increase his professional contacts.
◆ demonstrating an ability to perform the position into which he wants to be promoted

Practice Exchange with Abundance

PowerTip

One of the key differences between employees who are promotable and those who just keep their job is "exchange with abundance." Exchange with abundance is the belief that doing the extra is a part of doing the job.

Exchange with abundance is the difference between a company which succeeds and one which fails. It is the extra donut you get when you buy a dozen, the Disney toy in your child's meal and the free ice cream cone you get when you drop yours.

Exchange with abundance is the difference between the employee who merely maintains his job or is let go and the one who is promoted. It is seen in the waitress who memorizes her regular customers' names and how they like their coffee, so they are made to feel important, in the receptionist who recognizes clients' voices and the assistant who stays late or comes in early so the project is completed for the big meeting.

◇ practicing "exchange with abundance"
◇ strategically pursuing the next position

Teach your candidates to collect "work credits" as a means of working for advancement. "Work credits" are unspoken points an employee acquires in the mind of their employer or supervisor for doing "the extra." Doing the extra includes:

◇ exceeding expectation by doing his job in an exceptional manner, continuing to learn so the company benefits from his additional knowledge, or establishing himself as the expert within a group as small as his department or as large as the entire industry,

◇ helping the boss with her work load by coming in early or staying late, volunteering for special projects, minimizing personal problems and consistently practicing exchange with abundance, and

◇ making the boss look good by thinking of better ways to get the job done, making the company money, representing his department at company functions or speaking positively about her to her superiors and to key customers.

To earn work credits, the candidate must work hard and smart. "Work credits" are only granted if:

◇ "the extra" meets the employer's need,
◇ the employer is aware of "the extra" and who is doing it. Timing and visibility are important. For example, an employee who wants to gain "work credits" by putting in extra time should come in early if the supervisor works early, and should stay late if she works late, and
◇ "the extra" is perceived as part of the employees' work ethic and the employer believes that it would have been done whether or not she became aware of it.

"Work credits" can be cashed in by employees for benefits such as not having to work a holiday, getting first pick at vacation days, being permitted to leave early on a Friday or if his child gets sick, getting a better office space or being given a raise or promotion. The difference between work credits and "kissing-up" is an employee's attitude overall, the consistency with which the extra is done and the subtleness with which the employer is made aware of the extra.

Teach A New Skill

Sample Solution

The employee must learn to subtly make the employer aware of the extra he is doing. He should be aware of his employer's priorities, choose the most impressive to share with the employer, look for the appropriate time and mention it. The following are a few examples:

◇ "Last night while I was working on the report, I realized ..."

◇ "Tuesday when I took it home to work on, I noticed..."

◇ "I completed most of it over the weekend, then ..."

◇ "I did some research on my own and discovered..."

◇ "I called a friend who has expertise in this area. She suggested..."

◇ "I was telling Marty in the President's office, how much I have learned under your supervision and about the team approach you developed..."

We suggest that if your goal is to assist the candidate to establish a career so he can become truly self-sufficient, rather than just get a job, that you offer at least one year of follow-up counseling. The follow-up can be used to deal with on-the-job problems (benefiting your candidates, your employers and your reputation), assist the candidate in getting raises or promotions, return to school and update his resumé. Most importantly, use the time to help the candidate become his own Career Developer.

The only barriers which cannot be solved are those which you do not take the time to address, or those which the candidate is unwilling to address.

ADDICTION

In this barrier the candidate is male and employer is female.

The employer's concern is that the addict is still drinking or using, or will begin again, resulting in sick days, absences, safety hazards, accidents, a Worker's Compensation claim, poor quality work, damaged or stolen merchandise or company property, and disruptive attitudes. Other concerns include that he will begin dealing drugs on the job, influence other employees to use, or that the company will be required to pay for a recovery program. The employer may also be concerned that the addict will attract the "wrong type of people" to the business, damaging the company image. These occurrences cost employers thousands of dollars every year.

The candidate's concerns may include fear of having to explain a gap(s) in his work history, having been fired, a decrease in responsibility from one job to the next and short job retention. If the addiction led him to the streets, he may lack current work history, current job skills, official identification and a valid driver's license. He may be experiencing fear and anxiety about approaching the business world, fear that having a regular paycheck will create a desire to use again and feelings of self-doubt, especially because he is "clean" now and must relearn to function in various situations.

In General, Addiction

Addiction is a major problem in the United States. Most employers have had to deal with it on some level, whether with employees, family members, friends or personally. Due to its effect on the candidate's ability to work, it cannot be ignored. Candidates must be prepared to take drug tests before being hired, as well as on the job. Those who are still using are not ready to work.

Understand that there is a difference between sobriety and recovery. Sobriety is not using; recovery is a change of attitudes and lifestyle which occurs as the candidate begins to take responsibility for his life and deal with the problems which led to the addiction. Be sure the candidate is actively "recovering" and discover the tools he uses to maintain his recovery—usually the 12-steps of Alcoholics Anonymous or religion. During your meetings, ask him how his recovery is going. Make sure he is attending meetings or religious services weekly and is in regular contact with his sponsor or mentor. Stress the importance of replacing old habits with new habits and old friends with new friends. In our experience, the primary causes of relapse are the stress of an unhealthy relationship, taking on too much at one time, lack of a support network and boredom. If you can refer the candidate to groups, club, community volunteer organizations or churches where he can make friends with people who live healthy, fun, drug-free lives, you will give him the opportunity to see the new habits and attitudes he needs to learn. This will greatly decrease the possibility of relapse and increase his job retention rate.

Provide A Resource

Non-Recovering, Addiction

The candidate who is not in recovery and has caused any of the problems listed in the employer's concern, poses major concerns above, poses major concerns for the employer. To overcome this barrier(s), the candidate must be willing to admit that he has a problem and get help. Remember, both the job seeker and the employer are your clients. Therefore, it would be unwise to refer the candidate, and set the employer up for imminent disaster and the candidate for one more failure. Almost every community has recovery programs. You can find listings for private and free recovery programs, such as The Salvation Army and rescue missions, in the yellow pages of your local phone book. Many of the rescue mission and The Salvation Army recovery programs have excellent facilities and highly qualified staff. We encourage you to visit those in your local community. If the candidate is unwilling to change his attitudes and habits, you can be of no further assistance.

Good Answer...

Recovering, Addiction

Unless the candidate is applying for positions for which former addiction and active recovery are strong selling points (i.e., drug counselor or youth drug/gang prevention), he should not mention his addiction and recovery to the employer. It is common that the candidate will want to answer the question, "Tell me about yourself," with, "I am a grateful recovering addict....," to which we respond, "Great answer, wrong meeting!" This is personal information which the employer does not need to know. Ask the candidate if he thinks it is appropriate to answer the question with, "Well, I have a problem with bad breath," or "I am more attracted to blondes than to red heads." Hopefully he will quickly answer, "Of course not!" Explain to the candidate that if he is actively recovering, has created a strong support system and can pass a drug test, the addiction should not be mentioned to the employer. However, if the employer has had problems with this area in the past, she may ask whether the candidate has used drugs. The candidate must NEVER lie. Rather, he must be prepared with a good answer. Use The Ten Step Process as a guide in developing your answer.

If the candidate fears that a regular paycheck will prove too great a temptation to relapse, have him ask the employer to direct deposit or mail his paychecks to the bank. If he does not have a checking and savings account, assist him in opening them. He might choose to attach the ATM card to a one-signature checking account, which maintains only enough money to pay monthly bills and provides a weekly allowance. He may also want to establish a two-signature savings account which is not attached to the ATM card, and automatic transfer so any remaining funds from the checking account are moved directly into the savings account. Then, anytime he wants money from the savings account, the second signer, chosen by the candidate, must be present. Advise the second signer NEVER to refuse to sign for a withdrawal, because it is the candidate's money and the candidate's life. However, the signer should always ask what the money is for. This will make the candidate accountable for how and why he spends his money. It will help him learn to save, plan for major purchases and give him a chance to think again before relapsing. This will allow him to develop habits so he can hold himself accountable in the future.

Why do You Ask ?

A candidate of ours was asked if he had ever used drugs. He responded by saying, "Why do you ask?' After the employer shared the numerous problems the company has experienced due to drug use on the job, the candidate said the following:

"I won't lie to you, although someone who is 'using' would. Over a year ago I checked myself into a recovery program and have been clean ever since. I am determined never to return to that crazy world—my wife and family are too important to put them through that again. If what you want is a "clean shop," then I'm your man. As an employee, I will know who is using and who isn't. I can help to create a friendly environment for those who do not want to use, as well as help those who want to quit. You will never have to worry about me being late or calling in sick. In fact, on my last job, I always beat the shop foreman to the plant. You will find me to be a very honest, safety conscious, and productive machinist. As you can see by my resumé, I have over 8 years experience…"

Related Topics, Addiction

- ◇ ADDRESS: in a residential recovery program
- ◇ BUSINESS CULTURE: lacks comfort with the business culture
- ◇ IDENTIFICATION: lacks current identification
- ◇ RESIDENTIAL INSTABILITY: homeless or in residential recovery program
- ◇ SELF-ESTEEM: anxious about working again
- ◇ WORK HISTORY: lacks work history, has gaps, has only short-term work history or has been fired

ADDRESS, Lack of Current

In this barrier the candidate is female and employer is male.

The employer's concern is that the candidate may be unstable, undependable, have hygiene problems and thus not represent the company well, be tired on the job, be susceptible to illness or be desperate for money, making theft more likely. The employer may also have concerns about what led her to be without an address.

The candidate may be concerned about submitting applications and resumés without an address because she realizes she will be screened-out immediately. She may fear questions regarding her lack of address and the situation which led her to be without an address and may have already given up trying to get an interview.

Provide A Resource

In General, Address

We suggest that the candidate use the address of a dependable friend or local relative, your office or the shelter at which she is staying (without giving the shelter's name) until she has a permanent, reliable address of her own. When asked, the candidate should give the address at which she receives all job search related correspondence or the address of the office of the organization which is assisting her. If possible, avoid using a P.O. Box, as not having a street address may create questions about stability and where she lives. However, P.O. Boxes are becoming more acceptable for job searching.

Related Topics, Address

- ◇ MESSAGE SERVICE: does not have a phone
- ◇ RESIDENTIAL INSTABILITY: in a residential recovery program or shelter
- ◇ DEPENDABILITY: living situation causes lack of dependability

APPEARANCE

In this barrier the candidate is male and employer is female.

The employer's concern is that employees project the carefully chosen company image because the company image is part of the company's marketing strategy. Applicants who do not match the company image, in appearance and presentation, are given less consideration. Remember, the employer is in the business of making money, not creating jobs. A significant part of making money is the ability of the company to distinguish itself from its competition. If the company begins to stray from the marketed image, they may lose target customers, which translates into lost revenue.

The candidate wants to be judged on "his ability to do the job," not his looks. Often, the candidate does not realize how his appearance affects the employer's perception of his ability to represent the company effectively—and thus to do his job. The candidate may not have the resources, knowledge, awareness or desire to adjust this image.

In General, Appearance

Matching the company image becomes increasingly important the higher up the corporate ladder a candidate climbs. Although candidates must possess the required competencies, when employers are dealing with two applicants who are equally competent, image often becomes the deciding factor. Only for positions for which there are very few qualified candidates, image cease to matter.

Therefore, a candidate who does not closely match the image may easily secure an entry-level job but may not be considered for promotion, regardless of his qualifications. Always strive to match the candidate to companies whose image he matches, or which he is willing to develop so that career advancement is possible. For additional information, see *WNTS' Career Advancement & Business Acculturation Workshops, Teacher's Edition.*

Image is Everything!

A friend of mine was hired for a corporate level management position with JC Penny. Even though her competition had more experience and proven skills in the area, she was hired because she had "the corporate image." Her boss later explained that they were confident that she could learn the needed skills, but that her mid-west upbringing was irreplaceable as it matched the corporation's honest, friendly, all-American image. Her competition had the curt professionalism of a big city trained manager.

Body Language, Appearance

The way a person stands, sits, walks, uses his hands and his facial expressions creates a perception about his lifestyle, education, ability and personality. Remember that the employer and the customer make decisions based on perception, not "truth." Discuss with the candidate the image of the company or industry he wants to pursue. Then discuss whether or not his body language depicts that image. For example, most sales people must be perceived as confident, honest and as caring about the customer. If the candidate does not smile, maintain eye contact and hold himself confidently, he will not be perceived as projecting the correct image.

If the candidate's body language does not match the company image, but he is willing to learn, provide him with specific suggestions. Teach the candidate to observe and mimic the body language of the employees in the company or industry in which he wants to work. For example, is a big smile considered friendly or a sign of someone you cannot trust? Do they sit up in a chair or kick back and get comfortable? Are they animated when they speak or are they controlled? If he does not want to learn the new image, begin looking for companies or positions in which his present body language is acceptable.

Sample Solution

Adjusting The Candidate's Outlook

Mike had spent the last twenty years as a tough street hustler and had that hard expression that says, "You talk to me—you die." He had a moment of clarity and decided to change his life, with WorkNet's help. At first, many of the staff were afraid of him, but as they got to know him, they grew to love him. The staff had the benefit of time; an interviewer has only her first impressions. We wanted to soften Mike's look, but he decided he would rather do it his way. When this did not work, he allowed us to teach him to smile (he had a great smile!), to wear a shirt and tie with his jeans even for maintenance and gardening positions, to remove his earring and not to stare-down the employer. He also came up with the idea of wearing a pair of non-prescription glasses during the interview to make him look more intellectual. These changes minimized the harsh impression made by his intense stare, shaved head and prison-buff body. He was more approachable. Within a week of making these changes, he was offered two great jobs, each paying over $8.00 an hour with excellent benefits and room for advancement.

Change Where You Look

Disfigurement, Appearance

Obvious physical disfigurements must be addressed up front. Here are the steps we suggest. First, do not match the candidate to a position in which his disability hinders his performance. Second, identify possible employers by brainstorming what industries would not be disconcerted by the disfigurement. In fact, you may be able to turn this "lemon into lemonade" by identifying industries which would be sympathetic to the barrier. Third, begin marketing the candidate to those employers, focusing on how he will make or save the company money. Once the employer express interest, set an appointment. Before hanging up the phone or leaving the employer's office, in a pleasant nonchalant voice say, "There is one more thing I need to tell you about the candidate. It has nothing to do with his job performance, but I don't want you to be caught off guard when you meet him...." Then mention the specific disfigurement and give brief information if necessary. For example, "....During the Vietnam War his face was burned when a bomb exploded. He can see and work just fine, but there is some scarring...." End your comment with something positive, "... It is amazing to meet someone who has been through so much and is so positive. I know you'll like him." Never allow the employer to be caught off-guard. She may feel resentful that she was not prepared. Remember, it is human nature not to want to hire someone with whom you are uncomfortable. Informing her beforehand will make the interview more comfortable. Fourth, in the interview, the candidate must show the

Sew Creative!

A colleague told me about a candidate who is an excellent tailor but has a serious facial disfigurement due to extensive burns. It was unlikely that he would be considered for tailor positions requiring a lot of customer contact (such as a tailor's shop, up-scale retail clothing store, bridal shop, tuxedo shop, or up-scale men's clothier) because company image and customer service are so important. The employer may assume that the disfigurement would make customers uncomfortable and she would lose business. Moreover, finding an equally qualified tailor who better represents the company image would not be difficult. However, a position with a company who needs his skills and has customers who are compassionate toward the barrier would be a good match. In this case, the candidate was hired as the staff tailor for a large hospital. Other possibilities include groups which wear uniforms and are less concerned about the disfigurement and public image, such as the fire department or police department. The candidate could also open his own tailor shop targeted toward medical and emergency service workers.

employer that his attitude, personality, ability and determination far outweigh the impression the disfigurement may have on staff and customers. The candidate should be a joy to work with.

> CAUTION
>
> NOTE OF CAUTION: Do not sell the candidate's disability, rather sell his skills and benefit to the company. Few employers will hire entirely out of sympathy. They are in business to make money, not create jobs. However, compassion may compel them to consider the candidate or to turn the decision in the candidate's favor if all other considerations are equal.

Hair Cuts, Appearance

Provide A Resource | Adjust Candidate's Outlook

A good haircut will help to create the impression of economic and personal stability. The style of the cut should match the company's image (i.e., trendy for a modern art gallery, conservative for a finance company, elaborately styled for a job in the fashion industry, casual style for a trucking company and no-fuss for an athletic equipment retailer. We suggest you find a few local salons and barber shops to volunteer two or three haircuts a month for your candidates. Remind them that soon your candidate will be working and will need a regular barber or hair stylist. When setting up the free hair cuts, be sure YOU are the one who calls to schedule all appointments to ensure that the relationship with the stylist is not abused. Be sure to have your candidates write thank you notes or continue to use the hair stylist once working.

Looking The Part

Disney requires all of its theme park employees to be clean shaven with traditional haircuts and hair colors. This is important to create their fantasyland image in which everyone is a child—regardless of their age. Children do not have facial hair, nor do they make political or social statements with their hair (i.e., skin heads, bright colors, ornate decorations).

Provide A Resource · Teach a New Skill

Hygiene, Appearance

Generally, when a candidate has hygiene problems, he is unaware of how offensive they are and of how to resolve them. Just because hygiene is common sense to you does not mean it is common sense to him. A few important hygiene issues include physical cleanliness, regular brushing of teeth, having fresh breath (no cigarettes or coffee before an interview), clean, combed and styled hair, daily use of deodorant, clean and ironed clothing, shined shoes, clean finger nails, no visible nose hairs, no ear wax build-up and getting rid of or covering obvious blackheads or pimples.

The best way to deal with this issue is to discuss it individually with the candidate in an honest and constructive manner. If you have the opportunity to introduce these issues in a group setting, use that time also to give a few specific examples of inappropriate habits to make the class laugh and begin thinking. Let the candidates know that you may have to mention difficult issues, but that it will help them succeed. When in conversation, always ask permission to discuss this type of personal issue. Once permission is granted, proceed in a direct manner as if you are teaching new material. Offer SPECIFIC examples on how to resolve each relevant issue. Maintain good eye contact during the conversation, keep it brief, ask what he thinks or how he feels after you have expressed your concern and remind him that you believe in him and are on his side. Once he has had a chance to respond, turn the conversation to something he does well.

A second option, although far less effective, is to create a handout of hygiene tips to give to the candidate who needs specific direction. This is less effective because the candidate may not be aware of which topics relate to him, nor will he be given a comfortable forum in which to discuss it with you. A handout is best used as a supplement to your face-to-face conversation.

If you are working with a candidate who is living in a shelter, ask if he has access to a washing machine, laundry detergent, soap, shampoo, deodorant, toothpaste, a tooth brush and shower. Most shelters provide these items free of charge. If you assist candidates from a shelter which does not, call your local food bank, Salvation Army, rescue mission or community service organization to ask if they have these resources and whether your candidate can have access to them. If you find that you regularly need certain hygiene resources for your candidates, contact local retailers and social service programs which accept these types of donations to gather a generous supply for your candidates.

CAUTION *NOTE OF CAUTION: We recognize that confronting candidates about hygiene can be embarrassing for them and uncomfortable for you, but you do them a great disservice by avoiding obvious barriers which need to be addressed. You may think you are being "nice" by not mentioning the problem, but their success depends on the resolution of these issues. If they do not resolve these issues, they will not be hired and promoted!*

Adjust The Candidate's Outlook

Sample Solution

To discuss difficult topics we usually ask their permission to talk about it, then proceed to offer practical advice in a non-judgmental tone, such as:

"Remember when I told you that I might have to say difficult things sometimes? Well, this is one of those times. Believe me, it is easier just to say nothing, but I want you to do well. May I tell you about some of my observations? [wait for permission] Liz, you have great skills, you have a great personality and you are nice-looking, but you have a distinct body odor. I have some ideas on how to deal with it. Can I share them with you? [wait for permission] There is a type of underarm deodorant strong enough to be used only every five days; I suggest you get it and use it every day. Also, you should probably wear clothing only once between washings. To determine if a blouse or pair of pants needs to be washed, run a hot iron over the underarm and crotch area. If you smell anything, don't wear them again until they have been washed. Also, you might take the advice of a friend of mine who uses panty-liners every day because she sweats so much. She changes them a couple of times a day to stay fresh. What do you think? [wait for response]. I only mention these things because I would hate for something as silly as a little odor to stop you from proving what a great payroll clerk you are."

Provide A Resource | Teach a New Skill

Presentation, Appearance

To be hired the candidate must possess the company image. The higher the position, the more strictly he must conform. For example, in a large law firm, the mail room manager may wear shoes that are battered, but a senior partner's shoes will always be shined. Company image and presentation extends beyond clothing to include body language, facial expressions, hair style, jewelry, purse or brief case, car, education level, alma mater, hobbies, etc. Assist the candidate in researching the industry and the specific companies he wants to approach to determine the image required to get hired and promoted. Assess whether he matches the image. If he does or can easily adopt it, have him incorporate this into his presentation. If he does not match the image and is not willing to cultivate it, change where you look.

The candidate will need at least five outfit, including two for interviews, appropriate to the type of work he is pursuing. We recommend that the candidate's interview outfits be of the quality and style worn by those in the position into which he wants to be promoted, so he will be viewed as promotable from the beginning. Get creative! Solicit donations from staff, board members, local business professionals, service clubs and donors to begin a professional clothing closet. One clothing drive a month by a large corporation will give you plenty of suits. This will allow the candidate to select two or three outfits. Or, take the candidate to a thrift shop, discount store or consignment boutique near a wealthy neighborhood so he can buy a few like-new designer outfits, then upgrade one item at a time until he has enough for five to ten days.

Sample Solution

TEACH A NEW SKILL

I had a very bright and personable candidate who had spent the last five years on welfare. Her dream was to be a paralegal in a plush law office, but she had no professional clothing and did not perceive herself as a "professional." To move her toward her goal, I listed her transferable skills which included organizational skills, friendliness, physical stamina, dependability and ability to remember names. We determined that she would be a great match for a a office mail room clerk. To assist her in seeing herself as a "professional" and to determine the image she needed, I had her close her eyes and picture a mail room clerk in a plush law office. I asked leading questions, such as "how is she dressed?," "what does her hair look like?," and "how is her make-up done?," "what jewelry is she wearing?," "what do her hands and nails look like?" I was sure ask questions about specific problem areas. We then discussed the image we would cultivate. To further help her, we looked through some working women's magazines to get ideas. From my clothing closet we selected three designer suits with blouses. From a discount store we purchased one pair of black and one pair of neutral shoes. I made sure that she had hose and that her shoes were shined. I instructed that jewelry should be limited to a watch, simple gold or silver or pearl earrings and one ring. I got a local hair stylist to donate a free cut and style and a local beauty consultant to provide a free make-over and some make-up. The consultant enjoyed helping the candidate and hoped to gain a new customer once the candidate was working. Lastly, I had the candidate imagine herself walking the halls of a law firm, delivering mail, interacting with the staff and doing an excellent job.

Tattoos, Appearance

Change Where You Look

Adjust Candidate's Outlook

Tattoos create a very distinct image. The type of tattoo, where it is located and the physical appearance of the candidate in general, will determine whether the candidate is perceived as a gang member, an ex-con, a biker, military personnel or a "rebel" (we define "rebel" as a person who is economically secure and lives in the mainstream of society, but wants to do something a little "non-conformist," like getting a tattoo that is not readily seen).

For the most part, a candidate perceived as a gang member, ex-con or biker will create great concern for the employer. This type of candidate rarely portrays the desired company image and is assumed to be associated with trouble. For him to be employable in white-collar jobs, nothing about him can hint at his past or present associations—including his image or attitude. If possible, conceal tattoos under long-sleeved shirts and high collars. You may suggest concealer make-up for small facial tattoos. If the candidate is interested in having the tattoos removed, investigate where in your community free tattoo removal is offered. In Los Angeles, several cosmetic surgeons have gotten together to offer this service to former gang-members and prisoners. If your city does not have such a program, you may try to start one, or partner with a single medical office to assist your candidates. In return for their participation, you could assist the medical office to get free publicity through the local news or a story in the daily newspaper to help them build a customer base and positive reputation. If the tattoos cannot be concealed or the candidate does not want to have them removed, help him investigate employers for whom the tattoos are not an barrier. Some possibilities include construction, warehousing, long-haul truck driving, factory work, auto mechanics and machine shops. You can also ask parole

Professional?

If the candidate does not want to conceal or remove the tattoos, look for employers who don't mind or even may feel employees look proper with this image. Recently, on a business trip to New York, I ate lunch at a trendy hot-spot. As I ordered, I surveyed the decor and the staff. I realized that although I had waitressed my way through college, I would never have been hired at this restaurant. Their waitresses were rail-thin, darkly-clad women with a lot of tattoos and jet black hair. I am the all-American girl. They would never hire me—after all, they have an image to maintain!

and probation officers, Gang Task Force officers or a local pastor who works with this population where their candidates get jobs. In most cases, the candidate will need to develop a good answer to address the employer's concern that the gang or criminal lifestyle is no longer a part of his life.

Sample Solution

SAMPLE SOLUTION: DEVELOP A GOOD ANSWER

The following is a sample good answer for a candidate with noticeable tattoos who has adjusted his attitude and wants to enter the mainstream: "I know it was stupid of me to get these tattoos, but I was a kid and all my friends were getting them. Now that I'm married with a child of my own, I am more responsible and I am saving money to have them removed—but it's expensive. Another of my goals is to become a finishing carpenter. That is why I would like to be a Helper in your shop. I know I will learn a lot just by watching you. You will find me to be an eager student. I will always be to work fifteen minutes early, will do whatever tasks are needed, and ... "

The rebel may face difficulty if he is applying for an upper-level management position or pursuing a conservative company which is not interested in hiring "rebels"—provided, of course, the employer finds out about the tattoo. If the candidate is interested in these types of positions or companies, conceal the tattoo and develop a good answer in case the issue arises. Also, realize that the stigma associated with tattoos is fading with the "under 40 crowd" and may not necessarily be perceived negatively.

NOTE OF CAUTION: Do not allow the candidate to feel that he can get only low-skilled, low-paying jobs due to his tattoos or past affiliations—it can reinforce a sense of hopelessness. Always assist the candidate to identify and pursue his goals, and view himself as employable and promotable, while pointing out what he can improve and how he can get the results he wants.

Related Topics, Appearance

- ◇ CRIMINAL RECORD: has tattoos which announce his stay a prison
- ◇ DISABILITY, Physical: disfigured
- ◇ EMPLOYER BIAS: looks too old or too young
- ◇ GANG MEMBER: has tattoos which announce his past gang affiliation
- ◇ OVERWEIGHT: if extremely overweight

APPLICATION/RESUME, Ineffective

In this barrier the candidate is male and employer is female.

The employer's concern is finding the candidate who best meets her needs. She uses the application and resumé to screen-out candidates who do not clearly match her needs—NOT to determine who to hire (which is decided during the interview). So, if the candidate's application is incomplete, messy or does not show the skills that, he has requested, the employer will not even take the time to read it.

The candidate generally has little concern about the application because he does not understand its CRITICAL role in the process and often feels that it is just another piece of unnecessary paperwork standing between him and a job. The candidate may not want to "waste time" doing a great job on the application, may not have the requested information and assume guessing is good enough, or may not know how to constructively and honestly answer incriminating questions such as those regarding a criminal record, firings, major illnesses or gaps in work history.

In General, Application/Resumé

There are many "red flags" employers look for on an application including: ability to follow instructions, thoroughness, neatness, education, intelligence, whether the candidate has the qualifications, knowledge of the field, stability, honesty, whether the candidate has had progressive responsibility, whether they can afford the candidate, the candidate's availability to work the hours or shifts needed and self-confidence. An application reveals all this information and more.

Assist the candidate in developing a "model application" which he can carry with him when completing applications. The model application should include all the necessary personal, employment, education and reference information requested on any application, as well as his Quantified Selling Points for each position he is pursuing. Make sure your candidate's application and resumé SELLS! We have seen hundreds of people lose out on great jobs for which they were very qualified, because they fail to market themselves on the application. Once his model application is complete, evaluate it as if you were the

No Good Applicants!

Recently, I heard an employer on a radio talk show complain about not being able to find a single good applicant. She said that out of 50 applications, including one from a recent high school Valedictorian, not one was complete, and all had misspellings or were messy. She was disgusted to find that not one appeared to be qualified for her entry-level position.

employer. You should also conduct a full reference check to verify that the information is accurate. Share your impressions with the candidate so that the application can be improved. Using the model application will save time and greatly increase his chances of getting an interview. For additional information on creating model applications and developing Quantified Selling Points, see WNTS' *Creating A winning Application & Resumé Workshop, Teacher's Edition* and Step 6 of The Ten Step Process.

We recommend that you create a resumé for each candidate. Not only will this help market him to the employer, but it is an important self-esteem builder. Often, the candidate is surprised to discover how many skills he has. A good resumé can restore the confidence needed to successfully approach employers. For most of our candidates, a skills resumé is most effective because it highlights present and transferable skills, rather than illuminating poor work history. The process of writing a skills resumé allows you to discover and quantify the candidate's selling points. Use your counseling time to ensure that the candidate can articulate and give examples of his selling points and defend the information on the resumé. Be sure the resumé:

◇ uses words with which the candidate is familiar, and does not oversell or undersell him for the specific job
◇ presents how the candidate meets the employer's need for each different job title
◇ is one page (2 pages for a professional level position)
◇ uses bulleted phrases with Quantified Selling Points, and present tense action words
◇ is printed on high quality paper using a laser printer
◇ ALWAYS includes a cover letter addressed, by name, to the person who hires

For more information, we recommend *The Damn Good Resumé Guide* and *Blue Collar & Beyond* by Yana Parker, available at many book stores.

Illiterate, Application/Resumé

Often, employers will allow the candidate to take an application home and return it later. If this is possible, the candidate should get someone who reads and writes well to assist him in transferring the information from his model application. If the employer will not allow the candidate to take an application home, the candidate must be prepared to copy from the model application himself. Teach the candidate to recognize key words in each question so he can answer them when asked in various forms. Have him practice filling out various sample applications. Be sure he writes carefully and neatly, as writing will not be a comfortable action for him. If interviews can be arranged by faxing a resumé to the employer or through networking, the difficulties of filling out an application can be avoided until after the candidate is hired or has at least made a personal impression on the employer. Also, assist him in enrolling in a literacy class as soon as possible to permanently address the barrier. Your public library or community adult education program should have information on free literacy programs in your area.

> **NOTE OF CAUTION:** *Be sure to match illiterate candidates ONLY to jobs which do not require literacy. The purpose of the "model application" or resumé is not to assist the candidate to get a job for which he is not qualified, but rather to assist him to get a job which matches his skills and interests.*

Incomplete, Application/Resumé

Employers are looking for reasons to screen candidates out. If the candidate's application is incomplete, the employer may assume that the candidate's work will be incomplete. Therefore, every blank should be filled in, including "N/A" if the question is not applicable to the candidate. Identify information the candidate must gather to prepare his "model application." Have him call former employers to get employment dates, starting and ending wages and addresses. If the candidate does not have access a telephone, allow him to make these calls from your office. Discuss the job description of the position for which he is applying and which selling points will meet the employer's needs. Then quantify each selling point. Review how he will complete hard questions regarding reasons for leaving, major illnesses, having a criminal conviction, being fired, etc. Be sure the candidate does the following:

1) answers "open" or "negotiable" for questions regarding salary desired
2) lists all seminars, certificates and company-sponsored trainings which apply to the job being sought under "additional schooling"
3) answers "open" for questions regarding hours available, unless specific hours are non-negotiable
4) offers "reasons for leaving" which are consistent with the other application information. For example, if it says "for better opportunity" but his next job paid less or did not start until four months later it sounds like a lie.

Messy, Application/Resumé

There is no excuse for submitting a messy application, unless the candidate really does not want to be hired. Have the candidate write himself a reminder note about neatness on his "model application" and schedule extra time to fill out applications so he does not feel rushed. Remind him to PRINT and use only one style of writing, either all caps or upper-lower case. Have him write at a consistent angle so the application looks neat, and concentrate on writing on the lines provided. Copying information from his "model application" will allow him to concentrate on the appearance and not what to say next. Another option is to take the application home so he can take more time to complete it neatly or have someone else fill it out for him—although this will be misleading if he needs to write legibly on the job.

No English, Application/Resumé

Applications must always be filled out in English—unless the employer directs the candidate differently. Help him fill out his "model application" in English. Teach him to look for the key words in each question, and recognize common questions in various forms so he can identify them on any application and can copy the correct information from his "model application." Have him practice filling out sample applications. For additional information, see the *WNTS' Career Development Workshop Series in Spanish, Teacher's Edition*.

Poor Spelling, Application/Resumé

There is a false myth that people who cannot spell are stupid or uneducated. If spelling is a problem, help match the candidate to jobs which do not require that he spell well. Then, to create the perception that spelling is not an issue, be sure all the words on his "model application" are spelled correctly. Have him pay close attention as he copies the information onto each new application. In addition, on the back of the model application, create a correctly spelled list of additional selling points and information which might be needed. The candidate may also want to get the pocket-sized *Misspeller's Dictionary* by Webster's New World.

Selling Points, Application/Resumé

Teach a New Skill

In an effort to get the application process over with, the candidate may not market himself on the application, assuming he can just tell the employer in the interview. Unfortunately, without marketing himself on the application, the candidate may never get an interview. Spend time with the candidate identifying and quantifying his selling points. He must have three to six succinct Quantified Selling Points for each job title for which he is applying. Have him write all his selling points on his "model application" so he can choose the most appropriate for each application he submits. Train him to read the entire application before starting; this will allow him to determine the best place to use each selling point. For more information see Steps 6 & 7 in THE TEN STEP PROCESS.

Related Topics, Application/Resumé

◇ ADDRESS: no current street address
◇ CRIMINAL RECORD: has been convicted of a crime
◇ MESSAGE SERVICE: has no reliable means of getting phone messages
◇ OVER-QUALIFIED: has more schooling or education than the job requires
◇ REFERENCES: has few, only recent or poor references
◇ TRANSPORTATION: does not have a car
◇ WORK EXPERIENCE: has never worked, has limited experience, has no legal work experience or has no U.S. work history
◇ WORK HISTORY: appears unstable due to work history
◇ WORKER'S COMPENSATION CLAIM: has filed a Worker's Compensation claim

ATTITUDE, Bad

In this barrier the candidate is female and employer is male.

The employer's concern is that his employee's attitudes represent the company, facilitate a positive atmosphere and make the customer want to return. In all the employer surveys we have read or conducted, attitude is listed as a top concern with respect to new employees. Generally, the employer agrees that it is a misuse of the supervisor's time and personally frustrating to resolve employee conflicts, deal with dissatisfied employees, motivate uninterested employees and persuade lazy or self-involved employees to act in the best interest of the company. We are repeatedly told by employers that they are more likely to hire someone with a great attitude and the ability to learn than someone who has all the skills and a bad attitude, because teaching skills is easier than changing attitudes. The employer perceives that employees with bad attitudes cost them money through poor customer service, reduced employee efficiency, increased need for supervision or intervention costs, fraudulent Worker's Compensation Claims, law suits, excessive sick days, theft, and damage to merchandise or company equipment.

The candidate is often unconcerned about her attitude and does not realize the impact it has on her career. The candidate may have a bad attitude for a number of reasons. It may be the result of unresolved personal problems which are revealed in occasional anger, paranoia, self-sabotage, emotional instability, jealousy, pettiness or a controlling or judgmental nature. It may be a deeply-rooted character trait which consistently will be an issue, as she is unable to control her urge to lie, steal, destroy, etc. Also, consider that it may be perceived as a "good attitude" by the candidate because it is appropriate in her "culture." NOTE: In this book "culture" does not necessarily refer to ethnicity, but is just as likely to refer to regional, ideological, economic or generational groupings. To illustrate, among inner-city youth it is often considered unacceptable to allow anyone to "dis" (disrespect) you. However, what they perceive as disrespectful and what the mainstream work world perceives as disrespectful are very different. A few examples of "dissing" include, a supervisor giving an order rather than asking, a customer complaining about the service or product received, someone correcting their work, a supervisor testing their knowledge or skills, anyone maintaining direct eye contact with them, a member of the opposite sex talking to their girlfriend or boyfriend without permission or a supervisor requiring them to take a drug test. In their eyes, being "dissed" mandates a strong and immediate reaction. We have seen them swear at a customer, slug a co-worker, threaten their supervisor or quit. Obviously, these attitudes which are accepted and respected in their culture cause problems in the working world.

In General, Attitude

Attitude, most often, is a function of self-esteem and confidence. It is difficult to fake. How the candidate feels about herself will affect how others feel about her. If she has low self-esteem, her attitude will reflect it and compel others to treat her poorly. If the candidate is confident, her attitude will allow others to see that she is bright and capable. Usually, employers hire attitudes not credentials. If the candidate feels like a winner on the inside she will naturally reflect the attitude of a winner on the outside, making her more employable. The candidate's real attitude can seldom be hidden, which is why, though complex, this barrier must be addressed.

Discovering bad attitudes is easy. This can be done by reviewing the candidate's past work history and reasons for leaving, watching her verbal and non-verbal presentation for attitudes which might hinder her from getting hired or promoted and asking situational questions. You should also conduct a thorough reference checks and discover what she disliked most about her last job. As you look for attitude barriers, realize that employers will assume "whatever she has done before, she will do again." The best way for the candidate to offset a negative past, is by displaying a current positive attitude.

The greatest successes we have seen in changing a candidate's attitudes have come when the candidate gains a sense of purpose and value. We have found that assisting the candidate to discover her *spiritual identity*, the realization that God has created her for a purpose and has equipped her with the ability to carry out his wonderful plan for her life, will give her a new attitude of confidence and facilitate growth. NOTE: Understanding one's *spiritual identity* is not the same as becoming religious. There are many religious people who are oblivious to God's plan for their lives. *Spiritual identity* is found through an inward search for God, not an outward one, though outward changes usually follow. If you are uncomfortable with addressing spiritual issues, a second option is to refer the candidate to someone who can mentor her in this process.

A third option is to look for other things which could give her a sense of purpose and value such as her relationship with her children or husband, a worthy cause or even a 12-Step group. However, be prepared for a loss of identity if her family rejects her, the worthy cause no longer needs her or her 12-Step sponsor returns to the old lifestyle. To minimize the chance of this happening, encourage the candidate to gain new skills by going to parenting classes, family counseling or drug education classes. To minimize the damage of negative occurrences, encourage the candidate to expect the unexpected. Discuss how she can work through differences which arise and help her broaden her support base by joining a support group, building a network of people within the worthy cause or having more than one sponsor.

Once the candidate has begun to gain a sense of purpose and value, begin to deal directly with her bad attitudes. Remember, we have our attitudes, good and bad, because they have served us in the past. You must show the candidate how a new attitude is of greater value than the old one and offer specific examples of how the new attitude should be demonstrated. Honestly and gently point out specific incidences in which her present attitude is perceived negatively and offer alternatives. The specific barrier issues addressed in this section will provide you with some ideas.

Teach A New Skill

Sample Solution

If the candidate projects a bad attitude which does not accurately reflect who she is, teach her to correct the perception others have of her by adding or subtracting a single ingredient to her personality. This can be done for any wrongly perceived attitude, by asking what action makes you perceive a similar attitude as either positive or negative.

◇ If the candidate is perceived as stuck-up rather than shy, teach her to smile, make eye contact and say good morning.

◇ If the candidate is perceived as arrogant rather than self-confident, teach her to ask questions and show a desire to learn from others.

◇ If the candidate is perceived as talking too much rather than friendly, teach her to consciously ask questions of others and wait for their response before allowing herself to talk again and to keep her comments the same length as her listener's.

◇ If the candidate is perceived as controlling rather than organized, teach her to ask others if they want her advice, rather than telling them what to do. If she is a supervisor, teach her to clearly identify the goal she wants achieved, but to allow subordinates to suggest their own path to accomplishing it.

Have the candidate practice positive, resourceful answers using a pleasant voice. Instruct the candidate to observe her non-verbal behavior and to practice smiling, sitting up straight, making eye contact and shaking hands. As she becomes more confident and secure, these traits will occur naturally. When helping the candidate to improve these non-verbal behaviors, always be positive and affirming, NEVER critical. Video tape mock interviews so the candidate can see for herself the attitude she projects and ask her how she thinks she might change it. For more information, see *WNTS' Career Advancement & Business Acculturation Workshops, Teacher's Edition*.

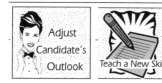

Anger, Attitude

The candidate who reveals anger to the employer, whether through non-verbal reactions or direct answers to interview questions, will usually be screened out. Anger has a way of destroying things around it, and the employer will work hard to keep the candidate's anger from damaging his company. Even if the employer is sympathetic to what caused the candidate's rage, he is usually unwilling to turn his company into a group-therapy site. So, the candidate learn to keep her anger out of the work place.

Do not ignore a candidate's anger. It must be dealt with and will not simply go away. To address the anger, you will need to understand the root cause—which may be outside your area of expertise and require professional counseling. We encourage you to collect information about local anger management groups so you can refer candidates. For our purposes here, we will focus on the job search services you can offer the candidate.

First, discuss the anger with the candidate so she can become aware of her anger and its negative impact. To do this, discuss past incidences of anger and the ensuing results (i.e., was passed over for a promotion or fired, got divorced, lost a friend, went to prison, etc.). Get her to agree verbally that she did not enjoy the outcome and wishes her anger had not caused the negative results. As you identify other options for behavior, be sure to discuss the results of each. Often the candidate feels like the situation mandated her action and she had no other options. Help the candidate to identify or speculate as to other ways she could have responded and what the result would have been. Also, help her to see the patterns which will continue in the future if she does not make changes.

Second, explain the employer's concern about hiring volatile employees and how her anger greatly limits the number of employers who will consider her. Help her create a plan for not allowing her anger to affect her work life negatively such as calling, leaving room or learning to say "okay." Ask if she would like your help in holding her accountable for implementing the plan.

Third, discuss which of her actions, facial expressions, voice tones, etc. communicate anger. We have been amazed at the number of candidates who argue about whether we perceived them to be angry, saying that they really were not angry. We always fall back on, "The issue is not whether you are truly angry, it is whether the employer perceives you as angry! As the employer I perceive you to be angry, and would not hire you. So what can you do to correct that perception?"

Fourth, help her develop means to deal with her anger more constructively in the future, as in the sample solution below or identify the situations in which she becomes angry so she can avoid them. For example, if the candidate has a problem with men in authority, refer her only to female-dominated industries or positions where she would have a female boss. If you know the candidate has problems working with whites, concentrate on companies which predominantly employ minorities and where her manager is a minority. It will also be important for her to find a mentor who can teach her how best to handle different situations. If your ultimate goal is to help her overcome her anger so she is not limited by it, help her deal with the root issues. This will seldom be achieved alone. You will need the help of other professionals who regularly deal with anger issues.

ADJUST CANDIDATE'S OUTLOOK

Sample Solution

Make an agreement with the candidate that when she STARTS to feel angry she will go to the restroom to refocus on her goals and how this job helps her attain them. This will take a great deal of self control, which is the very quality anger overrides. Therefore, it is important that you help her identify the early signs of irritation, before they boil over into anger. Also, teach her to remind herself not to allow any harassment from the sidelines to get her off her game and that "success is the best revenge." Require her to call you before doing anything rash. At WorkNet we have a rule that the candidate must talk to her Career Developer before quitting a job. If she does not, we will not help her for a year. If after talking with her Career Developer she still wants to quit, she may and we will assist her to find a new position immediately. This allows us a chance to resolve difficult situations and reinforce new coping skills.

Adjust Candidate's Outlook

Dishonest, *Attitude*

Dishonesty is a large problem for most employers. In fact, employee theft is the number one reason for loss in the retail industry in America. Dishonesty is not limited to employee theft, however. Employers must also deal with:

◆ candidates who lie on resumés and applications
◆ employees who cheat the company by having others clock-in for them, misuse sick time, take long lunch hours or charge the company for personal expenses
◆ employees who falsify records, such as timesheets, accounting records, statistical records or sales reports
◆ employees who lie to customers to get a sale

Employers tend to respond to dishonesty with strong and immediate action. Lying, cheating and stealing are grounds for immediate termination. In fact, we have seen employers lay-off an entire shift of ten to sixty workers when employees will not tell them who is stealing and demonstrate more loyalty to the thief than the company which pays them. To teach the candidate the employer's point of view, ask her how she would feel if she threw a party and one of her guests stole her TV, but no one would tell her who took it, saying, "I'm not gonna be a narc," "it wasn't my job to be security," or "it's only one little TV and you have another." She would probably be furious and change the guest list for her next party. Explain that this is how the employer feels. Employers hire people they believe they can trust and who will be loyal.

Once the candidate understands the gravity of dishonesty, recommend that she stay totally away from it. As with most addictions, this will be very difficult and take a lot of inner strength. Often, the candidate has lied so often in the past, it comes more naturally than the truth. Remind her how quickly one "little" dishonesty mushrooms into several. If the employer discovers or perceives that the candidate is dishonest in even one instance, he may assume she is dishonest in others. Carefully review the application with her to find discrepancies which can be corrected. Assist her to develop good answers for difficult interview questions so she will not be compelled to lie again. If a candidate insists on lying, refuse to give her job leads, and do not directly refer her. Also, refuse to refer a candidate who sees nothing wrong with stealing from the company.

CAUTION

NOTE OF CAUTION: This is a very difficult attitude to change because all segments of our society consider some form of dishonesty which they deem acceptable—from the corporate President to the street thug—as long as they are not caught. Outrage occurs when the attitude one deems acceptable interferes with another's quality of life.

Lack of Initiative, Attitude

Adjust Candidate's Outlook

Lack of initiative is often a sign of depression or low self-esteem. If the candidate views herself as incapable, then in her mind there is no reason to take initiative, because she will only fail. To assist her, you must first address her self-esteem barrier, because the candidate who will not take initiative in her job search will probably take very little initiative on the job. Remind yourself that this is her life, her job, and must remain her job search. Unless you intend to drive her to work each morning and do the work she does not complete, *giving* her a job will only enable dependency rather than make her independent.

Inform the candidate who shows little initiative, that she will set the pace for the job search. Explain that you will put forth only as much effort as she does. It is important that you are consistent and do not do things which she could do for herself. Use a Weekly Action Plan to show what tasks each of you have agreed to do. Praise her generously when she completes tasks, even if she does not do them as well as you would.

If the candidate's lack of initiative is due to disinterest in the type of job for which she is searching, find out what field fascinates her and identify jobs in that field for which she is currently qualified. People always work harder and learn more when they work in positions they enjoy. Determining what motivates her, such as time with her family, helping people, controlling how much money she makes or what others think about her will help you select a position which meets her needs.

Very INTEREST-ing

I had a candidate who felt he was confined to manual labor jobs because he had never graduated from high school. He dreaded job searching and did not want to return to a boring job. When I asked him what he enjoyed doing, he said spending time with his girlfriend, reading and watching wildlife shows. I also discovered that he read four to six books a week! We decided to change where we looked. I assisted him to get a volunteer position at the public library, which we hoped would turn into a full-time paid position. Next, we used his volunteer work at the library to prove that he loved books, making him more attractive to bookstore owners. He became very excited about his job search. Within a few weeks he was employed as Stocker for a large book store. Everyone is motivated by something. If you can help the candidate discover what they love and then secure a job doing that, he will show more interest in the search and on the job.

Negativity, Attitude

Adjust Candidate's Outlook

Negativity is most often the result of discouragement, hopelessness or upbringing. It is easy to become discouraged during the job search process when you are constantly being rejected. It is normal to feel hopeless when you have no goals or don't believe your dreams will ever come true. It is natural to see what is wrong with the world when you have been conditioned to see it this way since childhood. Regardless of the reason for the candidate's negativity, the employer cannot afford the disruption which negative people create among staff and customers, or the additional supervision needed to keep people focused on their jobs.

As with other attitude barriers, negative attitudes require time and conscious effort to change, and cannot be dealt with until the candidate chooses to address them. Again, a new understanding of her spiritual identity or gaining a sense of purpose and value will precipitate the greatest change. Hope is a powerful tool. Help the candidate identify these attitudes by pointing them out one at a time and explaining how it might be perceived by the employer. Help the candidate practice optional ways of viewing and talking about situations. Review interview questions which solicit negative answers, such as, "What did you like least about your last job?," "Why did you leave that job?," and "How have you gotten along with previous employers and co-workers?" Inform the candidate that if she speaks badly about past employers, the interviewer will believe she will be negative on the job and speak badly about him too. Few employers will knowingly hire someone who is going to "bad-mouth" them. Teach her that if she cannot say something nice she should say nothing at all, and help develop positive answers to these questions. This may mean concentrating on what the candidate has learned, or what she is looking for in her new job. Have her practice these positive responses. Remind her if she follows up her good answer with a bad story, it will defeat the purpose. Teach her not to talk too much. Send her on a few mock interviews before providing a direct referral. Always debrief her interviews to see if her negative attitudes seep through in other answers.

> *NOTE OF CAUTION: Teach your candidates to NEVER say anything bad about a past employer, co-worker, or ethnic group in an interview or on the job. If they want to be promoted, they should never even join in with another person's gossip. This is part of being politically wise, and is ESSENTIAL in upward mobility.*

Sample
Solution

DEVELOP A GOOD ANSWER

If the candidate tells you she left her last job because she knew more than the "new boss" did, and got tired of him constantly looking over her shoulder telling her how to do her job, you must determine if she is a "know-it-all" or just had difficulty adjusting to the new boss' style. Discuss how she plans to deal with her boss at the new job and identify specific ways she plans to get along with the new boss, such as just saying "okay" or asking if she can offer a suggestion rather than getting mad. Teach her to answer the question "Why did you leave your last job?' by saying: "I felt that I had learned all I could from my last position and I wanted a new challenge. I know that your company is on the cutting-edge and encourages employees to take initiative. I want to move on with my career and I believe the XYZ company will provide me that opportunity."

Helping the candidate to view the job search process more realistically will decrease the feelings of discouragement and hopelessness which lead to negativity. Explain that in outside sales, as in the job search, it is common to get only one positive response in ten attempts, so there is no reason for her to get discouraged until she has had ten unsuccessful interviews. It has been our experience that candidates rarely need more than ten interviewers before being hired. This will also be true for your candidates. Examine all the possible reasons she has been told "no" and help her to remove those barriers, so next time she sells herself more effectively. To combat hopelessness, assist the candidate with Life/work Planning so she can determine her dreams and design a realistic path to achieve them.

Rudeness, Attitude

If the candidate is rude to you, assume she will be rude to the employer. No employer will hire someone who is rude and disrespectful. Often, the candidate is shocked to learn what is perceived to be "rude" in the business culture. A few common examples include, entering an office without knocking, interrupting a conversation, using inappropriate greetings such as "Hey Baby" or "How's it hangin'?," leering at members of the opposite sex, or talking loudly in an office where people are working. Review how the employer will interpret and respond to the candidate's particular rude behavior. Ask permission to point out the rude behavior when it happens again. When it does, remind her of other options for handling the situation. These habits are not easily broken; be patient and consistent. The candidate may also need to practice being pleasant and speaking in a pleasant tone of voice.

If the candidate refuses to change her rude behavior, brainstorm with her about which industries or companies would permit it, and seek positions only in those industries. For example, construction, product transportation, some manufacturing, refinery industries and other fields are all tolerant of behavior which most industries would never permit. If necessary, you can refuse service until she agrees to conduct herself in a more appropriate manner. See *WNTS' Career Advancement & Business Acculturation Workshops, Teacher Edition.*

Unprofessional, Attitude

Each industry has it's own standard of "professionalism." Professionalism is not based merely on appearance, but also on interpersonal skills, tact, timeliness, quality of work, initiative, dependability, and other factors. To assist the candidate who does not appear to be professional to determine the definition of "professional" in her chosen industry, ask employers, NOT WORKERS, what an ideal candidate looks, sounds and acts like. For example, when we asked construction workmen what they thought they should wear to an interview, they assured us that jeans and a t-shirt was best. However, when we asked this same question of construction company employers they agreed with us that a candidate should wear a dress shirt with a tie and jeans. The jeans, rather than t-shirt, show that he is a working man, and the tie says he is promotable. Many employers also suggested that the candidate wear a t-shirt underneath the dress shirt so he could begin working immediately if needed. For more information, see the Related Topics list below, or see *WNTS' Career Advancement & Business Acculturation Workshops, Teacher's Edition.*

NOTE OF CAUTION: The definition of professionalism varies with different industries and employers. Be sure you are familiar with the expectations before you develop new attitudes in the candidate. For example, to transform the attitude of an industrial construction worker into that of an Ivy League professor, believing the second is truly professional, would lessen his professionalism in his chosen industry because, as my brother informs me, "no proper, soft-bellied, high-faulting sophisticate would make it on our construction site."

Unwillingness To Learn, Attitude

Adjust Candidate's Outlook

Inform the candidate that today's good employees never stop learning. The employer needs candidates who understand current technology, the importance of keeping up with the fast-paced business market, and how to embrace change so that the company remains competitive.

If a candidate seems unwilling to acquire new skills and knowledge, find out why so you can address it. Perhaps she is illiterate, afraid she will look stupid, thinks she is too old, is uninterested in the particular field, or is afraid of responsibility. As with other attitude issues, clearly articulate the benefits of changing her attitudes and the consequence of not changing it—then allow her to make her own choice. Also, help the candidate determine which methods of learning work best for her (i.e., classes, hands-on experience, discussion with an expert, audio-video presentations, reading) and help her find a "mentor" who will take an interest in her progress and offer encouragement when she feels overwhelmed.

If the candidate is unwilling to learn, you must examine the skills she currently has and brainstorm about companies in slow-change areas which need those skills. For the candidate who is unwilling to learn, but has good people skills, look for positions which are oriented toward customer service, rather than technical skills which must be updated constantly.

Related Topics, *Attitude*

- ◇ ADDICTION: attitude is a result of addiction
- ◇ APPEARANCE, Body Language: non-verbal communication creates a negative impression
- ◇ BUSINESS CULTURE: attitudes stem from not understanding the expectations of the business culture
- ◇ CANDIDATE BIAS: demonstrates prejudice
- ◇ COMMUNICATION SKILLS: lacks interpersonal skills
- ◇ CRIMINAL RECORD: attitude is a result of imprisonment
- ◇ DEPENDABILITY: lacks timeliness
- ◇ FEAR: demonstrates a bad attitude due to fear
- ◇ GANG MEMBER: attitude is a result of gang membership

BUSINESS CULTURE, Lack of Knowledge about the United States

In this barrier the candidate is female and employer is male.

The employer's concern is that his employees understand the basic rules of how the U.S. business culture functions, what it values, and how successful employees interact. Some rules apply to all industries (i.e., maintaining eye contact during a conversation), while others vary from industry to industry (i.e., style of acceptable dress), or even employer to employer (i.e., penalty for being late). The employer needs employees who understand these rules and abide by them so the company can successfully function in the U.S. business culture.

The candidate who has grown up in a non-management family may not be familiar with how the business world functions from the employer's perspective. She may be unaware that the protocol of the business culture is different from that of her home, neighborhood or school. Even if she is familiar with some of the rules, she may fail to understand the consequences of not following them. She may also feel uncomfortable and out-of-place in a professional environment—low self-esteem keeps one in a narrow "comfort zone." If the candidate was raised in a welfare family she may feel uncomfortable in any work environment, and may find it difficult to have people tell her what to do.

In General, *Business Culture*

It seems reasonable that a woman coming from another country would not know how the United States' business culture operates because she was not raised around it. However, we forget that there are millions of people in the U.S. who have not been "raised around" the employer's perspective—and after all it is the employer who makes the rules. Their parents did not sit around the dinner table and talk about what made their business succeed or created problems. They didn't require their children to shake hands with the adults who visited their home, or learn to comfortably converse with business associates. Their parents may not have taught them to value timeliness, how to ask good questions, or the importance of building a reputation and network to help them in the future. In short, they were raised "outside" the U.S. business culture. Realizing this will remind you that there is no reason why the candidate should know the "expected" behavior or attitudes and will allow you to be less judgmental when teaching about the culture and adjusting his outlook.

As you notice actions or attitudes which reveal the candidate's lack of knowledge about the expectations of the business culture, point them out. We recommend teaching Business Acculturation as one of your regular job preparation classes. This will allow you to review the Business Acculturation material or discuss basic rules of the business world individually with the candidate as needed, allowing him to ask specific questions about situations or practices with which she is unfamiliar. Be sure she understands that she must remain very observant—because each company and each employer may view the situation a little differently. It is important that she consider the concerns and needs of each new employer as she searches. See *WNTS' Career Advancement & Business Acculturation Workshops, Teacher's Edition.*

Yankin' my Chain

For over 20 years my candidate had been a successful drug dealer and numbers runner. He was used to being treated with the utmost respect. However, as he endeavored to move into the legal economy he was treated like all the rest of the "flunkies." He rushed into my office one evening, furious. He said he was going to quit his job because the boss was "yankin' his chain." When I asked what happened, he explained that his supervisor's boss had singled him out to take a test which entailed memorizing dozens of 5-digit numbers. After hearing the whole story, I told him it sounded to me like they were considering him for a promotion, not trying to harass him. He agreed to allow me to help him study for the test. The next morning he took the test and scored 100%. The boss was so surprised by the perfect score that he had him take it again the following morning. Again he scored 100% and was promoted.

Fear of, Business Culture

Teach a New Skill

Most of us are afraid of things we do not understand. As the candidate learns to control how she is perceived within the business culture, her fears will diminish. However, learning the rules and protocol of a new culture takes time. Teach the candidate the most obvious rules first, such as the importance of:

- ◇ a good hand shake
- ◇ good eye contact
- ◇ matching the company's image and attitude
- ◇ maintaining a friendly disposition
- ◇ always learning
- ◇ being dependable and on time
- ◇ being trustworthy
- ◇ doing the job better than required
- ◇ asking good questions
- ◇ learning the boss' priorities

Then teach the candidate how to develop mentor relationships so she can continue to learn. A mentor can be a formal or informal relationship in which an expert will answer questions, evaluate her work and offer suggestions, offer advice on decisions and even introduce the candidate to people she should know. This will help the candidate to be more confident in the business culture. Here are a few tips on building mentor relationships:

- ◇ Don't be afraid to ask, people are flattered to know you think they are the expert.
- ◇ Don't waste the mentor's time. Prepare good questions, use their advice, follow-up on their contacts and keep them informed.
- ◇ Make them proud to be your mentor. Your success is their success.
- ◇ Always say thank you!

The entire process of educating the candidate to the business culture will be much easier if she is working in a field which fascinates her and is using skills she enjoys. Assisting people to discover and pursue what they love is called Life/work Planning. For more information on this topic read *The Three Boxes Of Life and How to Get Out of Them* by Richard Bolles, or review *WNTS' Introduction to Life/work Planning Workshop, Teacher's Edition.* For more information about teaching U.S. Business Acculturation, see *WNTS' Career Advancement & Business Acculturation Workshops, Teacher's Edition.*

Adjust Candidate's Outlook

Harassment (sexual, racial, religious), Business Culture

What is acceptable behavior in the candidate's daily life may not be acceptable in the U.S. business culture. Sexual, racial and religious mythology which is circulated, joked about, or used in decision making is inappropriate and often illegal. If the candidate acts inappropriately toward you, another staff member or other candidates, she will likely do the same in an interview or on-the-job.

Hey Baby!

One day as I walked into the lobby of my office, I had a man turn and begin overtly staring up and down my body, undressing me with his eyes. When he saw the shocked look on my face he just smiled and kept doing it. After I regained my composure, I asked what he thought he was doing. He proudly stated that he was paying me a compliment. I told him that I was not complimented. Later, I took him to one side and explained that his action was inappropriate for the business world. If other women he worked with felt as I did, he could face sexual harassment charges or be fired. To avoid these possibilities, I taught him to practice a simple on-the-job rule— "Do not to do anything to a woman that he would not do to a man". Unless he would be caught undressing a man with his eyes, he should not be caught undressing a woman with his eyes. Over the next few weeks I had to kindly confront him several times on various infractions of this rule. For example, he would lean on my desk, look deep in my eyes with a knowing smile and tell me I looked very nice today. I would say, "thank you," and ask whether that is how he would compliment a buddy on a new suit. Another time I overheard him ask one of the female staff for her phone number, so I leaned over and asked if he would ask a man for his phone number. Slowly he learned.

Immediately take the candidate to one side and explain that in the business world there are spoken and unspoken rules which guide communication between members of the opposite sex, different races and religions. In a manner which says, "you may not be aware, but....." explain what was offensive, the likely consequences in the business world and how you expect her to act while in your office. Be straight forward and honest. Often she will explain that she "didn't mean anything by it." Point out that saying this in the business world will not change the results. If she responds with, "at my last company everyone spoke like that," or "if someone doesn't like how I am, that's their problem," remind her that it is her problem as well because that type of behavior is unacceptable in your office, and is becoming less acceptable in the business community. Let her know that in order to receive your help, she must promise to keep those actions and attitudes out of the workplace.

If the candidate's efforts to correct her mythology about a certain group progress slowly, you should place her in a setting which allows for little contact with that group and which is not offended by her views.

NOTE OF CONCERN: Strongly discourage candidates from dating people they work with. It can cause a lot of problems, even beyond charges of harassment.

ADJUST THE CANDIDATE'S OUTLOOK

Sample Solution

I had a foreign candidate complain after an interview about the large number of "negroes" at the company. He explained why he did not want to work around "these people" and asked if I could refer him somewhere else. I said that I would be willing to refer him elsewhere, but that it was unrealistic to eliminate all his interaction with African Americans. I also informed him that to be successful in the United States he must gain an understanding of and ability to work with people of many races. I went on to explain some things he could do to minimize the perception that he is prejudiced, such as replacing the Spanish "negro" with the English "African American," maintaining eye contact and a pleasant facial expression when talking to African Americans, not making derogatory comments in English or Spanish, and making an effort to get to know an African American co-worker. I realized at the end of our conversation that his mythology ran deep and it would take several positive interactions with African Americans to change it, even though he said he would try to act appropriately on the job. I decided that until he changed his attitude, the most successful match would be a job site where he had limited interaction with African Americans. It would also be helpful for him to build a friendship with an African American to begin to change his mythology.

Inappropriate Behavior, Business Culture

Adjust Candidate's Outlook

The word "inappropriate" lends itself to interpretation. In the business culture, "inappropriate" refers to any consistent behavior which creates doubts about the candidate's promotability or gets her fired. Inappropriate behaviors may include disgusting habits (i.e., nose picking, belching, chewing with her mouth open), annoying habits (i.e., finger tapping, talking too much, not cleaning up after herself), childish habits (i.e., interrupting conversation, touching things which are not hers, looking around when being spoken to) or unprofessionalism (i.e., always being late, making excuses for mistakes, promising things she does not deliver). Point out the problem, explain how it is viewed by others, discuss optional ways to handle the situation and help him to gain a tool or plan to deal with each issue. Ask permission to point out each time she acts inappropriately, and get a commitment that she will try to change.

Sample Solution

Adjust The Candidate's Outlook

The third time the candidate arrives late for an appointment, announce in a loud voice, "YOU'RE FIRED!" Once the shocked look leaves her face, inform her that if you were her employer she would no longer have a job. Explain that most employers interpret consistent lateness as a lack of interest in the job or a lack of respect for the boss. Assure her that not only do you want her to get a great job, but you want her to be promoted, which means she must learn to be prompt. Require that she be at your office fifteen minutes before each scheduled appointment and help her figure out when she needs to leave and which route she should take to arrive on time. Inform her that if she shows up less than ten minutes before the appointment, you will not provide her with any job leads during that meeting.

Related Topics, Business Culture

- ◇ ATTITUDES: has attitudes unacceptable in the U.S. business culture
- ◇ EMPLOYER BIAS: fears being discriminated against
- ◇ IMMIGRANT: from outside U.S. and unfamiliar with U.S. business culture
- ◇ WORK EXPERIENCE: entering a new field or has never worked in U.S.

C

CANDIDATE BIAS

In this barrier the candidate is male and employer is female.

The employer's concern is that her employees project the company image and attitude to the public. If the candidate demonstrates biases which differ from the company's image and attitude, the employer may believe that he will not represent the company in a positive light or, worse, compromise the company's image through unacceptable actions or comments. She may also be concerned that the candidate's bias toward others, or feelings that others have bias toward him, will create a need to constantly deal with disgruntled employees and customers.

The candidate may feel it is his constitutional right to express his opinions, regardless of how others feel. He may even feel obligated to promote his point of view. However, this group is in the minority; usually the candidate is unaware that his biases are offensive. Often, the biases are based on mythology he was taught when young which have never been reconsidered, such as "blondes are dumb," "Mexicans are lazy," or "fat people are not athletic." Still others may hold mythology because of traumatic incidents in their lives, such as the belief that all inner-city youth steal because his father's market was held up by a gang of kids; all male employers are unfair because a friend was told she would never get promoted if she wasn't "more friendly" with the boss; all whites are angry racists because a few have called him "chink" (a derogatory term for people of Chinese descent); or that under-qualified minorities are taking all the good jobs because one was hired into a position for which he had applied.

In General, Candidate Bias

Adjust Candidate's Outlook

Explain to the candidate that even if the employer agrees with his bias, it is unlikely that she will risk losing money, alienating customers and employees, or compromising the company's image to allow his bias. Do not argue with the candidate about whether his views are right or wrong; simply insist that the workplace is not the appropriate forum to discuss them. During the discussion, be specific about what could be perceived as offensive and offer alternative ways of handling various situations. If the candidate is receptive, challenge his mythology with the facts. Remind him of the goals he wants to reach and how continuing to share his bias in the workplace will have a negative impact on those goals. Have the candidate practice answering interview questions concerning biased attitudes until the answers developed would not offend the employer.

If the candidate insists on promoting his views, brainstorm about jobs in which he will have limited interaction with the population he dislikes. For example, working in a minority-owned business is an option for someone who does not like whites; working in the suburbs or in a business which does not interact with teenagers would be an option for someone who is fearful of inner-city youth; self-employment as a truck driver, gardener, freelance data entry operator, or in-home child care provider are options for someone who does not want a boss. See *WNTS' Career advancement & Business Acculturation Workshop, Teacher's Edition.*

Related Topics, Candidate Bias

◇ ADDICTION: fears the employer will show bias due to his past addiction
◇ CHRONIC ILLNESS: fears the employer will show bias due to his illness

⬦ CRIMINAL RECORD: fears employer bias due to his criminal record
⬦ DISABILITY, Physical: fears employer bias due to his disability
⬦ EMPLOYER BIAS: fears employer bias due to his age, gender or race
⬦ GANG MEMBER: fears employer bias due to his previous gang affiliation
⬦ IMMIGRANT: fears the employer will show bias due to his nationality
⬦ OVERWEIGHT: fears the employer will show bias due to his weight

CHILD CARE, Lack of Reliable

In this barrier the candidate is female and employer is male.

The employer's concern is operating an effective, profitable business. Employees who are late, leave early, miss days or take long lunches in order to care for their children cost the company money. This loss is measured in misuse of paid "sick time," lost production, fees paid to temporary agencies, and lower efficiency. Although the employer may be sympathetic to child care dilemmas, he cannot afford to allow the candidate's personal life to make a negative impact on his business.

The candidate's concerns usually focus on cost, quality, hours and location of child care. If she has several children in child care, she can easily spend almost her entire paycheck on child care costs— particularly if one or more child is below the age of two. Of equal concern are the stories in the news of abuse and neglect of children by day care providers. For a single parent, child care is of particular concern, because she may have a smaller income, fewer resources and no spouse to help when the children are sick or need to be picked up.

Have a Plan

This is the answer a candidate of mine gave when she saw concern in the employer's eyes after he learned she was a single parent.

"My daughter is great! And, I am so lucky to have a great neighbor who works at home and can watch her if she's sick. In return, occasionally I watch her kids in the evening."

Good Answer...

Provide A Resource

In General, Child Care

The candidate is generally well aware of this barrier. If she has not resolved it herself, it is probably because she does not know how to resolve it without your help. To assist her, you must realize that the candidate CANNOT conduct a job search without at least part-time child care. She cannot make inquiries over the phone with children crying in the background demanding her attention and she must NEVER take her children with her when she goes to request an application or to be interviewed. Suggesting that the candidate job search without developing a child care plan is setting her up for failure.

Develop a plan which addresses who will watch the children when they are sick as well as when they are healthy, since most child care centers will not accept children who are sick. Also, keep in mind that the greatest need for child care money will occur during the job search and the first month of employment— before the candidate can afford to pay. The child care plan must accommodate the job search schedule and work schedule once the parent is employed. It may take any number of different forms, including:

◆ an agreement made with a family member, a friend or neighbor. Often these untapped resources are available and affordable, but the candidate has not thought to ask.
◆ an agreement between shelter residents to alternately care for each others' children at a public library, playground, or community center.
◆ accessing low-cost or subsidized programs (i.e., churches, community centers or synagogues.)
◆ accessing a government or community sponsored education/employment program which provides child care for participants (i.e., Job Training Partnership Act (JTPA) programs or a community college.)
◆ researching companies which, as a part of their benefit package, provide on-site child care or child care reimbursement for employees.

Familiarize yourself with the resources in your community to become aware of the options and obstacles, such as long waiting lists for subsidized child care, geographic stipulations and income requirements. Begin your child care research by contacting a local child care referral network, service providers which work with families, child welfare programs, and Head Start programs. To contact government-funded programs, call your city hall and request the phone number and contact person for Job Training Partnership Act (JTPA), Community Development Block Grants (CDBG) and the local youth task force.

Provide A Resource

Sample Solution

If you are a non-profit service provider and find that quality, affordable child care is a consistent need for your candidates, you may want to do more than research options for individuals. The following are alternatives your agency may want to consider:

◆ negotiating with local child care providers to offer free child care during the job search and sliding scale payment once the candidate starts working. Carefully monitor who you refer. Determine how many referrals the provider will take, establish the maximum weeks of free child care a candidate will be allowed and express your appreciation.
◆ writing a joint grant for funds with a non-profit child care center.
◆ establish an in-house day care center for your candidates. This

center should be state certified and could also serve as a vocational training program to train candidates who want to be child care workers or in-home day care providers.

◇ writing child care expenses into any employment program grants you submit so that you can provide monies for child care during job search and the first month of employment.

This barrier issue should be resolved before the candidate begins job searching so that the employer is never given a reason to be concerned. If the candidate is asked in an interview or on the application whether she has children and how old they are, a good answer must be given. NOTE: Although these are not legal questions they may be asked. The good answer should include the candidate's emergency child care plan for when the children are sick.

 NOTE OF CAUTION: Until the candidate has a plan for child care, DO NOT refer her to an employer. The candidate is not stable enough to work—too many problems could arise. You will be reinforcing a sense of failure and hopelessness in the candidate and may lose the employer.

Related Topics, Child care

◇ PUBLIC ASSISTANCE: receives Public Assistance
◇ WORK HISTORY: raising family has caused gaps in work history
◇ WORK EXPERIENCE: this is a first job, or is going into a new field
◇ WORK RELATED SKILLS: does not believe she has any marketable skills

CHRONIC ILLNESS

In this barrier the candidate is male and employer is female.

The employer's concern is that she have dependable, healthy employees who will be at work every day, doing what they were hired to do. She may be concerned that the candidate will cost too much in medical benefits, that the illness will recur, resulting in excessive absences or an inability to work at full potential, that he will infect others or will file a worker's compensation claim for aggravating a previous illness. All of these concerns are daily realities which cost American companies millions of dollars each year.

The candidate's concern is that the employer will not believe that his illness is in remission or is no longer an issue, and that he truly is capable and wants to work. He may also be fearful of his co-workers' reactions if they find out about the illness. This is particularly true for illnesses with apparent symptoms or social stigma such as syphilis, epilepsy or AIDS.

In General, Chronic Illness

The candidate should not apply for a position which he is unable to perform to the employer's specifications. If the illness excludes him from continuing his past profession, help him to identify his transferable skills and select a new profession. If the illness will not hinder him from doing the job, he is not obligated to disclose any information about it—this includes AIDS. On an application, "major illnesses" is defined as those which result in four consecutive days in the hospital or at least two consecutive weeks of missed work. To build a perception of being healthy he should avoid calling in sick, asking for time off to visit the doctor, or showing signs of fatigue. To address questions regarding major illnesses, have the candidate write, I have had no illnesses which would hinder me from doing this job. For consistency, be sure the candidate answers all questions on the application in complete sentences, so that this particular answer does not stand out. Below is a list of the only four ways the employer can find out about past illnesses, along with a few tips about each one:

1) if the candidate writes medical reasons or health reasons under "Reasons for Leaving" on the application, or has unexplained gaps in his work history which would likely cause questions in the employer's mind. If the candidate wants to avoid discussing the illness, he should not allude to the health problems on the application or in an interview.

2) if the candidate tells the employer or tells a co-worker who then tells the employer. Remind the candidate that his past illness is a part of his personal life which does not affect his ability to do the job and, therefore, should not be discussed with anyone at work. Teach him to keep his personal and professional lives separate.

3) if a past employer or personal reference mentions the illness during the reference check. To avoid this, have the candidate call all employers and personal references who may be aware of the illness to assure them that he is healthy and capable of performing the job for which he is applying, and request that they keep the information confidential.

4) if the candidate applies for health insurance through the company and his previous illness increases the insurance premium, or he is rejected for coverage. To avoid this problem, you may encourage the candidate to secure coverage through a personal policy or his spouse's employer so he can decline the insurance offered by the company. However, if he needs the coverage offered by the company, the employer may become aware of his illness.

The best way to deal with this situation is to match the candidate to a position in which he can perform well, eliminating the need to mention the illness. However, the candidate should be well-prepared to answer any direct questions the employer might ask. In a positive, confident manner have him explain why the illness will not affect his job performance—it is not necessary to give details or even name the illness. After giving a brief explanation as to why the illness will not affect his ability to work, the candidate should redirect the conversation to highlight his skills, experience and qualifications for the job. Have the candidate practice discussing the issue until he can comfortably disarm the employer's concern. Having a good answer will make the candidate more confident and minimize the perception that he is hiding something.

Sample Solution

DEVELOP A GOOD ANSWER

Below are some sample answers regarding various illnesses. It is often advisable NOT to mention the illness by name.

"The doctors were concerned about my ability to combat infection, but it has never hindered my work performance, which is attested to by my work history and employment references."—AIDS

"I had some respiratory problems, but since I had surgery, I'm fine. It has not caused problems in years." —Lung cancer

"Due to my accident, I am not able to lift more than 40 pounds, which is what encouraged me to leave carpentry and pursue a new career. I have always been fascinated with computers so when I tested very high in this area, I knew I should take advantage of the opportunity to retrain and pursue computer programming."—Back problems

Related Topics, Chronic Illness

- ◇ DISABILITY, Physical: has a noticeable disability.
- ◇ MEDICAL BENEFITS: concerned about medical benefits.
- ◇ TRANSPORTATION, Disabled: disabled.
- ◇ WORKERS COMPENSATION: has filed a Worker's Compensation claim for his injury or illness.

COMMUNICATION SKILLS

In this barrier the candidate is male and employer is female.

The employer's concern is that her employees have the ability to communicate clearly, concisely and effectively. Poor communication could cost the company sales, create grounds for a law suit, undermine the marketing efforts, erode public trust, cause safety hazards, slow production or impede growth.

If the candidate is aware of his communication barrier, he may be embarrassed to talk with the employer, make phone inquiries or even submit applications and resumés. He may also be fearful that he will not be able to secure a position which is challenging and matches his skills, or that he will be viewed as less intelligent. If he is unaware of his poor communication skills, he may attribute his failure to secure employment to other issues such as nationality, gender, education, etc.

In General, Communication Skills

If a candidate lacks basic communication or interpersonal skills, he may miss opportunities for which he is highly qualified because he cannot articulate his qualifications. The employer will often judge how smart the candidate is based on his mastery of the English language and his ability to express himself. In this fast-paced age of satellite transmission and computers—mass media, teleconferencing, e-mail, the Internet and global communications—what we say and how we say it can be immediately transmitted without allowing the company time to edit. Employers need employees who will create the best image, whether talking with a customer on the phone, writing their own correspondence on a PC, communicating with co-workers in meetings, or making a presentation in front of a group.

Communication is a highly personal art. The candidate may view his communication style as adequate or preferable, yet the employer may not agree. It is important to teach your candidate that to meet the employer's needs he must understand that the employer needs a certain style of communication. Most communities have educational programs which can help the candidate to develop his communication skills, such as ESL to learn English or speech therapists to assist with impediments, Toast Master's groups to teach public speaking, and community colleges to teach English grammar, writing and comprehension skills. The higher up the corporate ladder the candidate wishes to climb, the more crucial his communication skills become.

Limited/Non-English,
Communication Skills

The candidate will need to deal with the myths and concerns the employer may hold about people who do not speak English well, as well as any myths about his ethnicity. It is a commonly-held myth that limited or non-English speakers are unintelligent or uneducated. To counter this, teach the candidate key sentences in English including, *"I am learning English"* or *"I am becoming bilingual in English and..."* rather than *"I do not speak English"*. Also, have him mention the language(s) he does speak fluently. A common, and valid, concern is that the supervisor and customers will not be able to communicate with the candidate. However, our experience has been that most limited English speakers understand far more English than they speak. If this is true of your candidate, he should let the employer know by saying, *"If you speak slowly, I will understand"* or *"I understand more than I speak."* To further facilitate communication, have the candidate use his English name, if he has one. This will increase the employer's comfort level and decrease the chance that she will become embarrassed by mispronouncing an ethnic name. See Step 8 for another sample solution.

NOTE OF CAUTION: When assisting a limited or non-English speaker to develop answers to employer's questions, select words which do not call attention to the accent. For example, several Asian languages use a similar sound for "l" and "r," so avoid words beginning with these sounds (i.e., replace "like" with "enjoy," and "require" with "need"). There is no "th" sound in Spanish, so avoid words with this sound (i.e., replace "think" with "believe," and "this" or "that" with the words to which they refer). Be sure your substitute words sound natural. Also, teach the candidate to maintain constant eye contact when he speaks to employers—it will demonstrate confidence, honesty and the ability to adapt to new customs.

Develop A Good Answer

"Hello. My name is Chuck. I speak three Chinese dialects, and I am currently learning English. If you speak slowly I can understand. I want to be a furniture refinisher for you. I have 12 years experience working with antiques in Taiwan. I am also very good at fixing intricate inlays, but will do whatever you need. May I give you my resumé?"

If your community has a large population of people who speak the candidate's native language there will also be businesses which cater to that population. The candidate can easily job search for himself within his own community. Have him use the ethnic yellow pages, newspapers and radio, and walk through the ethnic neighborhoods to locate prospective employers.

If his ethnic community is small or he wants to work outside his community, you will need to cultivate employers for him. Help the employer understand that the candidate can do the job duties and is occupationally fluent in English. Be sure the candidate has a basic industry vocabulary and is familiar with common questions and how to respond appropriately. For example, a housekeeper in a hotel must recognize phrases like *"more soap... shampoo... towels," "come back later," "don't touch," "dirty," "Where is the pool... the restaurant... the ice machine?,"* and be able to respond accordingly. For questions he does not understand, he must be able to respond, *"I do not know, let me check"* and then call the front desk so an English speaker can answer the question.

You will also want to help him learn the appropriateness of different slang terms which he may learn on the job. His English-speaking co-workers may teach him words which he will not want to use once he understands where they lie on the spectrum of appropriateness

Create the perception that your candidate is the exception to any negative myths about his community. Explain that he is very hardworking and reliable because he is grateful for the opportunity to work. Also, capitalize on positive stereotypes which are generally true about the population, such as loyalty, honesty, dependability, or friendliness.

If the candidate speaks enough English to conduct part of his own job search, have him walk into businesses, resumé in hand, to meet employers. This will be more effective than calling on the phone because of

He Said What?!

People who do not speak English as their first language must learn not only the meaning of terms, but also the appropriateness of terms. Case in point ... a friend of mine who had been helping me improve my Spanish asked one day if I would help him with his English. I happily agreed. He told me that he was having trouble determining which slang terms are acceptable and which are considered vulgar. In a quiet voice, he told me that he had overheard some co-workers talking when the topic of women's breasts came up. He wanted to be respectful, so he asked which of the following terms would be in poor taste in mixed company: chest, boobs, hooters, tits and breasts. Amused, I explained that on the spectrum of appropriateness, chest or breasts were the most acceptable, boobs and hooters were on the more offensive side and tits was the most vulgar to me. I had never before considered how important it is to teach bi-lingual speakers the appropriateness of words, if they are to smoothly integrate into our society. Without my help, he could have gotten into a lot of trouble!

the language barrier and because it is harder to disregard someone if they are standing right in front of you. Emphasize the importance and benefits of speaking English. Speak English during your meetings as often as possible so the candidate can practice. Encourage him to watch English TV and listen to English radio to improve his comprehension. Refer the candidate to English as a Second Language classes or English Conversation Groups.

 ## Limited Vocabulary,
Communication Skills

The employer may assume that the candidate's inability to express himself reflects a lack of intelligence. Employers whose companies project an intellectual image may scrutinize the candidate's vocabulary and use of language. The candidate's vocabulary becomes more important as he endeavors to move up the corporate ladder. **Help the candidate to become industry literate** so he can intelligently interact with the employer. This can be done by reading industry magazines and journals, attending seminars, watching documentaries or reading books. Encourage the candidate to find more descriptive ways of expressing himself and make sure he knows the correct meaning and pronunciation of words and how to use them in context. Teach him to listen to how successful people communicate and write down new words he does not know and look them up in order to expand his vocabulary. Have him select an entry-level job in the field in which he wants to be promoted. This will allow him to expand his vocabulary, begin to build his network and find a mentor. Spending time with people who have an expansive vocabulary will help him to become aware of and use new words.

 ## Speech Impediment,
Communication Skills
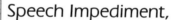

The candidate should not apply for jobs he cannot do well, so be sure the speech impediment in no way disqualifies him. Work hard to present him well on paper by creating a "model application," resumé, cover letter, employment proposals, and thank you notes for the job search process. Initial interaction with the employer should be done in writing or by you, rather than by the candidate over the phone. Be sure the candidate is comfortable articulating his qualifications to the employer. Use words that do not highlight the impediment. Remember, there are thousands of jobs that do not require direct verbal communication with customers or are in industries that are not concerned if the candidate has a speech impediment. For ideas, contact speech therapists to inquire about local industries in which their clients work.

Strong Accent, Communication Skills

If it is difficult to understand the candidate, do not match him to jobs which require extensive verbal communication with customers. Carefully observe specifically what about the accent makes him difficult to understand and have him work specifically on that area. Help him practice speaking clearly—especially when using industry vocabulary and articulating his selling points. Have him emphasize the fact that his comprehension and writing skills are very good. To minimize the effect of the accent, the initial interaction with the employer should be done in writing or in person, rather than over the phone. Even if the candidate has a large vocabulary and speaks confidently, if you have trouble understanding him, it is likely that the employer will too.

Often employment can be secured in companies which market to the candidate's ethnic community, such as local and long distance phone companies, utility companies and banks, because they need bi-lingual employees. Also, look for companies which have a large number of employees who speak the candidate's native language. The candidate can assist with this process by identifying businesses he patronizes, building a network within his community and discovering where others who speak his language and have his skills have been hired. For example, we have noticed in southern California that Kaiser Permanente employs a large number of Filipinos in the Accounting and Nursing Departments, and that AT&T is always looking for Mandarin- and Cantonese-speaking operators.

What was That?

I know a Haitian woman who has a beautiful but strong French accent. One day after a public speaking engagement in which she talked about the importance of being "available" (a-vah-lah-buhl) for God's use, she overheard a member of the audience comment on her unique analogy to be a "volleyball" for God. Surely the intricacies of her talk were missed because of her accent.

Uses Slang or Poor Grammar, Communication Skills

The North American Business Culture has its own language—Corporate English. To be successful in Corporate America, you must be able to communicate in Corporate English. Discuss with the candidate the limitations he puts on his career if he is unwilling to learn this language. If a candidate uses slang or poor grammar, he may be unaware of the problem or not realize the negative impression it makes. As a result, the employer may view the candidate as unintelligent, inexperienced, uneducated, flippant or unprofessional. Whether the candidate uses cultural slang or speaks with poor grammar—as is often seen in younger job seekers ("you know...," "all that...,"

"cool...") or those from inner-city areas ("homie" for friend, "dis" for disrespect, "aks" for "ask") encourage them to become "BI-LINGUAL" in Corporate English. Do not suggest that the candidate discard his everyday language, rather that he speak it only away from work. Speaking Corporate English, which is the language of most businesses and not just upper-level corporate environments, will create many more opportunities for him. Help him become aware of his most noticeable infractions and practice speaking in a different manner. Speech patterns are hard to break, so begin working on it immediately. Have the candidate listen to how successful people talk, and ask someone to help him on a regular basis at home.

Sample Solution

TEACH A NEW SKILL

To help the candidate become aware of slang expressions and poor grammar, agree to alert him by snapping your fingers each time he uses a particular phrase or speaks incorrectly. This will make him aware without interrupting the flow of the meeting or sounding like a nag. Choose one example to work on at a time so that you are not snapping at every other word.

Related Topics, Communication Skills

◇ ATTITUDE: communication problems are exacerbated by attitude problems
◇ IMMIGRANT: a limited/non-English speaker
◇ WORK RELATED SKILLS: lacks communication skills needed on the job

CRIMINAL RECORD

In this barrier the candidate is male and employer is female.

The employer may be concerned that whatever the candidate has done in the past he will do again. This may cause the employer to view the candidate as dishonest, untrustworthy, dangerous, and a threat to the staff, customers or company property. The employer may also be concerned that the candidate will attract "undesirable" people to the business, give customers the wrong impression of the company, or be strong-willed and unmanageable. If these concerns are not addressed, the employer will not hire the candidate, regardless of his abilities.

The candidate may fear that no one will give him a second chance. Although he has done his time and paid his price to society, society has rejected him. He may feel his only options are to lie to the employer about his past, or to return to the illegal economy.

In General, Criminal Record

The employer has a legal right to ask whether or not the candidate has ever been convicted of a crime. This question is almost always on the application. Often the candidate who has been convicted of a crime will want to lie and say "no." If he lies and the employer does a background check, he will disqualify himself from the position, regardless of his qualifications or the company's willingness to consider hiring ex-offenders. If he lies and the employer hires him without doing a background check, he will worry about whether the employer will check his background at a later date. It is common for employers to do a background check after hiring the candidate— usually for one of three reasons: 1) company policy is to conduct a background check only after the new employee has completed his probation period, 2) if the candidate has done a good job and is being considered for a raise or promotion, and 3) if the candidate does a poor job and the employer would like an easy means to terminate him. Lying on an application is grounds for immediate termination with no legal recourse. Over the years, despite our urging to always be honest, we have seen many qualified ex-offenders lie on their applications in order to get hired. Once on the job, they follow our advice and work for advancement and are often recommended for promotions, at which time they are fired because the company discovers the lie.

Promotion or Termination?

We had a candidate who applied for an excellent position with the power company. He was honest about his felony conviction and still got the job. Months later, upon the recommendation of his boss he applied for a promotion, but this time he took the advice of his friends and lied about the conviction. Not only did he miss out on the promotion, but he was fired from his original position when the lie was discovered. Even his supervisor's efforts to intercede on his behalf failed because of the company's policy that if an employee lies on the application he is immediately fired.

NOTE OF CAUTION: There is nothing more disheartening than knowing you are doing a great job, but getting fired because of a lie. This will often push the candidate over the edge and back toward hopelessness, drug abuse, or the illegal economy. Stay in close contact with your candidates so that you can redirect their energies toward learning from mistakes rather than repeating them.

To overcome this barrier you must match the candidate carefully to a job for which he is well-suited. Identify possible employer concerns about the specific offense, and address them. If the offense was particularly bad, you personally may need to contact employers to explain how the candidate has changed and why you believe his past behavior is no longer a concern. The better the

employer knows you, the more she will value your opinion. Remember, you are putting your reputation on the line, so be sure you believe what you are saying—you do not want to ruin your relationship with the employer.

Sample Solution

DEVELOP A GOOD ANSWER

We have seen many ex-offenders get great jobs and begin a career. *"Joanne, I have a great candidate for your driving position. He has a clean DMV record, has lived in the city all of his life and knows every side street. I have found him to be very conscientious, hardworking and great with the public. Can you use somebody with these kinds of skills?... [wait for response] Great, but I want to let you know that he is an ex-offender. I know you have had some good luck in the past with employees who are starting over. I think James will be one of these, but I wanted to be the one to tell you that he has been in jail. Since his conviction he has really tried to turn his life around. While in jail, he got his GED, became a supervisor in the maintenance department and was released early for good behavior. When he was young and stupid he joined a gang and allowed himself to be talked into helping with a kidnapping. The victim was returned safely, and James has changed. He really needs a second chance, and I know you won't be sorry if you hire him. I am confident that you will find him to be very loyal, hardworking and eager to learn. May I set up an interview so you can see for yourself what I mean?"*

As with many barriers, the more evidence you can show that the candidate's life is different today, the greater the chance he will be hired. Encourage your candidates to get involved in community activities, counseling or support groups, continued education, civic organizations or other activities which illustrate an improved attitude and lifestyle. Not only will this help him to appear more employable, but will also facilitate the building of new friendships, the improvement of self-esteem and offer new lifestyle options.

Adjust Candidate's Outlook

Arrests, Criminal Record

If the candidate has been arrested but not convicted, he should answer "no" without further explanation to any questions regarding criminal convictions. This is true even if he went to trial, as long as he was pronounced "not guilty." If the candidate is unsure whether he was found guilty, have him call the court in which his case was tried to find out what the record states. A few areas where candidates are often unsure include vehicle violations, unpaid child support and criminal convictions resulting in fines or probation, but no jail time.

Felony, Criminal Record

Good Answer...

If the candidate has been convicted of a felony, there are certain jobs for which he is ineligible, such as security work, law enforcement or selling firearms, and jobs for which he may be an inappropriate choice, such as working with children, accounting, money handling or working in a pharmacy. You must get the whole story in order to help direct him in his job search. Use THE TEN STEP PROCESS to develop good answers to any questions regarding the felony which are certain to be asked.

Remind the candidate that ex-offenders are hired every day. If other ex-offenders can find the right company and position, so can he. Your belief in your candidate will give him strength. We often share with the candidate that we believe God has a wonderful plan for his life. The question is whether or not we are willing to let God put that plan into action. If we are, we must trust that He will guide our steps, opening the right doors and closing the wrong ones. Most importantly, we must never give up. There are several great examples I draw from in the Bible, including King David, Joseph, Esther, and Paul.

Discuss the benefits of honestly securing a position with a company in which he can prove himself and be promoted. Most companies do not have a formal policy against hiring ex-offenders, nor do their policies require that they hire them. Each candidate is judged on an individual basis once he can get an interview.

Cooking up a Good Answer

We worked with a candidate who had been in prison for over 15 years. We identified the transferable skills he had developed and developed the following good answer.

Yes, when I was twenty-two I was involved in an armed robbery. So much has changed since then—my lifestyle, my friends, my priorities. Today, I am anxious to move ahead with my life. I am enrolled in a business management class at the junior college, I attend a great church and I am consciously trying to make a positive impact by tutoring young people. I guarantee that if you hire me as the cook for your boy's ranch, you will find me to be loyal, hard working and conscientious. More importantly, I will be able to tell the kids first hand why they want to change their lives now, before they waste their youth like I did. Also, if I can manage 28 prison inmates, I can easily manage 10 "tough" boys. As my resumé shows, while in prison I managed a kitchen with a staff of 28, prepared over 6,500 meals a day, am state certified in nutritional standards for institutional cooking and I can make great-tasting meals on a low budget."

One of the greatest challenges for ex-offenders who are job searching is to make it to the interview without being screened out. Here are several suggestions to help him get a face-to-face interview. Once he is in the interview and has built a good rapport, he must address the conviction. Have the candidate:

1) apply for positions which request a resumé rather than an application, because criminal records are not usually detectable on a resumé.

2) find openings by calling employers, briefly presenting the candidate's top three selling points, and asking if the employer could use someone with his qualifications. If she says "yes," fax his resumé and ask for an appointment to further discuss his qualifications. At no time during this phone conversation should his felony be mentioned.

3) request that a friend introduce him to the boss, allowing the candidate the opportunity to market himself and his skills before discussing his past.

4) walk into businesses and ask for the hiring manager. He should briefly present his top three selling points and ask if she needs someone with his skills. He should have his resumé and good answers ready so he can interview on the spot.

5) mail out proposal letters explaining how he can make or save the company money and follow up with a phone call to schedule a business meeting to discuss the proposal.

6) allow you to arrange interviews with employers who are willing to consider the candidate, as long as he has "turned over a new leaf" and is qualified.

To find him an interview, contact a local judge, his parole officer or professionals within the legal community for recommendations on employers who hire ex-offenders. They are often aware of these employers, because they have other "clients" who are working. Many have also already built special relationships with employers and are willing to share contacts with others.

If the candidate is unable to get an interview and must fill out an application, be sure he sells his skills, experience, attitude and availability. You may also want to include any related work experience and skills gained in prison, since you cannot hide his conviction. Do this by listing it under *Work Experience*, as you would any other job. If the candidate was paid, list the salary. If it was a training program or unpaid work assignment, write "volunteer" where it asks about pay.

When answering the question, "Have you ever been convicted of a crime?," the candidate has several HONEST options to choose from, including:

1) writing "Will discuss in interview," without checking "yes" or "no"

2) writing the criminal code number (i.e., #354786), and checking "yes"

3) neutralizing the employer's concern by offering a brief explanation, if it was a long time ago and things have changed (i.e., "Over 16 years ago I...," "Theft when I was 19," "Current work history very good." or "DUI—have not drunk in 8 years"), and checking "yes."

4) leaving the question blank and discussing it during the interview. This option

is recommended when the candidate refuses to check "yes," or has been unable to secure an interview using the first three methods. This will allow him to address the employer's concerns face to face. See Step 5 to review how to eliminate employer's concerns.

NOTE OF CAUTION: If you have to use the fourth option, remove the prison work experience from the application.

Prepare the candidate to talk about the conviction in an interview. The candidate must convince the employer that he is the "exception to the rule" regarding her fears about ex-offenders. He should honestly and straight-forwardly state his crime without going into detail about it. The candidate should focus on how he has changed, what he has learned, and why his previous action will not be a problem on this job. He should present himself as someone who went down the wrong road, suffered the consequences and has come to realize the importance of honesty, hard work and following the rules. Today, he is a very different person with a better understanding of the world. He is ready to work hard and be loyal to any employer who will give him the opportunity to build a future for himself. You must be sure that his answer truthfully reflects the changes in his life. The employer will judge the candidate's honesty and sincerity by his voice tone, eye contact, forthrightness, evidence of steps already taken towards improvement and whether his answer is consistent with the rest of his presentation.

Juvenile Conviction, Criminal Conviction

Adjust Candidate's Outlook

Juvenile criminal records can be sealed when the offender reaches the age of 18, so that as an adult he can start fresh. Instruct the candidate not to mention it on his application or during the job search process if his records have been sealed. If the candidate is unsure whether the record has been sealed, or if employers can retrieve the information through a background check, have him inquire at the court where he was convicted.

Misdemeanors, Criminal Conviction

Good Answer...

Legally, employers can only ask about misdemeanors which resulted in jail time. Instruct the candidate not to mention it on the application or during the interview unless it resulted in jail time. Remember that positions which require a high-level security clearance will necessitate an extensive background check. In such cases, providing straight forward answers upfront will increase the perception that the candidate is honest and trustworthy.

 NOTE OF CAUTION: Remind your candidates NEVER to lie or tell the employer that a question is illegal. Rather, instruct the candidate to answer a related legal question. For example, when asked if he has ever been convicted of a crime he can answer, "I have had traffic tickets and stuff, but nothing serious which required jail time."

Related Topics, Criminal Record

◇ APPEARANCE: appearance hints at a criminal lifestyle or record
◇ BUSINESS CULTURE: work history occurred in prison or the illegal economy and he lacks familiarity with the mainstream business culture
◇ GANG MEMBER: has gang affiliation
◇ SELF-ESTEEM: criminal record has caused a lack of self-esteem
◇ REFERENCES: lacks good professional and personal references.
◇ WORK EXPERIENCE: work experience occurred in the illegal economy or prison.
◇ WORK HISTORY: lacks formal, legal work history.
◇ WORK RELATED SKILLS: lacks skills or licensing needed on the job.

DEPENDABLE, Not:

In this barrier the candidate is male and employer is female.

The employer is concerned about keeping personnel costs low and productivity high. If an employee is not working, he cannot be productive, and other staff or temporary employees will have to be hired. Dependability includes not only whether the candidate shows up and is on time, but also whether he can be relied upon to complete tasks in the manner and time frame expected. If the candidate does not do his job correctly his supervisor is responsible to get it done in order to meet her boss' deadline.

The candidate may feel that time is not very important. With his family and friends it has never mattered if he was late, or changed his mind and decided not to show up. He may know that he "should" be dependable—like he "should" floss his teeth—but does not view it as important.

In General, Dependable

If the candidate is perceived to be undependable, he will not be hired for most positions. The only exception is when his skills are so rare and essential that the employer is left with no other options, but, usually, the employer can find someone with similar skills and experience to hire. In fact, most employers prefer employees who are dependable and willing to learn over employees who are highly qualified but regularly absent or late. This is particularly true in assembly line businesses in which one person cannot do his job until another person does his (i.e., in the restaurant industry, the dishwasher cannot wash the dishes until the busser clears the table, which requires the server to serve the food, which requires the cook to prepare the food).

Lack of Punctuality, Dependable

Adjust Candidate's Outlook

Illustrate the importance of punctuality by treating the candidate as the employer would. The third time the candidate arrives late for an appointment, announce in a loud voice, "YOU'RE FIRED!" Once the shocked look leaves his face, inform him that if you were his employer he would no longer have job. Explain that most employers interpret consistent lateness as a lack of interest in the job or a lack of respect for the boss. Assure him that not only do you want him to get a great job, but you want him to be promoted—which means he has to learn to be prompt. Require that he be at your office fifteen minutes before each scheduled appointment and inform him that if he arrives less than ten minutes before the appointment, you will not provide him with any job leads during that meeting.

Inform the candidate that "on time" is 5 to 15 minutes before the scheduled time. If he has an appointment at 2:00 p.m., he should arrive between 1:45 and 1:55 p.m.

I Don't Care How Good You Are!

I knew a young man who was hailed by his employer to be one of the best waiters they ever had. He trained other servers, was sent to Euro-Disneyland to help open a new restaurant, and was respected by other employees. However, he was consistently late. One day when he arrived (late, of course!), his boss said, "It has been a pleasure to work with you, but you are no longer employed here because you cannot be to work on time." When the young man responded, "You can't fire me, I'm your best waiter," the boss replied, "That's right, you are…and we cannot have our best waiter coming in late and setting a bad example! Good bye."

Have him bring a book to read, applications to complete, letters to write, or some other work which can be done easily on his lap so he is not wasting time.

When waiting for an interview, have him read material about the company found in the reception area, develop a rapport with the receptionist or simply observe how the company operates. Teach the candidate to be on time even after he is hired, whether going to a business meeting or arriving to work.

Sample Solution

Provide A Resource

If the candidate does not have a watch or an alarm clock, get him one. Contact the manager of a local department store with a jewelry department, explain what you're doing and ask for a donation of a half dozen watches or travel alarm clocks.

Adjust Candidate's Outlook

Numerous Sick Days, Dependable

The candidate who takes every allowed sick day appears unmotivated. Not only will he not be promoted or given raises, his poor performance could cause him to be the first one laid off when the company falls on hard times. Teach the candidate that sick days are not just extra vacation days, but are a means to provide him with a paycheck when he is very sick. Using all his days unnecessarily means he will not get paid if he becomes very sick or has an accident. Help the candidate realize the importance of investing in the company and letting supervisors know that he is committed to the company's goals and success. By carefully matching the candidate to a field and position he really enjoys, his desire to be at work will increase. See *WNTS' Introduction to Life/work Planning Workshop, Teacher's Edition.*

If a candidate must legitimately use several sick days, it is important that he make up the time and create the perception that his work is important to him and that he is dependable. Even if he is not misusing the sick time, the employer will likely doubt his commitment to the company and his promotability.

Working Smart
Not Just Hard

A young man I know was asked by his employer to work 12-hour days, Monday through Thursday, with an optional 12 hours on Saturday. He agreed gladly. However, after several weeks he got sick and had to take a Thursday off. He was concerned that being sick might create a bad impression, so he took care of himself, got to feeling better and decided to go in the optional Saturday rather than waiting for Monday. His employers were glad to see him and impressed with his commitment to the company. They showed their appreciation by promising to give him a raise. When they finally implemented the raise, several months after the promised date, they made it retroactive to the promised date. He received a check for over a thousand dollars.

Sense of Time, Dependable

Adjust Candidate's Outlook

The U.S. business culture has its own set of rules governing time. This refers not only to being on time and completing projects in the expected time frame, but also valuing time to the same extent the employer does. Generally, candidates who lack this sense of time have come from other cultures, have been unemployed for a long period of time, or have been in unconventional jobs which do not require adherence to normal business protocol. Failure to adhere to these expectations can be disastrous. A few interesting rules governing time in the U.S. business culture include:

Business people in the United States are willing to wait up to 19 minutes before they decide someone is too late or is not coming. In most of Africa and Latin America, parts of the Middle East, and portions of Eastern Europe, they will wait more than two hours.

In the U.S., being late communicates disrespect or that the meeting was not important to you. In portions of Latin America, if you are late it is assumed that you are a person of stature—you were detained by more important people or events.

In the U.S., time is generally measured in 15 minute, 30 minute and 1 hour increments. Arriving more than 15 minutes early may cause your associate to feel obligated to start the appointment early.

Related Topics, Dependable

- ◇ ATTITUDE: lack of dependability is due in part to bad attitudes
- ◇ BUSINESS CULTURE: unfamiliar with the U.S. business culture
- ◇ CHILD CARE: blames lack of dependability on children
- ◇ FEAR: reacting to subconscious fear
- ◇ MESSAGE SERVICE: cannot be easily and professionally contacted
- ◇ RESIDENTIAL INSTABILITY: residential unstable
- ◇ TRANSPORTATION: does not have reliable transportation
- ◇ WORK HISTORY: work history will make an employer believe he is not dependable

DISABILITY

In this barrier the candidate is male and employer is female.

The employer's concern is that the candidate with a disability may not be able to do the job to the fullest extent, and will miss work, work slowly, or expect special consideration due to his disability. The employer might also be concerned about increasing her exposure to law suits and government regulations. Lastly, she might be concerned that visible disabilities will make customers uncomfortable and discourage them from returning.

The candidate's concern is that the employer will not be able to see beyond the disability to his abilities. If the disability is visible, the candidate may also be concerned about the response of co-workers and customers, fearing alienation and condescension.

In General, Disability

The candidate should not apply for positions he is unable to do. If the disability is not visible and does not hinder him from doing the job well but could affect the employer's perception of his ability, it should not be mentioned until after the employer is sold on the candidate's skills. However, the employer may become aware of the disability due to a gap in work history, a reference check or comments made inadvertently during the interview. Prepare the candidate with a good answer, in case the employer asks. This answer should explain why the disability will not affect his job performance, steps he has taken to minimize inconvenience to the employer, and avoid giving details or even the name of the disability. Practice discussing the situation until the candidate is so comfortable presenting it that the employer will not let it affect her decision to hire. The candidate's obvious comfort with the disability will increase the employer's comfort. The candidate should then quickly return the focus to his skills, experience and qualifications for the job.

Sample Solution

DEVELOP A GOOD ANSWER

◇ "It has never hindered my work performance which is attested to by my work history and employment references."

◇ "It hasn't been a issue for me in years. I've learned new ways of doing things. In fact, some of these ways ended up working even better."

◇ "It is controlled by a prescription and has not caused problems in over 8 years."

The candidate with a visible disability must address it. Instruct him to begin the interview by building rapport, then directing the conversation toward eliminating the employer's concerns about the disability. This can be done by explaining why the disability does not hinder him from doing the job and, in fact, can be of benefit to the employer. In developing a good answer, you do not need to give details about the disability, but must address the employer's concerns. Again, practice discussing the situation until the candidate is so comfortable that the employer will not let it affect her decision to hire.

If the visible disability will decrease the candidate's job performance, the candidate must discuss how he will minimize the negative and what additional benefits the employer will receive by hiring him. This way he can still market himself as the best candidate for the job.

Emotional, Disability

If the candidate suffers from an emotional disability, be sure he is receiving professional help and that his doctor or counselor confirms that he is ready to work. If he is not ready, you should not try to place him—you will set him and yourself up to fail. However, you may want to spend time preparing him to work by creating a "model application," developing a resumé, and beginning to address other barriers. If the candidate's emotional disability does not hinder his ability to do the job for which he is applying, it should not be mentioned to the employer. Inform him that the interview is not an appropriate time to do this. If certain pressures or environments aggravate the disability or create additional problems, match the candidate to jobs where these pressures are not present. For example, a man who struggles with controlling his anger should be referred to a position which requires minimal people contact; a recovering alcoholic should not be referred to a position where he would be around alcohol; a woman who is fearful of men should be matched to a company in which her direct supervisor is a woman.

NOTE OF CAUTION: Often, candidates who are in counseling or twelve step programs are so focused on what they are learning that they want to share it with others—including the employer. Explain that not only is this unnecessary, but it may negatively affect their job search efforts.

Learning, Disability

There are thousands of learning disabilities, and nearly everyone has experienced at least one in their life. Learning disabilities occur when synaptic pathways in the brain are not developed during infancy and not because the candidate is stupid. If you suspect that a candidate has a learning disability, refer him to local learning center to be tested. These centers can identify and help treat the disorder by stimulating development in the pathways through regular sessions.

Teach the candidate the name of his learning disability and reinforce that it has nothing to do with intelligence, simply with how he learns. Chances are, he did poorly in school, perhaps even dropped out, and has been ridiculed his entire life as stupid. Calling the disability by name will remind him that it is actually a medical problem. To develop creative solutions, use the following steps:

1) Identify the specific task the candidate is unable to do and determine if that task can be done by someone else in exchange for one of their duties. For example, if someone with dyslexia works in a flower shop she could avoid writing by requesting that another employee take phone messages in exchange for doing the nightly clean up.

2) If the task cannot be avoided by the candidate, consider what specific aspect the candidate cannot do. In this case, answering the phone and talking on the phone are no problem—it's writing down the phone messages which is the problem.

3) Next, brainstorm about other ways of completing that task. For example, it may be done by using a hand-held dictaphone to record messages, which others can play back like an answering machine.

Develop A Good Answer

"As you can see by my portfolio, I have experience designing beautiful flower arrangements, with a special interest in exotic flowers. That is why I would love to work for the Island Flower Shop. I am applying for the designer and back room position, rather than the front counter because that is my true love, and also because I have dyslexia which makes it difficult to write down orders. I have found an efficient way to work around it when I need to take phone orders. I keep a small hand-held dictaphone with me and record the information as I repeat it back to the customer. The front counter clerk can then easily play back the message and complete the order form."

Mental, Disability

The mentally impaired candidate will need you to find the job for him, and will most likely require coaching on the job. Job Coaching means an employee of the placement program spends time with the candidate on the job teaching him to do each task, and remaining on the job until he is proficient. Mentally challenged candidates are usually most successful in jobs which are highly repetitive, such as packaging merchandise, stuffing envelopes, and unloading trucks. There are several successful workshops and placement programs around the country which work specifically with this population. We recommend using their expertise and program to assist your candidates. To contact local programs which work with the mentally challenged, call your state Mental Health Department.

Physical, Disability

The Americans with Disabilities Act (ADA) says that employers may not discriminate based on physical disabilities. Some key points of the ADA are presented in the Legal Guidelines to Hiring and Firing section of this book. The ADA does not mandate that employers hire the disabled, but requires that they not discriminate because of disabilities.

Begin by helping the candidate discover and articulate his strengths—whether physical, creative, or intellectual. Build his confidence by creating a strong resumé and developing good answers which address why his disability will not affect his ability to do the job. Next, actively locate employers who need his skills and experience. Matching will be very important. Be resourceful in locating companies already familiar with the value of physically impaired employees and will consider him based upon his skills, not allowing the disability to affect the hiring decision. To locate these companies, ask local advocacy groups where their constituents work, or talk with the HR directors of large companies to find out if they currently employ physically disabled people. If they do, ask what types of positions the employees hold and what types of

The "Exception to the Rule"

The year I was named one of *The Ten Outstanding Young Americans*, one of my co-recipients was a young deaf man from Hawaii who worked in a high-level position in state government. He was recognized not only for what he had achieved in his personal career, but for the in-roads he had created for other physically disabled people. He was responsible for many physically disabled people getting hired by local businesses. When I asked him why he thought he was so successful, he answered that he always knew he would be. He did not look at himself as "less than" because of his disability and he didn't allow others to either.

disabilities they have. This will give you ideas about where your candidates might work and the types of positions they might hold. Employers who are reluctant to answer these questions probably do not have a very good record of hiring the disabled. This may prove a perfect opportunity to approach them with a qualified disabled candidate who matches their needs. However, if the employer is not receptive, move on. There are other opportunities waiting.

Remind the candidate that during the interview he must always direct the conversation to his selling points, qualities, experience and why he is the best candidate for the position. Help the candidate remain positive and diligent. As with overcoming all barriers, first you must believe that employment is possible, then develop that belief in the candidate.

Sample Solution

DEVELOP A GOOD ANSWER

"I'm sure you've noticed that my left arm has been amputated. It does not impact my ability to be an excellent accountant. As you can see by my application my penmanship is clear. I have no difficulty using a computer, and can even lift and balance heavy ledgers. In fact, my last employer saw my disability as a plus, because in addition to getting a highly qualified accountant, it helped with her EEO (equal employment opportunity) requirements."

Related Topics, Disability

- ◇ APPEARANCE: disability is visible
- ◇ ATTITUDE: disability causes attitude problems
- ◇ COMMUNICATION, Speech Impediment: disability includes a speech impediment
- ◇ EDUCATION: learning disability has resulted in a lack of education
- ◇ FEAR: emotional disability includes fear of failure, rejection or responsibility
- ◇ MEDICAL BENEFITS: concerned about medical benefits
- ◇ TRANSPORTATION, Disabled: physical disability require special transportation arrangements
- ◇ WORK RELATED SKILLS: believes he has no skills

DISPLACED HOMEMAKER

In this barrier the candidate is female and employer is male.

The employer's concern may be that the candidate does not have any skills, does not understand the business culture, will be unreliable if she has young children or that her skills are out of date.

The candidate may be afraid of not "fitting in" with business people and may doubt she has any transferable skills. Also, she may not really want to leave her home for the business world, but feels compelled to do so due to financial demands. Often, displaced homemakers are women who are recently widowed or divorced who must now support themselves.

In General, Displaced Homemaker

Good Answer...

The major barrier for the homemaker re-entering the workforce after an extended period as homemaker/child care provider is that she does not believe she has any marketable skills. Usually, she will leave the Work Experience section of the application blank, leading the employer to believe she has no skills. In reality, she may have a lot of skills. Her volunteer work, community involvement, church activities and in-home work will attest to this. Instruct her to list these activities on her application as if they were paid jobs, writing "volunteer" where it asks about pay. Next, create a skills resumé by pulling from the skills she used as a homemaker and volunteer, and transferring them to her desired position. For example, if a candidate who has been a homemaker wants to go into office work, her transferable skills might include the ability to handle multiple tasks, phone skills, organizational skills, computer literacy, time management, money management, creating effective systems, and problem solving. It is amazing to see the change in attitude when the candidate sees her skills in black and white.

DEVELOP A GOOD ANSWER

Sample Solution

"I am very organized and am able to manage and complete multiple tasks simultaneously. I managed the schedules of five people while ensuring that all met deadlines and kept appointments. I have become very good at locating the resources necessary to complete projects, organizing and setting up for meetings and I am very comfortable communicating over the phone. I know Word Perfect 6.0..." Employer question] "I acquired these skills in my sixteen years of experience managing an active household."

Related Topics, Displaced Homemaker

- ◇ CHILD CARE: needs child care
- ◇ DOMESTIC VIOLENCE: has experienced domestic violence
- ◇ SELF-ESTEEM: lacks confidence or self-esteem
- ◇ WORK HISTORY: lacks formal work history
- ◇ WORK RELATED SKILLS: skills are out-of-date

DOMESTIC VIOLENCE

In this barrier the candidate is female and employer is male.

The employer's concern is that the candidate will be unable to focus on her job due to personal problems, will miss work due to injury or will come to work battered. He may doubt her ability to take initiative, act confidently or work well with men as a result of the abuse. He might also be concerned that the abuser will come to the job site and cause problems—this is a concern even if the woman has left the abuser.

The candidate's concerns, if she is still with the abuser, may include fear of his anger and violent reaction about her working, the safety of the children while she is at work, or the employer's reaction if she comes to work battered. She also may doubt her ability to integrate into the business culture, believe she has no skills, and worry about the shame and embarrassment of others discovering the abuse. She may fear leaving the abuser because she doubts her ability to financially care for the family, raise the children alone or protect her family if the abuser finds them. Even if she has left the abuser, she may still lack confidence, doubt her abilities, and be fearful that her abuser will find her job site and cause problems.

In General, Domestic Violence

In dealing with the candidate who has experienced domestic violence, you must be familiar with the whole situation and be sure the abuser is permanently out of her life. We recommend that you not job search with her until she has left him because she is too emotionally, psychologically and physically unstable to deal with the stress of working. You should refer her to domestic violence resources, such as a safe house and group counseling. Whenever dealing with this type of candidate, always include a domestic violence professional in the dual case management plan to ensure that special needs are being met.

Domestic violence has NO place in the job search process—it should be kept out of the interview and not mentioned on the application. Help the candidate realize that the employer does not need to know about the abuse; it has nothing to with her ability to do the job. If the employer raises questions about gaps in work history, a lack of work history or other issues resulting from the abuse, attribute them to reasonable causes which are true about the candidate, such as the candidate's decision to be a homemaker and raise her children, that her husband had a good job so she did not need to work, that she was a student or that she had a home business.

Develop A Good Answer

Sample Solution

"I believe in doing everything to the best of my ability, so while my children were young I stayed home with them. Now that they are in school, I am continuing my career."

Change of Identity / In Hiding,
Domestic Violence

Good Answer...

The candidate who is "in hiding" from her abuser is forced to cut all ties with her past, which may include a change in name, social security number, etc. As a result, she may not be able to give proof of her education level, licenses and certifications and employment history, and may have no personal references before she went into hiding. Lack of any verifiable past is the only reason domestic violence would be mentioned to an employer. Help the candidate develop a brief, professional explanation that includes the steps she is taking to ensure it does not affect her future, and prepare her to answer any additional questions the employer might have. Assist her to prove her stability, experience, education and reliability through other means. For example:

1) to prove the candidate's character and expertise, gather current references who can attest to who she is today, i.e., pastor, social worker, neighbors.

2) to gain an employment reference, suggest that the candidate volunteer during her job search.

3) to prove that she is skilled and certified (especially if the certification is inaccessible), have the candidate clearly articulate her skills and experience in a way that proves her

Prove It!

One of my strangest cases was a woman who refused to give her real name and could not give proof of her medical licensing because she had been in hiding. She told employers: "I have more than ten years experience as a Nurse Assistant with the developmentally disabled. For four years I worked in a 75-bed, facility and oversaw the care of 9 severely disabled adults, trained new staff, and wrote monthly reports. But I have been forced to leave my home state, change my name and start a new life, due to an abusive relationship. I am unable to present my license but am presently pursuing recertification in my new name. I am confident that as we talk, it will become apparent that I have the experience presented on my resumé, and would be an excellent candidate for this position." An employer agreed to hire her for a week to observe her and saw that she was excellent. She was promoted to manage a 12-bed facility.

expertise, and briefly explain why there are no references available. If the formal certification is necessary, have the candidate retake the test to get certified in her new name.

4) to demonstrate her abilities, have the candidate offer to work without pay for one week.

Adjust Candidate's Outlook

Self-Esteem, Domestic Violence

The candidate who has left her abuser must be taught that the abuse is not her fault, so ensure that she is in counseling and support groups. As an employment counselor, you may also want to educate yourself on the issues and psychology surrounding domestic violence. Local domestic violence programs can provide this information for you. This will increase your ability to assist the candidate to market herself confidently as the best applicant for the job. Prepare the candidate by assisting her to develop Quantified Selling Points (see Step 7 of THE TEN STEP PROCESS for instruction), strengthen her interpersonal skills, and present herself as enthusiastic and directed. Pay special attention to eye contact, volume of speaking voice, and nervous habits. If the candidate acts afraid, timid, or unsure of herself, it is unlikely that she will be hired. Do not set the candidate up to fail by not thoroughly preparing her. Keys to rebuilding her self-esteem include:

1) helping her to feel safe again by assisting her to meet her immediate needs, i.e., food and shelter
2) helping her to envision a new and better future for herself and her family
3) assisting her with setting and planning to achieve manageable goals
4) assuring her of your partnership in the process and your belief in her
5) taking small steps and celebrating the small successes.

Related Topics, Domestic Violence

◆ RESIDENTIAL INSTABILITY: living in a shelter.
◆ SELF-ESTEEM: lacks confidence or self-esteem
◆ WORK HISTORY: lacks good work history
◆ WORK RELATED SKILLS: skills are out-of-date or believes has no skills

---

EDUCATION

In this barrier the candidate is male and employer is female.

The employer's concern is that her employees are able do the job, and will continue learning as job requirements change. As we approach the 21st century, we are moving away from the Industrial Age which required an inter-changeable mass labor force, and toward the Information Age which requires specialized workers with the ability to efficiently find, assimilate, disseminate, and apply information. This type of employee will be the backbone of and the key to a company's success.

The candidate is concerned about obtaining employment which matches his skills, experience and intelligence, but may not accurately understand how his education, or lack thereof, affects his employability. A candidate who lacks the formal education required, but is otherwise qualified, may not realize that his skills, experience and knowledge can be marketed as a substitution for education. Another candidate may not understand the value of continued education, and, consequently, not be interested in learning new skills, may not want the pressure of learning new skills, may believe his old way of doing things is just fine, or may have disliked school and has no interest in returning.

In General, Education

In business, education represents two desirable elements to the employer. First, it assures a certain level of knowledge. Secondly, it demonstrates an ability to learn. A professor once said, "School teaches you to learn, so that when you graduate you can begin your education." When discussing education with the candidate, be sure he understands the two roles and knows how to demonstrate that he meets the employer's need in both. For example, if the candidate does not have the requested degree but does possess the appropriate level of knowledge which matches the employer's need, authenticate his knowledge using experience and self-taught expertise. If the candidate does not have a high school diploma he must demonstrate his ability to learn by giving examples which may include mention of something he is learning currently or sharing his plan for getting his GED.

Many believe that education is linear—that you must complete your education before you can get a job; but in reality, most people get their first job before they get their high school diploma. There are opportunities in the work force, although diminishing, for those who have not completed high school. However, as we enter the Information Age, those who are not educated in basic reading, writing, math and computer literacy will be relegated to low-skilled, low-paying jobs with little opportunity for advancement. To be promotable, employees must continue some form of learning while they are working. Education may mean formal study at a college or university, certified or licensed vocational training, seminars or workshops, on-the-job training, the ongoing processes of improvement by reading industry publications, watching specific documentaries and news shows, or perfecting skills through volunteer activities or hobbies. Self-teaching is one way to upgrade present skills or remain current, but is less marketable as the sole source of education.

Computer Literacy, Education

Currently, almost every job requires some computer knowledge. This trend will increase as we move further into the Information Age. As a greater percentage of the work force becomes computer literate, employers will no longer be forced to provide on-the-job training because they can easily hire competent employees. Emphasize the importance of becoming computer literate and provide the candidate with a referral to an Adult Education Program, community college, or JTPA program where he can quickly learn computer basics. Often, large temporary placement agencies have computer tutorial programs which can be used by anyone who signs with their agency. The better agencies will schedule regular times for the candidate to come in and will provide technical assistance as needed. Another option is to start your own computer learning center. The Resource section of this book provides you with information about consultants who can assist you with the process.

While he is learning how to use a computer, carefully match the candidate to jobs for which his limited computer knowledge will suffice. Once he has upgraded his skills assist him with upgrading his position.

English Literacy, Education

The candidate who cannot read has a limited selection of job possibilities, and often faces embarrassment and fear when filling out applications or taking employment tests. The employer may assume that because the candidate is illiterate, he lacks other basic skills necessary to do the job, or lacks the ability to learn. This assumption, not the illiteracy itself, will persuade the employer to screen the candidate out.

Find out why the candidate is illiterate; perhaps he quit school and began working at an early age, or has a learning disability, or speaks English as his second language. Turn these into selling points:

◊ If he has worked from a young age, sell his work ethic, history and skills.

◊ If you suspect that he has a learning disability, call a local school district and arrange for him to be tested. Once the truth is known, develop a creative solution which will demonstrate the candidate's innovation and ability to problem solve by following the steps outlined in DISABILITY, Learning.

◊ If English is not his first language, assist him in enrolling in an English as a Second Language (ESL) class. We always require a limited-English speaker to be enrolled in ESL classes before assisting with job search. This demonstrates an eagerness to assimilate and a willingness to learn, which are attributes valued by many employers. Even if he quits once he starts working, he will have improved his English and will know of an additional resource to help him succeed in the U.S. business culture.

◊ If the candidate's written English is not good, teach him to market himself to the employer before filling out the application. A few methods he could use include walking in to meet the employer, submitting a proposal letter, sending a tailored resumé and cover letter, being introduced to the employer, or volunteering.

Create a complete resumé and a "model application" which clearly communicate the candidate's Quantified Selling Points. Sometimes, especially in small companies, a complete resumé which includes the address and phone number of past employers can take the place of an application. NOTE: to keep resumés brief, company addresses and phone numbers are generally not included; however, with this barrier, the purpose of the resumé is to eliminate the need for an application. Thoroughly review the complete resumé and model application with the candidate so he knows the meanings of each word and can give examples of each selling point. It is also advisable to help the candidate become "occupationally literate," which means understanding and being able to use the 40-60 words unique to his industry. Also, have him practice recognizing key words on applications so that if he has to complete one, he is prepared.

Carefully match the candidate to a job in which he can perform successfully until he has learned some basics and can move up. Persuade the candidate not to mention his illiteracy in an interview, reminding him that he has been matched to a position which does not require reading and writing. However, in case a question about literacy should arise during the interview, the candidate must have developed a good answer. The answer should explain that he is "occupationally literate," and move quickly onto his strengths. If he is presently in class he may want to mention that as well. Suggest not using the words "adult education center" because it can have a negative connotation. Rather, use "community college," since most adult education programs are overseen by or held at a community college.

GOOD ANSWER

"Although I am not a great reader or writer, I do stay current with the latest industry vocabulary by talking with other workers. I purposely selected this field because it values my ability to make things grow, keep the grass green, produce multiple blooms on flowering plants, and keep the grounds looking well-manicured. My references will vouch for the excellent skills I have gained over 8 years of working in the field. However, I am also improving my writing skills by attending a class at the city college."

Lack of GED, Education

There are several reasons why a candidate may have dropped out of high school: it was "too hard," the campus environment was too hostile to learn, he came from a social or family environment that did not value school, or may have experienced a personal crisis. Regardless of why he dropped out, the candidate must understand the importance of obtaining a GED.

◇ For the candidate who found school to be too hard, determine whether this was due to a learning disability, illiteracy, or poor study habits. Investigate community programs which can assist these candidates with obtaining their GED, i.e., local adult education programs hosted by the school district or community college. For more information about how to deal with learning disabilities and illiteracy, see the corresponding entries.

◇ For the candidate whose school environment was hostile, inform him that college and GED classes are very different from high school and help him enroll in a program in which he feels comfortable.

◇ For the candidate who came from an environment which did not value school, help him understand the benefit of getting his GED and the continuing limitations it will place on his future if her remains a "drop-out." Also, assist him in securing a tutor, as he will probably have poor study habits.

◇ The candidate who experienced personal crisis during high school such as teen pregnancy, drug addiction, death in the family, divorce or abuse, has often had to put his life on hold to address these issues. Persuade him to focus on his future. Remind him that completing his education is his first step in reaching his long-term goals. If these personal issues are unresolved, refer him to appropriate counseling or community resources.

In all cases, encourage the candidate to complete his GED. Help him overcome his fears by becoming a partner in the process. Provide him with information about where to call, take him to register for class, ask him often about how his classes are going, and plan a "celebration" when he graduates—even if the celebration is only lunch at McDonald's or a cup of coffee at Starbuck's. Once he gets his GED, encourage him to take at least one college course, on a topic which fascinates him, so he can use the name of the college on his application and resumé. It will make him appear more educated, able to learn, and interested in education. It may also spark a genuine interest in returning to school, since college is very different from high school.

Afraid to go to School

Often, urban youth are so focused on surviving that they cannot concentrate on school, making it very difficult to succeed. Many are consumed with avoiding beatings, stabbings, or shootings. If you think that parents, teachers, or campus police can protect children—you are wrong! I learned this the hard way. Jenny, a teenage girl who came to live with me, was being harassed by a girl twice her size, because the bully wanted her boyfriend. I was told by one of the teachers that if he or the school principal got involved, Jenny would look like a "narc" and could be harassed by the entire student body. Even her boyfriend could not protect her, because it would invite male friends of the bully to stalk and beat Jenny up. Jenny did not want to go to school because she was afraid. I even contacted the parents of the bully, but they were no help. Unfortunately, many parents in urban areas have no control over their children, are too busy with their own problems, believe that violence is an acceptable means of dealing with problems or do not believe their child would hurt another child. Luckily, I had the resources to move and enroll Jenny in a better school district—which many parents cannot do. If we had not moved, I honestly believe she would have refused to go to school and joined the ranks of high school drop-outs. I was shocked to learn that this is the world in which our children are growing up. It is no wonder they are not graduating.

NOTE OF CAUTION: Instruct a candidate never to lie on his application or anywhere else regarding high school graduation because you think the employer will not check it. Lying on an application or resumé is grounds for automatic termination.

Provide A Resource

Lack of Vocational/College Degree,
Education

Lack of a vocational certificate or college degree may create a barrier for one of these three reasons: 1) the employer or job requires a specific skill, certification, license, or educational degree which the candidate does not have; 2) the employer assumes the degree to be proof of a lifestyle of learning and growing, which she needs to propel the company into the future; or, 3) the candidate is convinced that it will keep him from getting a job, so he sabotages the interview.

If the employer or job requires a certain degree, license or certificate (i.e., forklift driver's license, Emergency Medical Technician license, security guard card, Bachelor's Degree in accounting or nursing) which the candidate does not have, he should not apply for that job until he has acquired it. However, we strongly recommend that he secure another position in the field for which he is currently qualified while he is completing the required education. This will allow him the opportunity to begin building his network.

Mastering the Possibilities

In the Real World

A couple years after moving on from my company, a former employee who did not yet have her bachelor's degree, was hired for a position which required a master's degree. She realized that the board of directors' only reason for requiring a master's degree was to ensure that they acquired a person with a specific level of knowledge, professionalism, self-discipline, ability to think well and learn. My former employee was able to persuade this board of business professionals that her years of experience in the field, avid personal reading and current mastery of the required skills matched their needs. She reminded them that a master's degree does not mean the person can translate theory into everyday answers that work. She was able to further cement her position by enlisting the support of well-respected community leaders. She presented herself with professionalism, intelligence, friendliness, good employment references and a tremendous amount of confidence and enthusiasm.

If the candidate lacks the education believed by the employer to illustrate a basic ability or knowledge of the job, work experience can often be presented to show that he is actually qualified. When using experience in place of education, be sure the candidate's employment references verify his skills and recommend him for the position. Remind the candidate that most classified ads and job listings are "wish lists," so he should not be put off by them. If the employer finds someone who meets all of her criteria, great. If not, the person who best meets her needs and can be trained will be hired.

Before beginning a job search, review whether or not the candidate has the skills necessary to do the job. To market him to the employer as the best candidate for the job, look at his work history, areas of expertise, work ethic and life experience. Have him emphasize how his experience and hands-on education in the field compensates for the lack of formal education, and exceeds that which he could have learned in school. He should also communicate to the employer that he understands the value of education, especially in today's changing market, and is currently attending XYZ class at ABC college. Many companies will hire or promote candidates who do not yet have the required education, if they are working toward that goal. This is true even if the company knows it may take the employee years to finish.

PROVIDE A RESOURCE

Sample Solution

Most employers want employees who are up-to-date in their field and are continually learning. Suggest that the candidate take an industry-related class, attend a seminar, watch a TV special or news report, or read an industry magazine. The ability to talk intelligently about even one or two industry articles during the interview will create the perception that the candidate is current and industry literate. Reading industry information is helpful in marketing himself during the interview and, more importantly, for promotions once he is on the job.

Related Topics, Education

◇ APPLICATION: a limited English speaker or illiterate
◇ COMMUNICATION SKILLS: a limited English speaker, has a limited vocabulary, uses slang or speaks improperly
◇ DISABILITY: has a learning disability
◇ IMMIGRANT: a limited English speaker or was educated in another country
◇ SELF-ESTEEM: illiterate or dropped out of school

EMPLOYER BIAS

In this barrier the candidate is female and employer is male.

The employer's concern is that the candidate get along with other employees so there is harmony in the work place, that she work toward corporate goals, and that she adhere to the company's marketing strategy. This does not necessarily mean that she must be of a particular gender, race or age, but that she supports and represents the vision of the company.

The candidate is concerned about being judged "fairly," but does not realize that the employer will judge her based on HIS need and priorities. All employers have different needs and priorities, which is why when a new supervisor comes into a department, the needs and priorities may change. Often, the candidate assumes he knows the criteria on which the employer will judge her and the importance of each. But usually, the employer's criteria and the weight he places on various aspects is very different. For example, a candidate applies for a receptionist position. She is computer literate, organized, pleasant and has good phone skills. She believes that these qualities should count for 75% of the employer's decision. However, the employer believes that his needs are best met by someone who has a specific image and attitude, to reinforce the company image when customers first enter the office. Thus, he gives company image a weight of 75% and skills a weight of only 25%. Unfortunately, candidates seldom take the time to discover why they did not meet the employer's needs or how they incorrectly prioritized them. It is easier to simply condemn the employer than to learn about and adapt to the employer's needs. However, those candidates who are successful are those who learn the art of meeting the employer's needs.

In General, Employer Bias

All of us have preferences, or biases. We use these preferences to determine where we eat, how we spend our time, whom we choose as friends or partners and, often, whom we hire to work with us. Biases can be based on past experience, social pressure (i.e., what is politically correct, trendy or the boss' preference), or information learned (both accurate and inaccurate). In this book, we call the biases based on inaccurate information, "myths." All of us hold mythology about others. Women have mythology about men; men have mythology about women; the young have mythology about the old, and the old have mythology about the young; the rich have mythology about the poor, and the poor have mythology about the rich; Asians have mythology about African Americans who have mythology about Hispanics who have mythology about Caucasians....get the picture? The employer, like the rest of us, is concerned with making the best decision possible based on his best understanding. Although, if his understanding is "flawed," his decision will be also.

Because we all belong to several sub-cultures (gender, age, race and national origin among others), we have all been subject to others' mythology. Obviously, some sub-cultures experience more than others, but NONE of us like it. The question is not *"Does mythology exist?,"* but *"How can you make it work for you rather than against you?"*

Mythology will work against a candidate if she allows it to defeat her by becoming a **Victim**—someone who gives up and goes along with the myth because of her belief that, as an individual, she is powerless. Or if she allows it to so enrage her that she becomes a **Rebel**—someone who seeks to destroy her present society and establish a new one based on her own personal myths—she will also be unsuccessful in the job market. If the candidate goes into a new job looking for prejudice, she will probably find it. However, becoming preoccupied with it will not benefit her, but only fuel her despair or anger, thus making it difficult to be a good employee.

Mythology can work for the candidate if she can become the "exception to the rule"—someone who rises above the stereotypes held about her sub-cultures. In order to be promotable, she must distinguish herself from the crowd. This means that in addition to being the "exception to the rule," she must also meet the employer's needs, which usually comes down to generating profit. Ironically, by conducting herself in the same highly professional manner as other employees who are not from her sub-culture, she may receive recognition because her action was unexpected, whereas the same conduct by other employees, from whom it is expected, may not prompt the same recognition. This can give her an advantage. Secretary Ron Brown, head of the U.S. Department of Commerce, is an excellent example of a person benefiting from being the "exception to the rule" to the rule—his talent caused President Clinton to appoint a qualified African American to a cabinet position, where he made money for the country and himself.

As the candidate moves up the corporate ladder, she will find that fewer positions exist, and the competition has become increasingly fierce. To succeed, her focus must shift from merely distinguishing herself from her peers, to proving that she is similar to those in positions above her. Often, a candidate who has been a corporate executive may decide that it is easier to use her expertise to start her own company, rather than vie for these limited positions. If her expertise proves to be valuable in the marketplace, her company may become a leading company of tomorrow, and she will determine how employees are judged.

Have You Heard the One about the Blond?

Several years ago at the end of an important business negotiation, a successful middle-aged businessman with whom I was dealing leaned back in his chair and said, "You're pretty smart for a blond." I am sure the look on my face conveyed my shock at being subject to the long-standing myth that "blondes are dumb." He immediately apologized. I looked him in the eyes with a smile and said, "I guess you haven't met many blondes." My challenging response to his mythology pointed out the ignorance of his statement. I became the exception to the rule. Perhaps he reconsidered his myth at that point, or maybe as he meets more intelligent blondes his myth will change. In reality, the businessman's mythology may have given me the advantage during our negotiations because he did not anticipate needing to be alert and savvy.

We call someone who becomes the "exception to the rule" a **Challenger**. A Challenger does not give up or give in, as does the Victim, nor does she try to destroy every company, employer or co-worker who does not agree with her, as does the Rebel. Instead, the Challenger realizes that mythology abounds and seeks to re-educate those around her. She realizes that although beliefs are not easily abandoned, **ALL rules have exceptions.** By becoming the exception to a rule, she raises questions regarding its accuracy. Remember, persuading people to change their mythology is a slow process. We do not let go of our mythology easily. When challenged, our first response is usually to defend it. Later, we may think about the new information and watch to see if it holds true. Once the candidate, as the "exception to the rule," is in a position of influence, she can find other "exceptions" and help them get started. This is called being a mentor. Once the market place is flooded with "exceptions," the rule changes. For example, in the last century the rules have changed regarding women in the fields of medicine and law, and African-Americans in professional athletics.

Here are the steps a candidate must take to become the "exception to the rule:"

1) Remembering that the number one goal of most employers is profit, she must articulate how she positively impacts the bottom line. To do this she must sell the employer on how she will make the company money, perhaps by opening new markets, having a higher success ratio, maintaining a strong customer base or developing new ideas. She must also sell the employer on how she will save the company money, for example, by doing preventative work which reduces present costs, decreasing staff turn-over, or accomplishing more work in less time. If there are selling points resulting from her sub-culture affiliations, the employer should be made aware of the ways in which these will benefit his company.

2) She must position herself as an INDIVIDUAL rather than as a representative from her sub-cultures, as her sub-culture affiliations will be noticed without her mentioning it. To do this, she must invalidate the employer's myths about her sub-cultures, as they apply to her, by offering Quantified Selling Points (see Step 6 in THE TEN STEP PROCESS) which demonstrate that they are not true about HER.

3) She must understand that she is not a "sell-out" for not immediately trying to eliminate the myth entirely. Have her hold strong to the realization that once she has proven her profitability to the company, she will have the "clout" necessary to introduce more "exceptions" and begin to re-educate the company until the rule is no longer a rule, and the myth has been abolished.

4) She must continue patiently to work her plan.

Sample Solution

ADJUST THE CANDIDATE'S OUTLOOK

People overcome mythology by keeping their focus on their goals, and not on the opinions of others or the problems around them. Never forget that it is possible to overcome bias! Consider the lives of:

◇ Oprah Winfrey, an African-American woman who has climbed to the top of the entertainment industry, an industry renown for its dominance by white males.
◇ Two twenty-plus college friends, who started Apple Computers, became a major competitor of IBM, a Fortune 500 company ruled by the old guard.
◇ Margaret Thatcher, a woman who became Prime Minister of England, triumphed over a notoriously male dominated society.

Age, Employer Bias

Good Answer...

It is not legal for the employer to ask the candidate's age, birth date, date of high school completion, or any other question designed to identify how old she is. However, he can ask if the candidate is under 18 or over 70 years old, and request that the candidate provide proof of age, if hired. This is allowed because some jobs legally require the employee to be over the age of 18 or 21. Although the employer cannot ask about the candidate's age, he can guess. His guess is often made subconsciously, based on over-all appearance, style of clothing, hair color, choice of words and phrasing, attitudes toward current issues, hobbies and interests, or actions and gestures. Also, the candidate may unknowingly provide the information by listing the date of graduation or military discharge, or by providing information on jobs held more than ten years ago.

NOTE OF INTEREST: Most employers only require a candidate's work history for the last ten years or last four positions. Job skills learned over ten years ago which have not been used more recently are usually considered out-of-date. Even the terminology used within an industry changes about every ten years.

The employer is generally less concerned about age than he is about the candidate's image and attitude, and the company's market niche. So he will judge the candidate based on the image and attitude she projects, not her actual age, as long as she is old enough to legally hold the position. Help the candidate to develop a work image which matches the employer's needs.

An older candidate must first dispel the myth that she is out-of-date, too slow, or unable to learn, by talking about current trends in the industry, showing she has up-to-date skills and ideas, and demonstrating excellent health and great stamina. She must also market herself as "one of the team," ready to continue learning and growing. Next, have her turn her "lemons into lemonade" by relying on her experience, not her age, as she presents herself as the best applicant for the job. She should market herself as an expert in the field, "older and therefore wiser," able to teach others so that the whole company benefits from her experience. Lastly, she should capitalize on the positive myths about older workers by promoting her great work ethic and reliability.

A young adult applying for positions which require an "older, more responsible image," may choose a mature hair style or the addition of white temples, or may wear clothing which is worn by mature workers or denotes financial success. Appropriate clothing can be purchased at reasonable prices at second-hand, consignment and outlet stores.

A young candidate must first address the employer's concerns about work ethic, punctuality, hard work, excessive absences, attitude, honesty, or a lack of professionalism. To counter this, have her talk about what she has learned from Business Acculturation workshops, one-on-one discussions with you, and extra-curricular activities. She must show an ability to take instruction, eagerness to learn and willingness to work. Next, be sure the candidate matches the company image. This may require that she get "work costumes"—the wardrobe, jewelry, hair style, etc. required to promote the image of the company. For a young woman, this may include not wearing nose rings to work, toning down her make-up, wearing conservative clothing and accessories and using traditional nail polish. For a young man, it may include wearing a tie and jacket, tying back long hair, avoiding baggy pants, and removing earrings. Lastly, the candidate should capitalize on the positive myths about young people by promoting his knowledge of computers, high energy, and desire to keep learning.

Good Answer

To eliminate the perception that all youth have short attention spans, are irresponsible, are always late and do not care about the quality of their work, a young candidate might say, *"I know I am young, but being on the school basketball team has taught me the importance of being on time, working hard and always giving my best."*

Young women should also be aware that sometimes the employer is apprehensive about hiring women who are eager to start families. He doesn't want to deal with the cost or interruption caused by having an employee on maternity leave. This is a concern few employers will ever discuss outright, but if it remains unaddressed the candidate could be screened-out. To counter this concern, the candidate could mention that her goal is to establish her career before starting a family, or that she is not married and does not plan to be in the near future.

Change
Where
You Look

Adjust
Candidate's
Outlook

Gender, Employer Bias

If the candidate wants to enter an industry or position generally held by the opposite sex, she must rely heavily on her qualifications and ability to work in diverse situations. The words or actions of others should not detract her from being "the best at the job." She must be persistent, patient and the "exception to the rule." The easiest means to overcoming gender bias is to find a mentor who will open the door for her and vouch for her abilities. A second option is to gain work experience by volunteering, starting at the bottom and working her way up, or by taking advantage of an Equal Employment Opportunity apprentice program or employer. She must keep a positive attitude, remain focused on her goal and seek out those who will help her achieve it. Once she is an expert, she may want to branch out and begin her own business. By the way, this is true for both sexes.

ADJUST CANDIDATE'S OUTLOOK

Sample Solution

All things are possible if the candidate remains a Challenger. History proves it. It does, however, take determination, hard work, patience, and understanding of the people whose myths she wants to change and a good network. In the 50's it was believed that women had no "money sense," and thus could not be successful in the field of sales. However, a few very determined and hardworking women became the "exceptions to the rule," proving they were excellent saleswomen. Today, women dominate the field of sales.

Race, Employer Bias

Change Where You Look

Adjust Candidate's Outlook

Unless the employer has spent a lot of time within the candidate's racial culture, he will probably have mythology about it. The issue, then, is whether his mythology will stop the candidate from getting hired. Try to identify the most commonly held myths about the candidate's race, then create a selling strategy which proves those myths are not true about your candidate. The strategy may include dress, hair, language, examples of past work situations, promptness, organization, interpersonal skills, ability to learn and an understanding of the company's dominant culture. Anger or "poor me" attitudes will not take her very far with most employers. Even employers who are sympathetic toward her attitudes usually will not have the time to deal with all the personnel problems which arise from someone who has a "chip on her shoulder" or always is looking for ways in which her supervisors, co-workers, and customers are offending her. Instead, encourage the candidate to approach each employer with a positive attitude that says, "I can represent your company. I can make you money. I am pleasant to work with. I am the exception to your mythology." Then once she has proven her profitability to the company, she can open the door for more "exceptions," until there are so many "exceptions to the rule" that the "rule" is no longer a rule.

When the Shoe is on the Other Foot...

I minority friend of mine once reminded me that if a qualified Caucasian person was hired into an African American owned and operated company, and tried to organize a white solidarity group, complained that the African attire of his co-workers is unprofessional, and grumbled because no one else enjoyed country music, he would have little chance of being promoted.

All people are alike in that we are most comfortable among people who think and act like we do. The more two individuals have in common, the more secure they are with each other..

As with gender, finding a mentor who can open the door is the easiest means to start. Remember that a mentor does not have to be someone of his same race, only someone who sees potential in the candidate and is willing to help her succeed. The candidate's success as their protege will make the mentor look more successful. It is easier if the mentor is at least aware of the myths which the candidate will face and is sympathetic to her struggles. If the candidate is unable to find a mentor or wants to be a pioneer in a new field, she should gain the skills by volunteering, starting at the bottom and working her way up, or joining an apprentice program as one of their EEO numbers. She must keep a positive attitude, remain focused on her goal and look for those who are willing to help her get there. Once she has acquired the necessary level of expertise, she may want to start her own business.

Sample Solution

ADJUST THE CANDIDATE'S OUTLOOK

Examples of other "exceptions to the rule" and challengers who have changed "mythology" will be an encouragement to your candidates:

◇ In just the last decade the belief that minority TV programming was not profitable has been changed. During the 60's, 70's and 80's very few minority programs existed—today minority programming is on our televisions nightly.

◇ Even during the civil rights era, few African American lawyers rose to prominence—yet, today most Americans know the names Johnny Cochran, Christopher Darden, and Clarence Thomas.

◇ Hispanics in California have traditionally been viewed as only laborers with little economic power, yet today they own and operate the most widely listened to radio station in Los Angeles with an impressive advertising base.

If the candidate is unable to get past her anger or fear to become the "exception to the rule" you may want to look for companies which already employ large numbers of people from her ethnicity. Many large companies even have social clubs based on race, which will help the candidate feel more supported. If the candidate's anger is too intense, you may want to place her in a company that is owned and operated by someone of her own ethnicity and marketed toward her own ethnicity. Most community services offer Anger Management classes or seminars, if the candidate is interested in dealing with his anger.

Related Topics, Employer Bias

◇ ATTITUDE: attitude has become negative due to the employer's biases
◇ BUSINESS CULTURE: unfamiliar with the U.S. business culture

◇ GANG MEMBER: is or has been a member of a gang.
◇ OVERQUALIFIED: an older worker seeking an "easier" job
◇ SELF-ESTEEM: self-esteem is eroded by employers' bias
◇ WORK EXPERIENCE: first job or changing fields
◇ WORK RELATED SKILLS: skills are out-of-date

FEAR, Candidate's

In this barrier the candidate is female and employer is male.

The employer's concern is that he have positive employees who are excited about their jobs, excited about the company and confidently driving the company toward the future. As the employer interacts with a candidate whom he perceives to be overly fearful (more than a healthy nervousness), he may be concerned that as an employee she will take little initiative, not endeavor to improve her skills and knowledge, not complete assignments, not ask good questions, not keep appointments, not follow-up with customers, be easily intimidated by others, overreact to situations on the job, not receive criticism well, or react defensively. He may even be concerned that her fear is the result of a mental problem, will result in a harassment or discrimination lawsuit, or create divisive personnel problems. To be sure his concerns do not become reality, the employer may conclude that the only way he can hire her is if additional or specialized supervision is provided.

Equally, the employer may be concerned if the candidate does not display a healthy fear and appropriate sense of judgement in dangerous situations, acting in an unsafe manner which could endanger the health and safety of herself, her co-workers, and the company. Millions of dollars are spent each year on worker's compensation claims and high insurance premiums due to workplace injuries.

The candidate's fear is that she will judged based on race, gender, ethnicity, religion, age, disability, socio-economic status, etc. rather than ability. She may also fear that she will be rejected or not respected, not being "good enough" or that her lack of knowledge will be discovered.

In General, Fear

There is a huge difference between showing reasonable nervousness in an interview, and being unreasonably fearful. If the candidate displays the debilitating traits described in employer's concern above, she is not employable. Often, the candidate's fear will cause her to sabotage opportunities by subconsciously saying or doing things to disqualify her from the job, such as telling the interviewer of her welfare status or prior history of fights, giving the employer ultimatums or refusing to dress appropriately for the type of job she is pursuing. Subconsciously sabotaging opportunities allows her to attribute her loss to the employer, and avoid facing her fear.. If by chance she is hired and continues to make decisions based on her fears, she will likely be dismissed— and the last thing the candidate needs is to be fired, reinforcing her fear(s).

 NOTE OF CAUTION: We do not relinquish our fears easily. Be patient with the candidate and proceed at a pace with which she is comfortable. Do not let her avoid dealing with her fear by avoiding you. Create a safe environment in which her fears can be addressed, and be persistent.

CHANGE THE CANDIDATE'S OUTLOOK

To identify the candidate's fears, discuss patterns you see in her behavior and ask her why she thinks they exist; ask her what is the worst thing that could happen if she started working this week; talk with friends, family members and other case managers to learn more about the candidate; or ask her point blank what she fears. Address the fears openly and teach her to visualize herself overcoming the each one and succeeding. Affirm her strengths and opportunities. Do not discount her fear, because, in her mind, it is a considerable barrier. Take small, **sure** steps and celebrate the successes along the way. Do many of the tasks with her first, and do not expect her to do them alone until she is comfortable with them. Make a deal with her that during her job search she will call you anytime she starts to talk herself out of good opportunities.

PROVIDE A RESOURCE

If the ideas given above do not help, involve professional counselors. If you do not have a professional counselor who voluntarily works with your candidates, check the yellow pages. Call each counselor, explaining your program and ask if they would be willing to volunteer time to provide twelve sessions to one candidate per year. Continue through the list until you have secured a half dozen counselors.

Failure / Success, Fear

The candidate who is afraid of failure has usually experienced negative consequences for failing in the past—whether the anger of her parents as a child or being forced into homelessness as an adult. It is the fear of trying and then "hitting the rocks below because there are no safety nets in place" which makes taking a risk so frightening. If you want to teach the candidate to risk failure you have to be willing to be her "safety net." Being a safety net means having a plan for picking her up if she fails so she can try again. If your program does not allow for mistakes, or you do not want the responsibility of helping her overcome a failure, then DO NOT try to assist her in dealing with this fear yourself; rather, find another program or person who will.

If you choose to work with her, the **first step** is to identify and discuss how other employment barriers can be removed. This is important because these other barriers are often used to mask the fear. Only when they are addressed can the candidate move on.

The **second step** is to adjust the candidate's understanding so she realizes that failing is an important step in succeeding. Share examples of famous people who failed before succeeding. For example, Babe Ruth who holds the world record for the most "home runs" in professional baseball also holds the record for the most "strike outs"; Walt Disney was fired by a newspaper editor for lack of ideas; Henry Ford failed and went broke five times before he succeeded with the Model-T car; and Albert Einstein didn't speak until he was four and didn't read until he was seven—his teacher described him as "mentally slow!" Redefine failure as a "practice run" for success.

The **third step** involves pointing out her own character strengths, transferable skills, employment selling points and successes that she may not be allowing herself to acknowledge. For example, character strengths may include remaining clean and sober, being liked or respected by other program participants, or having made significant positive changes in her life such as re-establishing ties with family, developing a personal relationship with God, creating a debt reduction plan, etc. Transferable skills may include having taken care of a sick parent, volunteering at her child's school or knowing how to work on cars. Employment selling points may include length of involvement (paid or unpaid) in the field of interest, having a clean DMV record, attendance record on previous job, or vocational training. And successes may include having graduated from high school, raising a family or being selected as a leader or award recipient.

The **forth step** is to encourage the candidate not to equate her self-worth with her failures and successes. This is critical because each failure reinforces her false sense of low self-esteem. Instead, encourage her to associate her self-worth

What Are You Afraid Of?

I worked with a woman who had been on welfare for over 15 years, had raised 5 children in the midst of poverty and abusive relationships with drug-addicted men, and had not held a job in over 20 years. While discussing the benefits of being employed, she gave several well-presented reasons why she was better off on welfare—she wanted to be there when her 9-year-old came home from school, she had no car to travel to work and she had no current work history. My first task was to determine how these initial barriers could be resolved.

We adjusted where we looked by locating positions within walking distance from her home which would allow her to work while her son was at school. I convinced her to work with me for 3 weeks to determine if a suitable job could be found. As she began to see how she would benefit from working, her outlook changed and we found that she was well qualified for and interested in child care—she had raised 5 healthy drug-free kids, taken child development classes, volunteered with Head start and been PTA President. We prepared a resumé using skills from her personal life and developed good answers for the interview.

A local child care provider needed her skills but wanted to hire someone with a car. She immediately assumed she was ineligible. However, after I learned that the car was needed to pick up afternoon snacks twice a month, we brainstormed how she could meet their needs without a car, such as covering for another employee while they get the snacks or bringing snacks with her in the morning. She scheduled an interview. I supported her by providing bus tokens, watching her son during the interview and debriefing her and the employer immediately afterward. She was hired. When I said, "Congratulations! Can you believe less than 3 weeks ago you were debating whether you were better off working or remaining on welfare?," she replied, "The only reason I said any of those things is because I was afraid no one would ever hire me." At that point, I realized that her real barrier was fear—the rest was merely a smokescreen!

with how she can make the world a better place by treating others, God and herself in a positive manner. Remind her of the qualities she will develop as she takes risks, such as courage for risking, perseverance by not giving up, and tenacity by learning from each encounter.

Regardless of the outcome, the **fifth step** requires that you support her after she has risked. Support is shown by your willingness to debrief her after she risks, help determine the next step, encourage her when she feels discouraged, believe in her enough to give her responsibility for her own life, use your network for her benefit and continue to cheer her on. We also recommend making the candidate feel respected and special by telling the receptionist in the candidate's presence that if she calls after an interview or other assignment, the call is to be put directly through to you. If you are in a meeting, take the call, keep it short and tell her you will call her back as soon as the meeting is over. If the meeting is with another candidate, an employer, a co-worker, or a donor, they will all be impressed with the level of interest you show in your candidates and will be encouraged by a good story.

Rejection, Fear

| Provide A Resource | Adjust Candidate's Outlook |

This fear often underlies the candidate's entire line of reasoning, whether she realizes it or not. Usually she has either a "victim" mindset which says, "I would rather remain unemployed than apply for a job and risk rejection again," or a "rebel" mindset which says, "I will hurt and reject you before you can hurt and reject me." Neither of these mindsets will get her hired or promoted.

In working with this type of candidate, you must first make sure she feels accepted and respected by you.

Second, remind her that the job search process is not about her personally, but rather about her ability to "market" herself. Inform her that in outside sales, such as the job search, most salespeople expect to hear "no" nine times before they hear one "yes!" So the first nine tries are practice sessions during which they can perfect their selling techniques. Since the candidate is probably new at outside sales, let her know it may take her more than nine practice interviews before she gets a job. In reality, it will probably take her less, but raising her expectation to nine attempts sets her up to be a great success when she is hired on the sixth interview!

Look Me in the Eye and Say That

Often, fear of rejection manifests itself in physical ways, such as poor eye contact. Helping the candidate minimize behaviors which raise "red flags" will reduce the employer's concern. Recently, I worked with a young man who had struggled for years with alcoholism and "fitting in." He was afraid of being rejected and, as a result, would not maintain eye-contact with people—unless he was drunk. Now sober, he prepared to enter the job market but found that because of his fear of rejection he could not look people in the eye. I knew his fear would not be eliminated in a couple of weeks, but he could learn some techniques to lessen the employer's concern.

First, I explained that in the American business culture, eye contact is perceived to communicate honesty and confidence, as well as respect and interest toward the person with whom you are speaking. These are necessary qualities if he wants to be hired. I told him it was highly unlikely that he would be hired unless he could "look em' in the eye." Once he understood the importance of looking the employer in the eye, I taught him that while in conversation, he could look anywhere within the area between the person's collar and the top of their head. Practicing with me, he learned to watch my mouth, look at my nose, glance at my ear and occasionally at my eyes, then back to my mouth while I was speaking to him. He continued to practice with friends and others. Also, I discovered that he had lived in Japan for a few years, and had also been in the Navy, both of which taught him NOT to look people in the eye.

We developed the following good answer he could use if the interviewer seemed concerned or frustrated that he would not look her in the eye, "Excuse me for not maintaining better eye contact. I lived in Japan for several years where direct eye contact is considered rude, so I am learning to get comfortable with it again." He was soon hired as a Stock Inventory Clerk at a local retailer. As he interacted with staff and customers, his eye contact continued to improve.

Third, be sure you spend time preparing and tailoring the candidate before the interview. This should include reviewing good answers to difficult questions, developing a minimum of six Quantified Selling Points for the position sought, reviewing the company culture and how she will represent them well, and ensuring that she is dressed appropriately.

Finally, debrief her immediately after each interview. This will allow you to determine problem areas in her interviewing skills and assist her to become better at marketing herself.

 NOTE OF CAUTION: As with all fears, the fear of rejection will not be removed simply by getting a job. Continue to talk with the candidate about things which happen on the job which might trigger her feelings of rejection...or help her locate a counselor who can help her work through this issue.

Responsibility, Fear

The candidate usually fears responsibility for one of the following reasons: 1) she has never been taught how to be responsible, so it is new to her; 2) she does not want to disappoint others by creating expectations she does not think she can fulfill; 3) others have accommodated her irresponsibility so she sees no reason to change; or 4) she is lazy.

First, point out patterns in her behavior which demonstrate irresponsibility and discuss to which of the four reasons listed above they are attributed. Most often you will find that the various behaviors all can be attributed to the same reason. I also recommend that before you determine that the candidate is merely "lazy," you closely examine the other options. Deciding she is lazy leaves you little to work with, and mislabeling her incorrectly can impede success—so be careful.

Second, if the candidate fears responsibility because she has never been taught or because she does not want to disappoint others by creating expectations she does not think she can fulfill, help her define or redefine what "responsibility" means. Rather than referring only to being perfect or to achieving major accomplishments, such as graduating from college or meeting all your family's expectations, "responsibility" refers to things she accomplishes every day, for example, being on time for a meeting, completing an assigned task, returning a phone call, or doing something else she agreed to do. This new definition will make "responsibility" attainable and allow her to see where she has taken responsibility in the past and been successful.

If the candidate is not responsible because others have accommodated her irresponsibility and she sees no reason to change, or because she is lazy, she probably already has a clear understanding of "responsibility" and will need a compelling reason to take responsibility. Motivating her will usually be met with a lot of resistance. However, having her complete some Life/work planning exercises to determine her career interests may help. If she is fascinated by the type of work she is pursuing and wants to build a career in it, she is more likely to take responsibility for tasks that help her achieve her goals. In general, as a survival skill, this type of candidate has learned how to deflect responsibility onto others. Do not allow her to make you take responsibility for the fact that she is not responsible.

Third, help the candidate learn the negative consequences of not taking responsibility and state in detail how taking responsibility will benefit her. DO NOT rescue her from experiencing the natural consequences of her irresponsibility. This must include strictly enforcing any negative consequences you agreed upon. For example, at WorkNet we have a 50/50 rule which states that if the candidate does not complete her agreed upon assignments, her Career Developer will not provide her with the results of her assignments such as job leads, reference check information, bus tokens or interview clothing. Deal with the candidate's behavior, but avoid punishing her with an emotional reaction, such as guilt, disapproval or anger, so that she continues to feel that you are on her side and is reminded that you believe in her. This will dissuade her from giving up and reverting to old habits. For example, calmly discuss why the assignment was not completed and help her determine what must be done to accomplish it before the next meeting.

Fourth, give her recognition each time she completes a task, risks trying something new or shows that she is taking responsibility for her life. Be sure the recognition is appropriate so that she does not get embarrassed, feel uncomfortable, or begin to expect a celebration each time she does something.

Throughout the process, require her to take ownership and responsibility for her own job search. Create a plan together, make her a 50/50 partner, discuss each step of the process, and give her regular tasks to complete. Have a highly structured accountability plan and always follow-up. Do not "role model" irresponsibility yourself by failing to hold the candidate accountable, or by rescuing her from the consequences she has created. Let her know that she, not you, will set the pace for the job search. This will encourage her to take responsibility for her job search if she wants to find a job, thus proving to herself that she can do it. She may need an entry-level position with close supervision until she gains more confidence.

TEACH A NEW SKILL

Sample Solution

A candidate I worked with displayed his irresponsibility in many ways, including being late for meetings. He showed up 30 minutes late for our first meeting so we began by talking about the link between being on time and taking responsibility. I discovered that he had never been taught to be responsible, and that, because he was charming, others had accommodated his irresponsibility so he saw no reason to change. We discussed that in the American business culture lateness is a sign of disrespect, lack of respect for the other person's time, or disinterest in the topic. We then talked about how being on time would benefit him, and how being late would hinder him from reaching his goals.

When he arrived 30 minutes late for our next meeting, I made him wait until I had completed the task I was working on before seeing him. I explained that due to his lateness we would not be meeting, and that he would not receive the information I had gathered from my assignments and that I could not look at the drawings he brought to show me (his long-term goal was to be an animator and we were setting-up investigative interviews). He was very disappointed. However, I never got upset, and although I shared his disappointment I remained firm—for his sake. I knew his future depended upon learning this skill, and that no matter how charming he may be, if he can not meet a publisher's deadlines he will be fired.

He needed new information and a lot of accountability to learn this lesson. As I asked leading questions, he came up with a plan to ensure that he would be on time for our next meeting. He decided on an early appointment so he would not get distracted and forget to come. He decided to set his alarm for two hours before the meeting so he could eat, get ready and catch the bus. When I asked how he would remember to set his alarm, he decided to write himself a note and place it in his picture portfolio and put it on his refrigerator as soon as he got home. He arrived to our third meeting on time with his assignment 80% done—he took responsibility for not having finished it and told me his plan to finish it before the end of the day!

Related Topics, Fear

◇ BUSINESS CULTURE: fears the unknown world of business
◇ DOMESTIC VIOLENCE: fears her abuser will find her.
◇ DEPENDABILITY: fear of responsibility manifests itself in being late or not showing up
◇ EMPLOYER BIAS: fears discrimination.
◇ IMMIGRATION: does not have the legal right to work in this country and fears looking for work
◇ SELF-ESTEEM: suffers from low self-esteem
◇ WORK HISTORY: has a poor work history

G

GANG MEMBER

In this barrier the candidate is male and employer is female.

The employer may be concerned that the candidate will lack a strong work ethic and knowledge of basic business protocol. She may fear that he will react in a belligerent or threatening manner toward staff, customers or supervisors and will invite a "bad element" into her place of business. She may also fear that he is still affiliated with the gang, or that rivals are looking to harm him. She may doubt his dependability, honesty, willingness to be taught, and willingness to follow instruction.

The candidate may be concerned that he will not fit in, be expected to change, be relegated to menial positions, not be paid what he thinks he is worth, or treated in some other "disrespectful" manner. He may also be concerned about what his "homies" (other gang members) will do or think about him working in an entry-level position for "the man" (any person who has power within the system—usually white), or working outside their gang-related enterprises.

Realize that if a gang member is compelled to look for a job, it is usually because he realizes the gang lifestyle will lead him to prison or death and he wants more out of life than that, he develops a personal relationship with God, he becomes a parent, or he loses someone close to him and reassesses his life. We believe that there are many who would like to work but are hindered because they want it on their terms or do not know how to be an employable, promotable candidate. These candidates often struggle with fear, lack of understanding of the business world, lack of job search skills and presentation barriers.

In General, Gang Member

The nightly news reports have given employers valid reasons to be hesitant when it comes to hiring gang members, former gang members or those who dress, talks and act like a gang member. At the same time, if systems are not established to assist gang members attain legal, living-wage jobs which offer them hope for the future, then our problems in the inner-cities will never improve. Employment programs, such as yours, which can mediate between the two sides—always remembering that both the employer and candidate are your clients—are the hope for this system. Both sides are proud and do not believe that they should have to endure any disrespect from the other, but both sides can be taught to respect and communicate with the other if the mediator is patient, diligent and earns their trust by always looking out for the best interest of each side.

The employer is usually focused on making a profit, which means ideally she wants workers who are good at their jobs, have the company image, learn quickly, have a great attitude, require little instruction, work cheap, and are dependable and hard working. Today, employers realize that finding this type of candidate is less likely so many are more willing to provide training or work with people who have completed a good training program. There are also many who would like to lend a helping hand, as long as it does not hurt their business.

In gang culture the two most important issues seem to be: 1) "being there for your homies, no matter what," and 2) not allowing anyone to "dis" (disrespect) you. To illustrate the extent of what is meant by "being there for your homies," let me share a story. I had an employee who had grown up in "the projects" in Oakland, but through hard work had graduated from the California State University at Berkeley with a BA degree. He came to me one evening and said that he might have to take a couple of days off due to personal problems. I later overheard him talking with other staff about one of his "homies" who was angry at someone for messing with his girlfriend. He explained that his "homie" wanted him to go along when he shot the guy, and said that if the "homie" decided to actually do it, he was obligated to go. I was shocked. I asked if he realized that he could go to prison if he took part in a shooting. He said, "yes, but homies stick together." I asked sincerely how he could so easily throw-away his hard-earned college education and bright future because a friend had a girlfriend problem. He responded that the friend was his "homie" long before he went to college. He went on to say that he was trying to give his friend other options for resolving the problem, but if, in the end, his "homie" decided to shoot the guy, he would go. As an employer, I was astounded that an educated man would view this as a reasonable option.

Equally confusing to the business culture, is the issue of not allowing anyone to "dis" you. Gang members, and others living in the street culture, define disrespect differently than the business community. To illustrate, the following are a few definitions of disrespect which candidates have given me: "my boss keeps telling me what to do," "he is always watching me and checking my work," "he talked to my girlfriend," "she gives me the dirty jobs"(even when they are part of his job description), or "he touched me." Although they may seem like minor incidences to us, the retribution for such disrespect can be anything from grumbling, to quitting, to physical violence against the individual or property. At the same time, they see no disrespect in doing things the business culture views as disrespectful, such as talking back to their boss, being late, taking things which belong to the company, being rude to customers or only doing the part of their work assignment they enjoy doing.

To begin bringing these different cultures together, you have to understand both sides and be able help each side understand the other and find common goals. However, a greater compromise is generally required of the candidate because he needs the employer more than the employer needs him. Consequently, more of your time will be spent assisting the candidate to adapt, while the work you do with the employer will be more subtle. Once the candidate is working, your focus will be on helping the employer interpret the candidate's actions and reactions as problems arise as well as continuing to mentor the candidate in how to be a promotable employee.

Former or Looks Like, Gang Member

In areas which have gang problems, the pressure for young people to participate in gangs is very high. Understanding what motivated your candidate to leave his gang, or never join in the first place, will help you determine what type of jobs best will move him toward his goals and enable you to keep him focused on his goals when he becomes discouraged. Remember that both of these types of candidates must have exercised strong will and persistence to have made this choice.

As with most barriers the best solutions moves the barrier enough that the employer is unaware that it was ever a concern. With this barrier it may take a couple of survival jobs in which the candidate focuses on perfecting new skills, rather then career development. There are three major issues you must address: image, attitude and safety. How easily they are overcome depends on how willing the candidate is to change. Image is probably the least difficult to address since it is superficial. The following are the steps we suggest:

1) Identify for yourself what the employer may perceive as an "image" issue, i.e., clothing, hair style, make-up, tattoos, speech patterns and language.

2) Assist the candidate in understanding why it may be a cause of concern for the employer. If he does not agree that it must be changed, it won't be. We would do this by asking him questions like, "How do you think a businesswoman would react if she walked into a landscape nursery and a young man dressed like you are now walked up to her and said, 'Yo, what do ya' want?" Usually the answer will include laughs about how scared she would be. Ask if he thinks it is a good idea to hire staff who scare the customers, and what he thinks he could do to be less scary. If this initial question does not bring about the desired response, ask another question regarding the reactions he gets when he goes to the mall or other places where there is a mix of professionals and kids. Another question could be, "Why do you hang out at … (a hangout for teens)?, rather than … (name a yuppie restaurant)?" His answer should highlight that he hangs-out where he is most comfortable. Ask why he is more comfortable at one place then the other, then talk about what types of things he could do to make customers feel comfortable in the type of industry he plans to enter. NOTE: It is

important that you do not tell him that his culture is bad or wrong, but rather that if he wants to succeed, he must be able to fit into the business culture as well as his home culture—he must become bi-cultural.

3) Help the candidate identify what he can do to meet the employer's needs. To do this, we usually have him close his eyes and imagine the perfect employee for the job he is pursuing. While the candidate has his eyes closed, ask a series of questions allowing him to think through each issue which is a problem for him (for a fuller explanation of this exercise, see the Sample Solution given in APPEARANCE, Presentation). For some candidates it is helpful to look through magazines to identify styles which he would be willing to take on. Discuss with him the types of industries where that "look" would be acceptable. If he wants to work in a different industry, use the magazine to show him what an acceptable image would be for that industry.

If he needs to learn corporate English, identify opportunities, i.e., through an English tutor at the public library, listening to television and radio shows in which the host uses corporate English, enrolling in a community college course, joining Toast Masters (a social group designed to gain public speaking skills), asking his mentor, friends, and family members who speak corporate English to help him learn.

4) Help him gather the resources to address each issue, for example, appropriate interview and work clothing, a barber to cut hair, a tutor to work on his English skills, a contact person for a local Toast Masters group, a plastic surgeon who will remove tattoos, etc. Do not expect the candidate to find or secure these resources himself. It will be more successful if you approach them on his behalf.

5) In your regular meetings, have the candidate practice being in the Business Culture. Require him to dress, speak and act like he is at work. Remember when teaching a new skill to **Tell** the candidate what you want him to know, **Show** him how to apply the information, **Watch** him do it, **Praise** what he does well, gently **Correct** specifically what needs to be improved and **Repeat** these six steps until he applies the new lesson comfortably. For more information about teaching a new skill, see Step 4 of THE TEN STEP PROCESS.

The second issue is attitude. As we discussed earlier the gang culture and business culture have very different rules. It is important that you always remember that there is no reason the candidate should understand the rules of the business culture if he has never been taught. It is also important to remember that there is no reason he should feel comfortable with them, or agree with them if they are new to him. Understanding this will put you in a better mindset as you begin to address this issue. Develop a means by which you begin teaching him the differences between his culture and the business culture. Do not infer that one is right and the other is wrong, rather that to succeed in either culture he must act appropriately. At WorkNet's programs, we present two four-hour workshops which deal with understanding the American business culture, conduct individual discussions with each candidate and provide employment mediation once they start working.

Assist the candidate to get involved with groups which function outside the gang culture, such as church groups, community college or city sports teams. Community involvement is also a good way for them to interact with working people who want to give back to the community by volunteering at the library, youth center, neighborhood clean-up program or gang prevention programs. There is a basic rule in cross culture studies which states, the more interaction you have with the culture you want to learn, the faster you will learn it. That rule certainly applies to the business culture also.

The third issue is safety—of the candidate and those around him. Generally, gangs have certain neighborhoods they control which they do not leave, because doing so means entering another gang's territory. Violence is almost always the result of being in another gang's neighborhood. If the candidate fears that a member of his previous gang or a rival gang will come to his place of employment to hurt him, assist him to find employment outside the area. Suburban and downtown areas are usually safer. Get a copy of the yellow pages for the selected area(s), and assist him with contacting employers in his desired field. If the candidate is going to ride the bus out of his neighborhood, you must also

Okay [period]

Mac had spent 20 years in the street/gang culture and had mastered the skill of intimidating people with "just a look." On the streets this is great, in business this is not so great; To counteract this, I had to teach him to smile during the interview (smiling in the street culture usually means you are up to no good). During one of our regular meetings, he told me about an incident at the restaurant where he worked. He was in the kitchen when his boss came up to him to correct something he had done wrong. Immediately he defended why he had done it his way and gave her "the look" when she started to argue with him. She stopped mid-sentence, quickly turned and walked out. She did not look at or talk to him the rest of the day. He knew this was not good if he wanted to get a raise at his upcoming review.

We talked about how his natural reaction when someone challenged him was to "put them in their place," but that in this circumstance her place was above him. To counteract this, I taught him the skill of saying "okay" and just doing it. "Okay," when someone gave him advice, "okay," when someone corrected him or gave him an assignment, "okay," even if he wanted to punch them or tell them to shut up. Because he clearly saw how saying "okay" benefitted him, and that he was not saying she was right—only that she was the boss and that he was being paid to do it her way—he was willing to change. He also realized that if he could not say "okay" with a pleasant look in his eye, he had to quickly look away so that his non-verbals did not speak louder than his verbal "okay."

consider the bus route and what neighborhoods it passes through. You will probably need to encourage the candidate to move out of the area and start over. Ask if he has a relative in a neighboring city with whom he could stay, or if he would be willing to move into a half-way house until he could save enough money to get his own place. In many of the large cities, local churches or ministries have begun discipleship homes for young men who want to grow in their faith while living in a communal setting and working on the outside, such as Victory Outreach. These programs may offer the new environment and support your candidate needs to start a new life.

For most candidates, initial placement is best found in a position which requires minimal attitude and image adjustment, so it can happen gradually. These positions should involve limited customer or professional interaction, such as warehousing, construction, manufacturing, etc. This will allow the candidate to learn to be on time, work a full day, take instruction and complete tasks, which are major first steps.

Present, Gang Member

Placing active gang members into mainstream businesses will likely bring to fruition all of the employer's concerns. In fairness to the employer, do not refer active gang members without fully informing her of the situation and gaining her consent. Few companies will knowingly hire active gang members, because the employer is in business to make money, not offer a training program for people who are resistant to developing good business practices. If you plan to offer your services to present gang members, we suggest that you start your own business in which you employ the candidates, so the primary focus can be to assist the candidate rather than on making money. We suggest that you avoid referring active gang members directly to employers for several reasons. First, because his loyalty and daily life is tied to the gang, he cannot be committed to his employer and will leave his job whenever it interferes with his gang activity. Second, he cannot give up his gang image, behavior and attitudes. Third, you risk bringing physical violence upon an unsuspecting employer, her employees, company property and customers.

There are several successful gang intervention businesses operating in major cities around the country. Contact your local Youth & Gang Prevention Services to see if there is one located in your area. To begin your own business, consider what type of business is needed in your community which could employ gang members, considering their barriers, and is feasible, given your resources.

Sample Solution

Provide a Resource

Dolores Mission/Proyecto Pastoral in Los Angeles, California, created Jobs For The Future, a gang intervention and employment program designed to offer jobs to gang members and "at-risk youth." As part of their program, in 1992 they established a tortilla factory called Homeboy Industries, which has expanded to include three subsidiaries: Homeboy Bakery, Homeboy Silk Screen and Homeboy Merchandising. They presently employ twenty gang members. For more information, contact Father Greg Boyle, Program Director at (213) 526-1254.

Related Topics, Gang Member

◇ APPEARANCE: projects the gang image.
◇ ATTITUDE: displays attitudes inappropriate for the U.S. business culture.
◇ BUSINESS CULTURE: unfamiliar with the employer's perspective and U.S. business protocol.
◇ CANDIDATE BIAS: has bias against members of your targeted clientele.
◇ COMMUNICATION: needs to learn business English.
◇ CRIMINAL RECORD: has been in trouble with the law.
◇ DEPENDABILITY: unfamiliar with expectations regarding time.
◇ EDUCATION: a high school drop-out.
◇ EMPLOYER BIAS: fears employer bias due to gang affiliation.
◇ FEAR: demonstrates a fear of rejection, failure or responsibility.
◇ SELF-ESTEEM: living in an non-supportive environment.
◇ WORK EXPERIENCE: this is first legal job.
◇ WORK RELATED SKILLS: does not think he has any skills.

IDENTIFICATION, Lack of

In this barrier the candidate is male and employer is female.

The employer's concern is that she adhere to federal and state laws governing her employees' "right to work," either because she is a good citizen or she does not want to be fined. Legally she is required to have each employee complete the Federal Form I-9 verifying his right to work in the US. If she does not, she can be fined thousands of dollars.

The candidate is often unaware of the necessity of proper identification, unless they have endeavored to get a job without it. The three groups which are most a effected by the I-9 requirement are illegal immigrants, first time job seekers and homeless individuals who have lost all their "important papers." These groups are usually concerned with how to get the needed documents, or how to find an employer who will risk hiring someone without appropriate identification.

Provide A Resource

In General, Identification

The Federal Form I-9 requires a candidate to show proof of legal residency or a work visa, and a photo ID as proof that they are who they say they are. An American passport, military ID or Green Card meets both requirements. A driver's license or state ID card and a birth certificate or social security card also give the needed proof. I recommend completing a Federal Form I-9 for each candidate before referring him to an employer to ensure they have the required ID. For further information or a copy of the Federal Form I-9, call your local Department of Justice or Immigration & Naturalization Service.

If the candidate does not have the proper identification, you must assist him in securing it before he can legally be hired. If he does not have a current photo ID, but is a U.S. citizen, the first step is to help him get a copy of his birth certificate or baptismal certificate. NOTE: The subheadings in this entry are listed in a logical order, rather than in alphabetical order

Birth Certificate - A birth certificate can be secured by writing to the Office of the County Clerk in the county where he was born and requesting an official copy. We recommend calling first as most counties require an administration fee which can range from $3 to $15. Determining the amount ahead of time will save weeks of correspondence back and forth. Send a cashier's check and letter signed by the candidate requesting the information. Allow two to six weeks for delivery.

Baptismal Certificate - The fastest way to get a copy of a candidate's baptismal certificate is to contact a family member who is still active in the church and ask them to contact the pastor. If that is not possible, have the candidate call or write to the church requesting a copy. Be sure to include the year he was baptized, his full name and the full names of his parents. The pastor or a staff member can review the church records and send a copy. When you write a letter, always make a follow-up phone call within a couple of days to be sure they received it and are looking for the records. Also, do not overlook the possibility the candidate's parents may have a copy of it in his baby book.

Social Security Card - Direct the candidate to the local Social Security Office, where he will be required to complete an application, present a copy of his Birth or Baptismal Certificate and show a photo ID. The Social Security Office can be fairly lenient about what photo ID is acceptable. I have had clients use any of the following: Student ID, Check Cashing Card, Workplace ID Card, as well as Driver's License or State ID. The candidate will receive a printout to use until the card arrives. Most employers will accept the printout.

If he has had a Social Security Card in the past, knows his number, and has a photo ID, the office will give him a printout to use until the replacement card is issued. Most employers will accept the printout.

If the candidate does not have a photo ID, the following steps may be taken:

Driver's License—The requirements for obtaining a driver's license may vary from state to state, along with the actual length of time it takes to receive the photo ID. In some states, the candidate can get it immediately. Other states may only give him a receipt which does not have a photo and will send the license within 30 days. To get a driver's license, the candidate must make an appointment with the Department of Motor Vehicles to take both a written and driving test. Upon arrival, he must offer verification of legal residence and pay a small fee. Verification of legal residence generally can established by a birth certificate, baptismal certificate, U.S. Residency Card, naturalization papers, U.S. Visa or U.S. Passport.

If he has had a license before but it has expired, he will not need to take the driving test again, but will have to take a written test, show verification of legal presence and pay a small fee.

If he has a current license but has lost it, he can get a duplicate by going to the DMV office and paying a small fee.

State I.D.—To obtain a state ID, the candidate must make an appointment with the Department of Motor Vehicles. Upon arrival, he must show verification of legal presence and pay a small fee. No testing is required. The length of time it takes to actually receive the photo ID varies from state to state.

Military ID—If the candidate is discharged from the military and wants a copy of his Military ID from previous service, have him contact the Veteran's Benefits Information and Assistance Office for local contact numbers for his branch.

If the candidate is not a U.S. citizen, he must obtain a Green Card or U.S. Work Visa which gives him the right to work in this country. Although replacing a lost Green Card is a fairly easy process, applying for a first time card is complicated. It is seldom a fast process and can result in deportation if he is denied. We suggest having your candidate talk with an immigration advocate before moving forward with a request for Alien Right To Work status.

Green Card—Permanent and conditional aliens are required to have an Immigration & Naturalization Service (INS) Green Card which shows his status as a legal immigrant with the right to live and work in the United States. If the candidate has lost his Green Card he should call his local INS office to get an INS Form I-90 application, and INS Form FG-98 for finger printing. He must complete and return these forms, along with two passport-style photos, to the INS office which has jurisdiction over his area.

If he has never had a Green Card but is the spouse, child, sibling, or parent of an adult child who is a U.S. citizen, or the spouse or unmarried child of a current

Green Card holder, the legal resident must fill out INS Form-130 and submit it to the local INS office.

If he has never had a Green Card but provides a specialized skill which an employer needs, and cannot find among American workers, he can ask a prospective employer to submit a Federal Form ETA-750A (Application for Alien Employment) and a Federal Form ETA-750B (Statement of Qualification for Alien) to the local State Employment Office which will forward it to the Department of Labor (DOL). If the DOL agrees that no U.S. worker could fill the position, it will provide a Labor Certification which the employer must submit along with the INS Form I-140 (Immigrant Participation for Alien Worker) to the local INS office. There are other specialized alien work applications which do not require that you go through the DOL, such as the I-526, if the candidate intends to begin a business in the U.S., in which he is investing over a million dollars and will provide ten or more jobs for U.S. workers, or the I-360 if the candidate has extraordinary ability in the sciences, arts, education, business, athletics or as a religious worker, professor, researcher, or is given "special immigrant" status. For more information about this process, call your local U.S. Department of Justice, INS office.

NOTE OF CAUTION: If the candidate is not eligible to gain the legal right to work, you will jeopardize your program and its reputation by referring him directly to employers. If you feel compelled to help him with job preparation, assist him in creating a "model application" and resumé, finding job opportunities, and practicing interview questions, but require him to contact employers on his own. This will ensure that any hiring agreement is strictly between the candidate and the employer, and that your program is not involved. It also means that you should not count this candidate in your placement statistics..

Related Topics, Identification

- ◇ ADDRESS: homeless
- ◇ IMMIGRANT: new to the United States
- ◇ MESSAGE SERVICE: without a phone
- ◇ RESIDENTIAL INSTABILITY: homeless, living in a shelter or residential recovery program

IMMIGRANT

In this barrier the candidate is female and employer is male.

The employer's concern is that he avoid issues which could encourage the federal government to get involved with the operation of the business. Over the last ten years the federal government has become increasingly interested in whether illegal aliens are taking jobs away from U.S. residents and placing an undue burden on tax payers by utilizing government-funded entitlements. Few employers are willing to suffer the cost of fines for breaking the law, risk the downtime in production if INS agents haul away a significant portion of their work force, or endure the embarrassment of an INS raid. As employers weigh the potential expense of hiring illegal aliens against their value as low-cost workers, they often determine that it is unprofitable.

Employers may also have other concerns such as communication if the candidate's English is limited, a difference in work ethic, a different view of "on time," problems with sexual harassment if they come from a culture which does not treat women as equals, or lack of knowledge about American business protocol. Employers may also be concerned that customers will not feel comfortable or relate well to a foreigner, or that customers may have mythology regarding other ethnic groups, such as "they have an unpleasant odor, dress funny, are lazy, are stupid, are argumentative or are dishonest."

The candidate may have concerns about language, relating to co-workers, being treated unfairly or taken advantage of, being physically abused, being cheated of payment for work she has done, being unable to get the same type of professional position she had in her country, understanding business protocol, or being discriminated against based on race or ethnic origin. It is important to realize that most candidates do not come to this country with these fears. She has bravely traveled to a foreign country with great expectations of starting a new life, but these realities soon become valid fears.

In General, Immigrant

When working with an immigrant, your initial tasks will include determining whether she has the legal right to work in this country. If she has the identification necessary to complete the Federal Form I-9 required for all new employees, she is considered to have the legal right to work in the U.S. Whether a candidate has or does not have the legal right to work will determine your next steps.

In most instances, the more you can do to assist the candidate in understanding the American business culture and becoming bi-culture the more opportunity she will have in the future. For those who do not want to adapt to the American culture, then working within their ethnic community, or for an employer of the same ethnicity is their best option.

If the country she comes from is a non-English speaking country, assist her with enrolling in an English as a Second Language class, particularly if she is young. Encourage her to practice English when she meets with you and assist her in memorizing a brief English "sales pitch" which tells the employer why she would be a good employee. If she speaks a less common language such as Hungarian, Thai, or Portuguese, and you are not familiar with where their "local community" is situated, call the local Court House and ask for the office which provides interpreters for court hearings. They should be able to give you the name of an individual who speaks that language and is familiar with that community. A five minute conversation with the entrepreneur will often provide you with a wide range of information about the specific target population, such as the name of local publication or news letters, where their business district is, industries which seem to hire a large number of this minority, etc.

WANTED: Immigrant

Nathan had been the Vice President of a large paper manufacturer in England. He had been trying to find employment in the U.S. while living in England, with no luck. When his wife became pregnant they decided to take an extended leave from their jobs, sell their home and move to the United States. They wanted their child to be an American Citizen. We began by determining what he could offer a U.S. company that most U.S. residents could not. The answer was knowledge of British business practices, how to complete the legal paperwork for doing business in the Common Wealth, and contacts in Europe. Armed with these selling points, he began researching both paper manufacturers who were already doing business in Europe and those who had not tapped into that market yet but were large enough to make the move. He created an individualized Employment Proposal Letter addressed to each CEO which presented how he could benefit the company. He followed up with a phone call the same week and arrange interviews for the following week. After creating great interest in his skills and how he would benefit the company, he then explained that he was in the process of applying for citizenship and that he would need the company to submit a Federal Form I-140 to the government so he could gain alien worker status so they could hire him.

Not only do immigrants have to deal with language and cultural barriers, but also with the myths which Americans have about people coming from their culture. Review EMPLOYER BIAS, Race and CANDIDATE BIAS, for information on this issue.

Legal, Immigrant

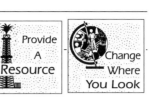

Provide A Resource

Change Where You Look

If the immigrant received her education and held a professional position in her own country, such as a doctor, nurse, engineer, accountant, or school teacher, she will not be allowed to practice her profession in the United States without gaining the additional training required and U.S. "licensing." If she is willing to go to school and gain the U.S. license, assist her with obtaining an entry-level position within the field, such as Medical Assistant, Nurse's Aid, Bookkeeper or Teacher's Aid, so she can begin to build a professional network. If she is unwilling or unable to return to school, examine her transferable skills and assist her with selecting another position within the field or a new field in which she could advance. Remember, this is a real emotional and psychological adjustment for her. It is common for candidates in this position to experience fear, anger and depression. Treat her with the greatest respect, help her logically examine her options, and stay positive!

NOTE OF CAUTION: It can be very frustrating to have worked as a respected doctor in your own country only to be told that in this country you can only clean-up after a doctor. The same is true for all professional positions. Therefore, unless the candidate is planning to immediately return to school to regain his right to practice his profession, it may not be a good idea for him to take an entry-level job in his old field. If he is going to school, the advantage of taking an entry-level position is to build the professional network needed to resumé his career once he is licensed.

CHANGE WHERE YOU LOOK

Sample Solution

Jose had owned a hospital in Guatemala, but to practice medicine in the U.S. he would have to complete almost eight years of schooling. He was a single father of two and could not afford to return to school, so we began looking at his transferable skills and interests. He was good at making people feel comfortable and gaining their trust. He was also a good businessman. While looking for a home, he discovered that there was great opportunity in real estate for native Spanish speakers, and that it would take him only a few months to get licensed. Within a year, not only was he working, but owned his own agency.

If the legal immigrant was not a professional before coming to the United States, placement will be easier. Look for companies which service her ethnic community, such as local restaurants, book stores, and theaters. Often, there are ethnic phone books, newspapers, newsletters, radio stations or television stations which advertise companies, such as long distance carriers, real estate brokers, and cable companies, which market to that particular population. The larger of these companies will often hire bi-lingual staff to target an immigrant population, You can also look for companies which have departments with bi-lingual supervisors, such as the housekeeping departments of many major hotels, field workers and assembly workers.

Sample Solution

PROVIDE A RESOURCE

Assist a company which is having difficulty keeping positions filled to convert one shift to a crew which speaks the language of the non-English speaking population you serve. Assist the company in finding a qualified bi-lingual supervisor, then follow-up by supplying the limited English speaking employees.

Change Where You Look

Illegal, Immigrant

It is not advisable to refer candidates who do not have the legal right to work in the U.S. to your employers, because you expose both your agency and the employer to negative repercussions. There are three options you could pursue if you want to service this population:

1) Assist the candidate in becoming legal, by reviewing with them the regulations for gaining legal status or referring them to agencies which assist with this process. One means of gaining the right to work in the U.S. is to find a U.S. employer who will petition the government for permission to hire the candidate because she possesses a skill which the employer has been unable to find among U.S. workers.

2) Teach the illegal candidate how to market herself and how the American business culture operates. Encourage her to tap into the underground job network which exists in most cities with a sizeable immigrant population by talking with friends and family, and asking immigrants from her country who are working in the U.S. Warn her that employers who use this network often pay below minimum wage, withhold pay checks, and can be abusive.

3) Assist the illegal candidate to explore starting her own business. Many illegal aliens become self-employed as maids, gardeners, mechanics, venders, etc. To do this, she may need additional training in marketing, bookkeeping, and other basic business practices. Most large cities have entrepreneurial training programs which teach these skills. Another option is to locate a "job co-op" of undocumented workers who market themselves to do day jobs and regular assignments for private homeowners. This would provide her with a support network and a steady income without the stress and stigma of soliciting work by waiting along the street to be hired for the day.

Related Topics, Immigrant

- ◇ APPLICATION: cannot complete an application in English
- ◇ BUSINESS ACCULTURATION: unfamiliar with how the U.S. business culture operates
- ◇ COMMUNICATION SKILLS: non- or limited-English speaking.
- ◇ EMPLOYER BIAS: fears employer bias because of his race or nationality.
- ◇ FEAR: fear of failure or rejection is debilitating
- ◇ IDENTIFICATION: lacks the necessary identification to work in the U.S.
- ◇ MESSAGE SERVICE: does not live in an English-speaking household
- ◇ REFERENCES: lacks U.S. references
- ◇ WORK HISTORY: has no U.S. work history

JOB SEARCH RESOURCES, Lack of

In this barrier the candidate is male and employer is female.

The employer's concern is that she be able to contact the candidate easily and that the candidate be able to return her calls the same day. She is also concerned that the candidate be professional and dependable.

The candidate's concern is that he will be able to conduct a professional job search by having access to a telephone, a message service, current job market information and leads, a professional-looking resumé and a means to create cover letters and thank you notes so he can secure an appropriate level job in his field as soon as possible.

In General, Job Search Resources

There are certain resources which candidates need to conduct a successful job search and to do industry and educational research. They include:

- ◇ a telephone to contact potential employers, past employers and personal references
- ◇ a message service, voice mail service or a message board so he can receive messages from employers daily
- ◇ current job leads from the open market, i.e., classified ads, local employment

listings, flyers about job fairs, job leads from other candidates.

◇ current job leads from the hidden market, i.e.,your contacts, the business section of the local paper, a professional networking group you attend, or a weekly networking group you arrange for candidates

◇ resource materials including local yellow pages and telephone books, local job market information, a listing of local employers, Chamber of Commerce publications, a listing of job hotline phone numbers, etc.

◇ reference materials including a dictionary and thesaurus, "how to" books for job searching, information about various industries and industry publications

◇ a street map of the local area, and public transportation schedules

◇ basic office supplies, i.e., paper, pens, stapler, tape, paper clips

◇ access to a computer and laser quality printer

◇ quality resumé paper, matching envelopes and postage

◇ access to a fax machine, a photocopier

We suggest that you create a candidate resource area which includes access to the resources listed above. Depending on your resources and the scope of your program, this may mean a desk in the corner of your office or a room which is monitored by a staff person. The resource area should provide a professional atmosphere and access to someone who can offer suggestions. Candidates should conduct themselves professionally while using the resources area, i.e., language, clothing, topics of conversation, no children, no personal business. The resource area should have regularly scheduled hours so candidates can plan when they will use it. We have seen agencies use anything from a large closet to a large room as their candidate resource area.

 NOTE OF CAUTION: If the resource area is in your office, you lose your privacy and cannot conduct individual meetings with other candidates while the resource area is being used. If the resource area is outside your office, it must be monitored by staff or volunteers to be sure the equipment and resources are being used appropriately.

The more tools you provide for your candidate, the more they can do for themselves. The fewer you provide, the more you have to do for them because they cannot succeed without them. If you are unable to provide any or all of these resources, partner with a local agency which already has an appropriate resource area, or has the space and resources to create one. In exchange, you could provide job search workshops, individual job search counseling or other services to their clients. Another potential solution is to write a grant to sponsor the project.

Related Topics, Job Search Resources

◇ ADDRESS: does not have a permanent address

◇ APPEARANCE: candidate needs interview clothing or hygiene resources

◇ MESSAGE SERVICE: does not have a reliable phone or message service

MEDICAL BENEFITS, Needs

In this barrier the candidate is female and employer is male.

The employer's concern is that he keep costs low while providing the benefits needed to attract the level of employees he desires.

The candidate's concern is that she have medical coverage for herself and her family. This becomes particularly important when she has small children or a member of the family has a major illness.

Welfare to Work

As a mother of two, Tasha was very concerned about moving from welfare to work, for fear that she would also lose her Medi-Cal benefits. She knew that working was important in being a good role model to her children and that welfare would never offer her more than a substandard living. After finally getting in contact with her welfare worker, we were able to get Transitional Medi-Cal for her first year of work. She obtained a job as a security officer. Because the security industry traditionally has a high turnover and because she practiced the "work for advancement" skills she learned in our classes, within a year she was promoted to a management position which offered full medical benefits. Note: It is important that the candidate know before they accept a position whether medical benefits are offered at a management level. Remind them to ask rather than assume.

In General, *Medical Benefits*

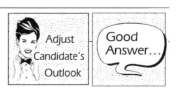

Adjust Candidate's Outlook

Good Answer…

Many of today's large businesses are focused on becoming "leaner," while entrepreneurial businesses are struggling to establish themselves. Consequently, employers often feel that they cannot afford insurance for their employees. However, employer's attitudes on medical benefits vary—some endeavor to provide for as many employees as deemed financially possible, others provide it only when necessary to attract "the right candidates," and employees of entrepreneurial businesses often must buy their own. Unfortunately, most companies with a large "minimum wage" workforce do not provide medical insurance to these employees, due to the substantial cost of paying for so many people (a family of three can cost the employer over $4,000 a year—equivalent to a $2 an hour raise.)

The job search process will be easier if you discuss with your candidate that medical benefits are, in fact, a "benefit" like a company car, uniform allowance, educational pay-back, or discount passes to local entertainment, given by the employer rather than a "responsibility". Understanding this will give the candidate a better attitude during the search. She can either focus her search toward companies and industries which are likely to provide this type of benefit, or look for a job which pays more so she can purchase her own.

Sample Solution

Change Where You Look

The types of companies most likely to provide medical benefits are as follows:

1) companies in the medical industry, such as hospitals, HMOs, doctor's offices and pharmaceutical companies
2) professional companies with only a small number of entry-level positions such as law firms, advertising firms and special effects companies. The entry-level positions may include parking lot attendants, office clerk, receptionist or mail room clerk
3) well-established companies which still feel a moral obligation to provide medical benefits to all employees

Related Topics, Medical Benefits

◇ CHRONIC ILLNESS: has recurring illness which may concern employers
◇ DISABILITY: has a physical disability
◇ OVERWEIGHT: is extremely overweight
◇ WORKER'S COMPENSATION CLAIM: has filed a claim

MESSAGE SERVICE, Lack of

In this barrier the candidate is female and employer is male.

The employer's concern is that his messages be received by the candidate and that the candidate return his calls promptly. If the phone is answered by someone who is rude, seems incoherent, or portrays some other negative personal trait, it may raise "red flags" about the candidate's personality, lifestyle or stability.

The candidate's concern is that she get her messages so she can become employed. At the same time, she may not have the money to buy an answering machine or rent a voice mail box, and she cannot depend on the people with whom she lives to take messages.

In General, Message Service

The candidate must have a phone number where she can be easily reached—employers do not schedule interviews by mail. Help the candidate realize that whoever answers the phone for her directly represents her to the employer. I have often called a candidate's home only to be greeted by, "Yo!," "What's up?," a foreign language, a mumbling two-year-old, a teenager who was irritated that I was tying up "her" phone line, or a voice which interrogated me and then yelled, "phone" to my candidate without giving her any of the information acquired. Ask the candidate who would answer the phone if you were to call her house right now, and how well they would represent her. Remind her that the employer will often assume things about her professionalism based on little things such as how her phone is answered. Also, the employer will not spend time trying to communicate with non-English speakers or rude people, nor will they endeavor to track down a candidate who does not return their calls.

If the candidate is living in a shelter or residential program, either her residence or your employment program should provide her with a phone number she can give to employers. It is important that when answered, her phone number does not announce where the candidate is living, but rather leaves the employer assuming he has reached a residence or for-profit employment center (unfortunately, many employers still hold a lot of mythology about the homeless and their prejudice could cost your candidate the job). Require that the candidate call in daily to get her messages and remind her that your phone number is to be used to job search only.

Sample Solution

TEACH A NEW SKILL

Have the candidate tell her family that employers will be calling, and that her family can help her get a job by answering the phone politely and professionally. To assist them, she should explain how she wants the phone answered, such as "Good morning, Lisa speaking," "Good afternoon, Smith residence," or simply "Hello." She should put a message pad and pencil by the phone, along with the questions to ask, i.e., "Who may I say is calling?," "May I tell him the name of your company?," "At what number can you be reached?," and "When can she reach you at this number?" Be sure she periodically checks to be sure the phone is being answered professionally and has a plan for enforcing it.

Sample Solution

PROVIDE A RESOURCE

If the candidate does not have a phone, lives in a shelter, cannot rely on those in her household to take good messages, or cannot rely on an English speaker always answering the phone, suggest she get a voice mail box or beeper. Most local telephone companies have voice mail boxes which they donate to homeless and non-profit employment programs. If your local telephone company does not provide this service, ask a local service club or the employee's association of a large company to provide the money to rent them.

Related Topics, Message Service

◇ JOB SEARCH RESOURCES: you need ideas on providing other job search resources
◇ RESIDENTIAL INSTABILITY: living in a shelter, residential recovery program or with family

OVERQUALIFIED

In this barrier the candidate is male and employer is female.

The employer's concern is that she only pay for the skills she needs. She may also be concerned that the candidate might become disgruntled with the lower wage and level of control, or that the personal problems leading him to seek a lower position might cause problems on the job.

The candidate may be concerned that he find work immediately, gain current work history or obtain a transitional position which will allow him to enter a new field. He may be focused on recovering from a traumatic personal problem, such as being fired, a death of someone close to him, addiction issues or divorce.

In General, Overqualified

Often a candidate struggling with self-esteem issues assumes it is easier to get a position for which he is overqualified. This is not true. Generally speaking, it is easiest to get a position which matches his skills and experience. However, we have identified four situations in which a candidate may want to pursue a lower level position: having a Master's Degree with no work experience to complement it, needing a job immediately, changing fields or titles, or needing to be re-certified.

1) Having a Master's Degree but no work experience to complement it. In most fields, a degree without work experience makes the candidate very difficult to place. The employer does not want to pay a Master's Degree salary to someone who has not proven that he can apply the information. My recommendation is to omit the degree from the resumé, not to mention it in the interview, and to pursue a lower-level position. If the interviewer asks a direct question about a Master's Degree, we tell the candidate not to lie, but to explain that he left it off the resumé because he realized that without actual work experience he was not yet "educated" enough to apply for a position which matches his degree. Once the candidate has acquired a year of work experience, he can begin job searching again, with both the degree and current experience in the field on his resumé. NOTE: This dilemma is particular to a Master's Degree, and not so true for a Bachelor's or Doctorate Degree.

2) Needing a job immediately, but having to wait too long to secure a position at his level. The length of the hiring process, the period between the first interview and when the candidate starts work, varies with the level of employment being sought. Traditionally, for unskilled labor it is less than two weeks; for skilled labor and entry-level professional positions it is one week to one month; for management level positions it is one month to six months; for upper-level management it is six months to one year; and for executive-level is a year or more. For candidates who cannot wait for the traditional amount of time to be hired, we suggest finding work assignments through a temporary placement agency or using his personal network to get consulting work while he continues to conduct his job search. If he only wants to look for full-time permanent work, consider entrepreneurial companies who often look for overqualified candidates, not yet realizing that overqualified employees will soon become unhappy in lower paying, lower-responsibility positions. Also, these smaller companies hire more quickly because the owner is also the Human Resource Director. Lastly, if the candidate decides to pursue a job for which he is over qualified, he may need to reduce the skills he lists on his Skills Resumé to match the employer's needs for the position.

3) Changing the field or industry in which he works. Today more than ever, we are seeing professionals desiring to make a transition from one field to another. In order for this to be done successfully, the candidate must identify his transferable skills and gain the specialized skills required by the new industry. For example, a candidate who is the Food Service Director for a large hotel could not move directly into the position of Manager of a travel agency. Although his management and marketing skills are transferable, he would need to gain the specialized knowledge required to operate a travel agency. He could gain this knowledge by working as a travel agent or a ticket agent for the airlines. We have found that the best approach in these situations is to have the candidate develop a compelling answer about why it is so important to him personally that he change fields. Usually, it revolves around quality of life, areas of fascination, or personal goals. Next, he must make the employer feel like she has won the lottery by having someone of his caliber and skill level want to "learn the ropes" from within her company. The candidate must approach the employer as a subordinate peer—one who is his equal, but is willing to submit himself to the other's expertise in order to learn. If he does not approach her as a subordinate, the employer may fear he will be to difficult to supervise, or that they will have power struggles; if he does not approach her as a peer, she may lose respect for him and question his value.

4) Needing time to become re-certified, re-licensed, or gain the most current skills. If the candidate's license, certification or job skills are invalid or expired, he will need to retest or return to school to gain the required documentation. This is a common problem for new immigrants who were professionals in their homeland, but find that they must gain a U.S. license before they can practice their profession. Expired licenses and out-dated skills may also be a problem for ex-convicts, formerly homeless or people who have been out of the field for years.

Another group which seeks positions for which they are overqualified, are those who have gone through emotional trauma. In general, it is in the candidate's best interest to secure a position at his former level, but he is often unable to move ahead until he rebuilds his self-esteem, views his present situation differently, re-thinks his employment barriers and develops good answers to the hard questions which are often the questions he needs answered, rather than the ones the employer will ask. Once the candidate's life makes sense again and he understands clearly why an employer would want to hire him, he can do well in interviews and easily get hired. As with all candidates, ask yourself whether there is anything about the candidate's resumé, references, presentation, or answers to interview questions which would raise a "red flag" for an interviewer. Then address each "red flag" issue using THE TEN STEP PROCESS for overcoming employment barriers and the ENCYCLOPEDIA OF BARRIERS contained in this book.

Riches to Rags

Daniel had truly gone from riches to rags. Once a very successful Personal Injury Lawyer, he was now homeless, penniless, temporarily disbarred and going through a divorce. He explained that he had hired a lawyer to handle his Spanish-speaking clients at his second office. However, he had failed to manage him, and before he knew it, the other lawyer had taken tens of thousands of dollars in payment for services never rendered and left the country. It was later discovered that the other lawyer had pulled the same scam twice before in other cities. Unfortunately for Daniel, as the owner, he was responsible for the entire debt. Everything he owned was seized to begin paying back the debt and his license was suspended until the debt was paid in full. He came to my office he embarrassed and disheartened.

To give him confidence, I reassured him that finding a job would be no problem. I began by defining his top three selling points: 1) an extensive professional network of vocational rehabilitation companies which referred clients to him, generating thousands of dollars each week, 2) 16 years experience practicing law and 3) the ability to give lawyer-quality work for a much lower price.

Next, I asked him to think back to when he had his own law office, and identify all the positions which did not require a license, but he would have loved to have had a lawyer do. Next, he listed every Personal Injury Lawyer he knew in the local area. Finally, we developed a good answer to why he could not practice on his own, but would be a great asset to another law office—he took responsibility for being a poor manager and judge of character, but stressed that he was a capable lawyer. He spent the next week contacting and asking each lawyer if they had an opening. If they said, "yes" he explained the situation and presented his business proposal. Within three weeks he was working…making considerably more than I did.

Sample
Solution

Adjust The Candidate's Outlook

Ann, a lady in her early fifties, was referred to our displaced workers program by her pastor. After nearly three years of unemployment her savings were almost depleted. She had worked for seven years as a medical Case Manager and had always received above average performance reviews (which she insisted that I review one by one so that I would know she did not deserve to be terminated), plus two promotions. She had become immobilized by her confusion regarding why she was fired, and her fear that her past employer would tell prospective employers lies about her. To resolve the latter of the two concerns, I conducted a reference check with her previous employer and received only the standard information, that she had resigned and, 'yes,' she was eligible for rehire. Hearing this shocked her. I then shared a story which a Human Resources Director had once told me. There had been a mid-level manager at her company who they wanted to get rid of, but they knew the normal means would risk a costly lawsuit. So, the company decided to eliminate all the positions below her and several lateral positions, in order to legally to eliminate her position and any other position she could claim based on her seniority. In the process, they terminated several very good employees who they would have liked to keep—but getting rid of the "bad apple" was worth losing a few good apples. I went on to tell her that just as those "good apples" may never understand why they were fired, so she may never understand why she was forced to resign. As she saw correlations between her story and the one I had told, it allowed her to find a reasonable explanation for her traumatic experience. To this day she has no way of knowing why she was forced to resign, but, in reality, it is not important.

Next, I began to develop "a good answer" which would explain why she had not worked in the last three years. The answer she had been giving employers, "I was wrongfully terminated from my last job and now no one will hire me," was not a good answer. I reviewed her activities for the last three years and developed this answer, "After I resigned from my position, I moved in with my mother to take care of her. Once she improved, I took a few months off to visit friends and recuperate, before beginning my job search. I am eager to get back to work, and look forward to the rewards of working with clients and their families." I taught her to never mention being forced to resign, since her past employer did not. Instead, she should focus on things she enjoyed about her job at which she excelled, awards or recognition she had received, ways she had solved problems and success stories about clients she had helped. Within a month, she was hired by a small company which had been searching long and hard for someone experienced in handling clients with head injuries. She started at a wage higher than the one she had left.

Related Topics, Overqualified

◆ APPLICATION/ RESUME: For tips on presenting the candidate on paper
◆ IMMIGRANT: skills and education were acquired in another country or she needs to be relicensed
◆ SELF-ESTEEM: suffers from low self-esteem in general or due to a recent personal trauma
◆ WORK EXPERIENCE: changing field or titles
◆ WORK RELATED SKILLS: wants to change his field or title and believes he has no transferable skills

OVERWEIGHT

In this barrier the candidate is female and employer is male.

The employer's concern is that he keep health insurance rates low (if they are accepted by the medical service provider, overweight and chronically ill people raise the rate for everyone on group plans). He may also be concerned that the candidate will be out sick often due to health problems caused by being overweight, or that she will not represent the company well to the public.

The candidate's concern is that she will be judged unfairly or kept from working, due to something which she perceives as having nothing to do with her ability to do the job.

In General, Overweight

America is a very visual society, and as a result, our initial tendency is to make decisions based on appearance. However, we are also a "politically correct" society, so many of us automatically reassess our obvious prejudices. Traditionally, extremely overweight men have been able to integrate into the workplace more easily than women. If employers hired extremely overweight women, they were placed in behind-the-scenes positions. Yet today, we are seeing more extremely overweight men and women in public and professional positions. If the candidate looks good in her clothing, is comfortable with herself so that others are made to feel comfortable, and is clear on how she will make and save the company money (including not using the company's medical plan), then her weight will be a smaller factor in the hiring decision. If any of these factors are missing, then the candidate's chances of being hired drop dramatically.

Good Marketing

I received a phone call from an articulate and pleasant sounding shelter graduate. Rene had secured an interview but needed some advice on how best to market herself. Even though she had told me that she was a large woman, I was taken aback when I met her. I began assessing my own reactions to her. I noticed that when she maintained eye contact with me, I focused on her face. As she became more comfortable with me, made humorous remarks, flashed an untroubled smile, asked good questions and articulated her selling points, I became less aware of her size and more intrigued by the person inside.

We determined that her best approach was to have a long phone interview, so the employer would already be sold on her personality, insightfulness and competency before she arrived at the interview. She would arrange this by sending her resumé, then following up with a phone call. During the conversation she would share her top six selling points, ask whether they matched the employer's needs, then ask good questions about the company and position. We agreed that at the end of the phone interview she should explain that she is a very "large woman," but that it will not hinder her ability to … (recap of her top three selling points for the position).

We decided that since she had already sold the employer on her skills, she would use the in-person interview to make him feel comfortable with her. To do this she would smile a lot, find things in common, tell stories of her past job successes and even bring up her weight so he could ask questions if he wanted. Her good answer for questions about her weight explained that on her last job she took far less sick days than most employees and that she did not expect to be added to the company's medical plan. She would also mention that she purposely selected positions which did not require a "model's body," but instead utilized the skills she possessed. We also decided that she should wear a solid colored dress with a colorful scarf at the neck to draw the focus to her pretty face.

As with any physical barrier, we recommend that the candidate market herself on the phone first. Once the employer is sold on her skills and personality, the candidate can move on to the face-to-face interview in which she must address her physical barrier. To prepare the employer, she should mention the physical barrier at the end of the phone interview by saying, "I am a very large woman." This will give the employer the opportunity to become comfortable with the idea before actually meeting her. It is also important that the candidate do "the extra" such as calling all previous employers to be sure she has good references, being 10 to 15 minutes early for the interview and following-up with a thank you note after the interview.

Related Topics, Overweight

- ◊ APPEARANCE: extremely overweight
- ◊ CHRONIC ILLNESS: experiences recurring illness due to weight
- ◊ DISABILITY: has a disability associated with her weight
- ◊ MEDICAL BENEFITS: may be screened-out due to the increase her weigh could cause in the company's insurance rates
- ◊ SELF-ESTEEM: self-conscious, negative or insecure because of weight

PUBLIC ASSISTANCE, Dependent upon

In this barrier the candidate is female and employer is male.

The employer's concern is that his employees are motivated and hard working, not afraid to ask questions and take initiative, and have personal lives that will not interfere with their commitment to the company. Employers hold many myths about those on public assistance: that they are lazy, incapable, uneducated, drug addicted, irresponsible, lacking in social graces, and do not really want to work. If the employer learns that the candidate is receiving public assistance, his mythology may lead him to screen her out immediately without considering her qualifications.

The candidate is concerned about entering the foreign world of work and losing her government assistance. She may fear that the employer will not consider her qualifications if he finds out she is on public assistance, or the opposite, that her desire to get off of welfare will make the employer hire her because he feels sorry for her, not realizing the strong biases employers often hold about those dependent on tax dollars. She may lack self-confidence, a basic understanding of the business world, necessary education, an appropriate wardrobe, and knowledge of how to transfer her present skills into selling points. She will likely be fearful of not being able to care for her family while she makes the transition from welfare to work, and of losing her medical benefits before she can secure other coverage.

In General, Public Assistance

Welfare dependency has no place in the job search process. To deal with this barrier, address all related topics, developing good answers to difficult interview questions and design a marketing plan for the candidate before beginning job searching.

In most states, single adults who receive government assistance receive so little that even a minimum wage position will pay significantly more. Unless the state also offers them housing or medical benefits while they are unemployed, these candidates are generally easier to work with because they have a financial motivation to work and do not have family responsibilities.

Better Off Working

One day as I presented why candidates are better off working, Angie, a welfare-dependent single mother began to argue with me that she truly was better off on welfare. She passionately argued why she should not get off welfare—she had no car so she could not get a job, she had an 8 year old who needed her, her mother was ill and might need her assistance someday, etc. I calmly listened and presented a few ideas on how she might manage these issues and still pursue work. I also pointed out that she had nearly 20 years of unemployment to her credit and would likely be forced into the job market soon as the welfare reform continued—and besides, there are many employers out there who would be lucky to get her.

She agreed to try it my way for three weeks. As we met together, I discovered that she had raised 5 children, developed a personal campaign to help children in her neighborhood avoid getting involved with drugs and alcohol, taken care of her ailing father, and had even done college course work in Early Childhood Development (which she failed to mention on her application!). We decided to seek a position within walking distance or a single bus ride from her home. I determined that a child care position would utilize her current skills and might allow her to bring her son to work when he was out of school. I also addressed various barriers by improving her telephone presentation, practicing filling out applications, creating a resumé, mock interviewing and getting her some interview clothing.

Her confidence grew. Within two weeks of our initial "discussion" about whether or not she was better off working, she was hired as a child care worker, within walking distance of her home, with hours that allowed her to pick her son up from school and bring him to work when he was out. When I called to congratulate her, I mentioned her passionate defense about why she should not work and she replied, "The only reason I said any of those things is because I didn't believe anyone would ever hire me."

This section of the Encyclopedia of Barriers deals specifically with candidates receiving Aid to Families with Dependent Children (AFDC or ADC). For our purposes, "welfare" denotes a monthly cash grant, food stamps and/or medical assistance given to a family with children.

Moving from welfare to employment poses many challenges, especially for long-term recipients. In addition to overcoming the mythology and concerns of the employer, you must work extensively with the candidate to overcome her fears. To begin, the candidate must see the benefits of getting off welfare and make a conscious decision to do so, or it WILL NOT HAPPEN. Begin by helping her to see the long-term effects of welfare:

◇ no retirement plan and no future; this is as good as it gets
◇ less respect from her children, negative role model for her children
◇ lessened respect from the community and a low sense of self-worth
◇ no control over what little she has

Next, help her to understand that if she works she can:
◇ build a brighter future for herself and her family
◇ gain respect as a role model to her family and children
◇ make more money　　　　◇ learn new skills
◇ meet new people　　　　◇ feel better about herself

Educate yourself about how the welfare system functions. Currently, federal legislation requires that 80% of recipients must be working within two years and completely off the system within five years. However, welfare to work programs and regulations vary greatly from state to state so you will need to research the programs offered in your state to encourage parents to return to work. As you acquire this information, you will also learn about other available resources (i.e., transitional child care, transitional Medi-Care, vocational training.) and the immediate and long term financial benefits of moving from welfare to work. Locate and call advocates to get the names and phone numbers of local organizations which provide these services.

In addition to understanding the system, you must determine what motivates each candidate—time with family, money, prestige, being a role model and/or positively impacting society—so you can use it to motivate them throughout the job search process, and teach them to motivate themselves. Continue to work with the candidate to help her realize that she is actually better off working than remaining on welfare, so she develops a willingness to pursue the process.

Being positive and encouraging the candidate to return to work is not enough. To help her succeed, you **must offer practical tools** which will make her job search DIFFERENT this time, such as how to market herself to employers over the phone, filling out applications in a way that makes the employer want to interview her, identifying and helping her to articulate her selling points clearly, how to interview successfully and how to follow-up with the employer. Design a skills resumé for her which presents her skills and experience. Because she may not have formal work experience, rely upon skills she uses in everyday life, community involvement, natural abilities, hobbies and volunteer experience. For additional information, we recommend using

Decisions, Decisions ...

I worked with a single mother on welfare who, after battling alcohol addiction, got her kids back, moved into a small apartment and began to put her life together. After discovering that she wanted to work in the medical field, I helped her begin her education to become a Medical Assistant. Because it was important to her that she make a better life for her children than she had for herself and that they be proud of her, she worked very hard—juggling full-time school, a heavy study schedule, getting three kids to and from day care on the bus, and single parenthood.

One night as she sat studying for an exam, her children asked her to come play. She decided that she could not because she had to study, but they persisted. After a moment she looked over at them and thought to herself, "What am I doing reading these silly books? I should put them away, forget this nonsense about school and go play with my kids. They'll never become what I want them to be if I don't!" As she began to walk over to her kids, she stopped and looked back at the books. She stood in the middle and realized that if she really wanted a better life for her children, she needed to sit down and finish her studying. Several months later she graduated at the top of her class and currently works at a local hospital where she plans to advance and become a Physician's Assistant. She is growing off welfare, and building a bright future for her family. It was important for us to understand what motivated her to finish school. When times got tough, I could always help her refocus by talking about her children and how her career impacted their future.

"*Blue Collar & Beyond*" by Yang Parker. Also, assist her in determining her dream job (the job she would love to hold within five years). Then identify several entry level positions in her dream field for which she is currently qualified, help her secure a starting position and design a career path which leads from the entry level job to the dream job. Take very small steps, and praise each accomplishment.

NOTE OF CAUTION: Fear is generally the major factor inhibiting a candidate's move from welfare to work. Fear—of the business world, not fitting in, rejection, failure, success, responsibility, etc.—is often what causes defensiveness, aloofness, or avoidance. Realizing that the candidate is most likely afraid will help you accurately diagnose the barrier and deal with it.

Two other aspects which need to be dealt with are Business Acculturation, and the role of education and new skill acquisition. Having come from the sub-culture of welfare dependence, the candidate will probably need to learn a lot about the expectations of the business culture. It is likely that she will need to learn to speak Corporate English, hold herself with poise, and interact with others in a different manner than is acceptable in her neighborhood. Help her to find a mentor in her field of interest who will help her learn the ropes, answer questions, introduce her to important people and advance in the business world. You will also need to consider how education and vocational training fits into the picture. Often education is a good first step because it is not as scary or as structured as job searching and employment, and it gives experience in an environment which expects her to use proper English, be on time and regularly complete assignments.

Making the transition off welfare is intertwined with many other employment barriers. Once you have brought the candidate to a place where she is willing to try, immediately begin to identify and address surrounding issues which could hinder her from securing and maintaining employment. You will find our recommendations on how to deal with those barriers in the related topics listed below.

Related Topics, Public Assistance

- ◇ ADDICTION: has been addicted to drugs or alcohol
- ◇ APPEARANCE: has poor appearance, limited wardrobe or poor hygiene
- ◇ BUSINESS CULTURE: lacks understanding of the business world
- ◇ COMMUNICATION SKILLS: lacks communication skills
- ◇ DOMESTIC VIOLENCE: has been a victim of domestic violence
- ◇ EDUCATION: lacks education
- ◇ EMPLOYER BIAS: fearful of the employer
- ◇ FEAR: fearful of success, failure, rejection or responsibility
- ◇ MEDICAL BENEFITS: needs benefits or is fearful of losing Medi-Care
- ◇ SELF-ESTEEM: lacks self-confidence
- ◇ WORK HISTORY: has a poor work history
- ◇ WORK EXPERIENCE: lacks work skills

REFERENCES, Poor

In this barrier the candidate is male and employer is female.

The employer's concern is that she select the right candidate for the position in her company, and gather all the information needed before making a hiring decision.

The candidate's concern is that his references will reveal his faults, mistakes and failures, causing the new employer not to hire him. He may also be concerned that the only people he knows are "from his old life" and that now he is a new person, with new attitudes and goals. Or he may be concerned that he is new to the area and does not know anyone at all.

In General, References

B ecause the prospective employer does not know the candidate, and does not know if her impressions are accurate, she will probably rely on references. For the most part, "employers trust other employers" and believe, for better or worse, that "if he did it before, he'll do it again." References from the candidate's former employers or professional acquaintances can make a great impression, and if the reference is given by someone the prospective employer knows and trusts, it will make her hiring decision more comfortable. It is also helpful to cultivate personal references who can describe when the candidate succeeded at relevant tasks or represented the prospective company's image and attitude.

There are legal guidelines governing what information an employer may reveal about a past employee. The most prudent employers will reveal only the following information in writing, if provided with an official request by the candidate: position held, start date, termination date, final salary, and whether or not the candidate is eligible for re-hire. Although the legal guidelines have been loosened, employers still fear the exorbitant cost in time and lawyer's fees to fight lawsuits levied by former employees.

If the candidate states that he does not have any references, you must help him brainstorm about who he can include. Once you have identified possible references, the candidate should contact each of them to ask if they will act as a reference and to prepare them to market him to the employer. He should explain the job for which he is applying and why he believes he would be excellent for it. A few possible references include: pastors, teachers, department heads, past co-workers, a volunteer supervisor, sponsor (identify them as a "friend" or by their job title, not as a "sponsor"), housemates who are working, work therapy supervisors, friends from church, friends from a 12-step group (identified as friends with no mention of the 12-step program), others with whom he volunteers, and long time family friends. As you discuss references, remind the candidate of the importance of building good relationships so that he will have even better references next time he needs them.

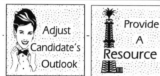

Business, References

Employers listen to other employers, so candidates need as many good employment references as possible. We recommend that you conduct a full reference check on the candidate to hear what potential employers will be told. For more information on how to conduct a reference check, see *WNTS' Career Developer's Manual*. The candidate should then call all past employers to let them know he is job searching and that they may receive calls regarding him. He should tell past employers what kind of work he is seeking and remind them of his accomplishments and skills which would relate to the new position. This will help the past employer to provide an informative reference. Have the candidate keep the conversation friendly and casual.

If the candidate left a previous employer on bad terms, he needs to turn the negative reference into a neutral or positive one. To do this, have the candidate call the employer, take ownership of the things he did wrong on the job and apologize for them. For many of our candidates this is very hard, but we remind them that they can keep their pride and remain unemployed, or apologize and get a good job. If this does not motivate the candidate, go back to basics and ask him what he wants and how his present attitude will hinder or help him to achieve it. Remind him that he is not exacting revenge on past employers by remaining unemployed, and that it only hurts him. Also, if he wants the employer to realize that she was wrong about him, and that he really is a "great guy," then his success is the best tool. Emphasize that the purpose of the apology is not to discuss what the employer did wrong or to get a reciprocal apology, but rather to make her feel good about him so she will give him a good reference. Removing the expectation that the employer will recognize that she also did things wrong will allow the candidate to stay focused on his task. Next, the candidate must follow-up his apology with an explanation of what has changed in his life that led him to see his mistakes and choose a new course of action. The answer may be as simple as, "I have just completed a Career Development course and now realize that I was hired to do it the employer's way, and that if I were the boss, I would expect others to do things my way," or as detailed, sharing briefly about a transforming experience such as completing a drug/alcohol recovery program, developing a personal relationship with Jesus Christ, or having a moment of clarity in which he realized where the path he was on would lead him. An honest explanation will validate his change of heart. The key to this approach is for the candidate to have really changed or gained a new insight. The candidate should conclude the conversation with a brief explanation about what he is doing now, which includes looking for a job. Be careful not to make the employer feel like the apology was "just an act" so that she would give the candidate a good reference. If there were tasks which the candidate did particularly well, he should casually mention them so that the last thing the employer remembers about him is why he was good at his job and how he has changed.

In all the years that we have been doing Career Development, the number of employers who responded negatively to an honest attempt to make amends can be counted on one hand. At least once a month a candidate who was sure the employer would not want to hear from him would excitedly announce that he had been offered his old job back, or that a past employer knew of an opening and would recommend him for it. When this happened, our major concern was to help him determine whether or not this job was the best one for him to take. Often, if it was associated with an addiction or other equally devastating problem, you may want to recommend he keep looking.

That Says it All!

A prospective employer called a prospective candidate's former employer during reference checks. The former employer said he would not give out any information about the candidate because he did not want to be sued. The former employer's response told the prospective employer as much about his feelings toward the candidate as if he had shared every mistake she had ever made. Needless to say, she was not hired.

NOTE OF CAUTION: Counsel your candidates against giving prospective employers derogatory information about themselves which they "fear" past employers might disclose. Assure the candidate that if the employer did not divulge the information during your reference check, chances are she will not give it to other employers. This is particularly true when it comes to reasons for termination. Often candidates would say that they had been "fired," when their past employer said they had "resigned" or "left by mutual consent." If the employer does not say he was fired, then use the term she uses—she's the boss.

Adjust The Candidate's Outlook

Sample Solution

A candidate who had just completed a one year recovery program was very hesitant to call his past employers due to the "bad" things he had done while using drugs. After much conversation, he agreed to start with the "easier ones." These conversations went very well and all of them stated that he was eligible for rehire, but they did not have an opening. Finally, he moved on to the most difficult one. He called to apologize and share how he had changed. A week later, he called again to just say, "Hi" and let her know he was job searching and that she might get inquires from perspective employers. A couple of days later he got up the courage to call again and ask if she knew of any openings in the field. The employer said she would keep her ears open. He continued to have regular conversations with the employer over a period of two months. In the end, the employer offered him his old job again at a salary of $35,000, explaining the reason he had been fired was because of his attitude—his work was always excellent. With the change in attitude that he had demonstrated consistently over the last two months, the company was willing to give him a chance once again.

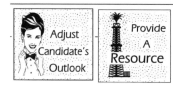

Personal, References

Opportunity and success in the American business culture is tied closely to the extent of your personal network—who you know, who knows who will return your calls, and who will do you a favor. Network and personal references play a significant role in the hiring process, For example, the young woman who is hired as a waitress because she is also a cheerleader and the football team hangs-out where she works and true of the president of a multi-million dollar company who promises to facilitate an important merger or bring in high-powered investors. Although the employer may not refuse to hire someone without a personal/professional network, it is often the deciding factor.

Ideally, personal references should show that the candidate has a strong network AND good character. Most employers peruse a candidate's personal references to see what type of people he has listed and how long he has known them. For this reason, the best personal references are given by people within the employer's industry, or people in "trusted" positions such as pastors, professors/teachers, doctors, business owners, professionals or public officials. If these references are not available, use working people who have known the candidate for a significant length of time. Feel free to write "full-time mom," "retired," or "student," if appropriate. Avoid using more than one drug/alcohol counselor, shelter provider, or social service provider, unless that is the candidate's field of interest. Also avoid using people who are unemployed if the application asks for the reference's employment information.

Related Topics, References

- ◇ ATTITUDE: references raise questions about attitudes
- ◇ DEPENDABILITY: references raise questions about dependability
- ◇ FEAR: fearful of success, failure, rejection or responsibility
- ◇ SELF-ESTEEM: feels that they cannot gather good references
- ◇ WORK HISTORY: references and application present a weak work history
- ◇ WORK RELATED SKILLS: references and application present weak qualifications

RESIDENTIAL INSTABILITY

In this barrier the candidate is male and employer is female.

The employer's concern, if she discovers the candidate does not have a home, will be his overall stability. In particular, she may be concerned about theft if the candidate is having financial problems, illness if he is living on the streets or in a dormitory setting, poor hygiene if he does not have easy access to a shower and washing machine, and a lack of focus if he is in the middle of a personal crisis.

The candidate's concerns differ, based on whether he is staying with a friend, staying in a shelter or living on the street. If he is staying with friends he is concerned that he does not "wear out his welcome" and end up on the streets. If he is living in a shelter with dormitories, his concerns may include lack of sleep. His concerns may also include limited access to showers, washing machines and ironing boards, adhering to house rules (i.e., required meetings, daily chores, meal attendance, curfews) while job searching, providing employers with an address and phone number and finding permanent housing before his time runs out at the shelter. Additional concerns may include running into a donor or volunteer from his workplace at the shelter, having a co-worker offer him a ride home as he waits for the bus, meeting the new financial obligations of a new home, and helping his family adjust. If he is living on the streets, his concerns will be the safety of his belongings, of someone taking his camping spot, cleaning himself up to job search, as well as most of the other concerns listed above.

In General, Residential Instability

Homeless candidates are often amazed to realize that employers will never assume they are homeless, unless they give them a reason to be concerned, such as appearing unkempt, having poor hygiene, wearing mismatched clothing, appearing weather-beaten or mentioning a problem regarding their residence. Employers will always assume that the people applying to work in their companies live a normal life, in a normal house, with a normal family, facing normal problems—they will never assume the worst unless given a reason. Teach your candidates to avoid drawing attention to their homelessness by not mentioning things which are specific to being homeless or in a shelter.

Sample Solution

Develop A Good Answer

Teach the candidate never talk about himself in homeless terms, but rather to use the "non-homeless" equivalent, for example:

◇ Rather than referring to other residents as clients, program men, residents or beneficiaries, he can say "I have several housemates (or roommates)."

◇ Rather than saying he lives in a transitional house or sober living home, he can give the location. For example, "I live in a big house on Hill Street."

◇ Rather than saying he lives at a mission or shelter, he can give the general area. For example, "I live off 5th street, near downtown."

◇ Rather than saying that the phone number he gives is the number for a local shelter, he can say, "This is my message phone."

◇ Rather than saying that he has a mandatory house meeting he must attend, he can simply say, "I have an appointment this evening."

◇ Rather than saying he cannot work evenings because he has to check in by 6 p.m. to get a bed, he can say "I prefer to work daytime shifts because I have other obligations in the evening."

◇ Rather than mentioning his counselor or sponsor, he can talk about his "friends."

 Adjust Candidate's Outlook   Provide A Resource

Shelter/Residential Recovery Program,
Residential Instability

Living in a shelter creates many difficulties for a job candidate, as noted in the candidate's concern above. To help alleviate these problems, advocate special considerations for residents who are job searching or working. Suggest that they be given priority for showers in the morning and for use of the washing machines and irons in the evening. If the shelter has private or semi-private rooms, suggest they be used for people who need a good night's sleep in order perform well on their new job. Special consideration may also be needed regarding required meeting attendance, completing house assignments, and adhering to set curfews. Encourage the shelter staff to consider the time needed each day to conduct a successful job search (particularly if candidates are using the bus or walking), and to be lenient when shelter obligations conflict with a new job. To protect the resident's privacy, encourage the shelter to train volunteers in the art of discretion and confidentiality. Inform them that if they recognize a shelter resident, they should reassure the resident of their silence and never mention it outside the shelter. Assistance in budgeting and referrals to permanent housing resources are necessary for newly working residents preparing to move out of the shelter. If the shelter does not provide these resources, either provide them yourself, find a volunteer to do it, or refer the candidate to a program which does.

PROVIDE A RESOURCE

Sample Solution

Create a Candidate Resource Room (CRR) where candidates can use private phones for job searching and retrieving messages, use computers to compose cover letters, thank you notes and improve their computer skills. The CRR should also contain classified ads, job leads, flyers about job fairs, reference material on various industries and jobs, and photos of those who are now working. The CRR should also be used by candidates and employed residents to complete required work assignments in peace and quiet.

Friends & Family, *Residential Instability*

Adjust Candidate's Outlook

If the candidate is temporarily staying with friends or a family member, it is important to discuss with him how long he has asked to stay. Get actual weeks or months, not a vague reply like "until I am on my feet again, " because you can be sure that his friends or family members have a date by which they expect him to have moved. Few people are willing to support someone else indefinitely. If the candidate has not had this conversation with his host(s), encourage him to do so. It will serve two purposes: one, it will allow you to determine how long he has to job search and save money to move out, which will determine whether he should pursue a survival job or career job, and, two, it will help to defuse tension at home by giving the host(s) a timeframe for when they will regain their privacy. Remind the candidate that not having the conversation will not extend his stay, it will only ruin the friendship by forcing the host to "throw him out" when he has over stayed his welcome.

To assist him with building a grace-period by which he could stay beyond the stated deadline, if necessary, discuss the importance of helping around the house, cleaning up after himself, buying his own groceries or giving money toward the household fund, not hanging around the house during the day, not tying up their phone with calls unrelated to moving out, not expecting to control which TV channels the family watches, and saying thank you often. Remind him that although he is building a grace-period, his goal must be to move out on time. Also discuss other job search related issues, such as using the phone to job search, the reliability of receiving phone messages, the way in which the phone is answered, and transportation from the new location.

| Adjust Candidate's Outlook | Provide A Resource |

On the Street, *Residential Instability*

Assisting candidates who are currently living on the street is very difficult because so often their personal problems are so great that they do not have the emotional stability to deal with the added pressure of being at work on time, learning new tasks, completing assignments, following instructions, pleasing the boss, or getting along with co-workers. These things often seem trivial next to the crisis issues they are facing. It is my belief that to refer candidates to full-time steady employment before they have dealt with their crisis situation is to set them up to "fail one more time." However, if money is needed to stabilize their situation, you may want to assist them in obtaining a casual labor position or temporary assignments which require less stability. More importantly, you should refer the candidate to a shelter or residential rehabilitation program where he could begin addressing his personal problems, have a clean place to sleep, take meals and maintain his hygiene before offering to do job placement with him.

Clean Cut & Homeless

John entered my office, not looking at all like a homeless man. He was shaven with a nice haircut, well-dressed in clean clothing with a sport jacket, and smelling of aftershave.

He explained that although he was homeless, he had rented a 4'x8' storage unit. He had hung a rod across the back of the unit so he could hang his freshly laundered clothes, and created shelves so he could keep all his belongings organized. He also kept a wash basin, soap, towel, mirror, razor and five gallon water jug so he could clean up each morning. Each night he would return to the storage unit and retrieve his street clothes, his sleeping bag and overnight gear in preparation for sleeping "on the streets." He informed me that, although he was not allowed to sleep overnight in the unit, its economical cost ($45 a month—same as one night in a hotel) allowed him to launder his clothes, keep his hair cut and save for a car.

He requested permission to use WNTS' mailing address, message service and phones for his job search. I realized that he could have rented a P.O. Box and voice mail box, and used pay phones to conduct his job search, but I wanted to support his ingenuity and effective use of his limited funds. So, although our policy is not to work with homeless candidates who are not in temporary housing, I agreed, as long as he continued to look professional. In this business, it is important to remember there are exceptions to every rule.

Related Topic, *Residential Instability*

◇ ADDICTION: has been addicted to drugs or alcohol
◇ ADDRESS: does not have a reliable address to use in job searching
◇ APPEARANCE: does not have a place to shower regularly, lacks an appropriate wardrobe or has hygiene problems

◇ DEPENDABILITY: living situation makes them undependable

◇ EMPLOYER BIAS: the employer may be concerned because of current living situation

◇ IDENTIFICATION: has misplaced important documentation while homeless

◇ JOB SEARCH RESOURCES: lacks job search resources

◇ MESSAGE SERVICE: does not have message service for job search

◇ PUBLIC ASSISTANCE: is or has been dependent on public assistance

◇ SELF-ESTEEM: lacks self-esteem

◇ TRANSPORTATION: does not have reliable transportation

◇ WORK HISTORY: has many gaps in work history or a poor work history

SELF-ESTEEM, Lack of

In this barrier the candidate is female and the employer is male.

The employer's concern is that the candidate may not take initiative, may not ask questions, may blame other people for her own mistakes, may be timid or overcompensate by acting arrogant. These problems can create conflict among the staff, tension in the working environment and personal problems which distract the employee.

The candidate may feel that she is never good enough and fear that others will think she is not good enough. Her focus is often on herself, rather than on doing excellent work.

In General, Self-Esteem

If the candidate lacks self-esteem it will be magnified in the job search process because job searching requires her to market herself and face rejection. The job search process is like sales—and most of us have trouble articulating why the employer should "buy" us. Teach the candidate that it is not the person who is most qualified for the job who gets hired, but the one who convinces the employer that she is the most qualified. To rebuild her self-esteem, consciously treat the candidate with respect: Always be on time to appointments, call in advance if you are unable to meet and stand to shake her hand when she arrives. Also, rephrase negative statements in the positive and help her to do the same. For example, "I'll probably never be a …" becomes "When I become a…," and "I can't…" becomes "I'm working on…" Highlight her skills and accomplishments by creating a skills resumé so that she can see how qualified she actually is.

Sample Solution

PROVIDE A RESOURCE AND ADJUST THE CANDIDATE'S ATTITUDE

Create a skills resumé for every candidate. Even if she does not believe she needs one or you suspect the employer will not ask. It is the best tool we have found for building self-esteem during the job search, because it visually articulates her value to the employer in a manner which cannot be easily discounted.

Looks Aren't Everything

I knew a beautiful young lady who had decided that she was not pretty. To support her belief she subconsciously developed an elaborate philosophy of why people complimented her—men wanted sex, women wanted her to think she was pretty so she would remain ugly and pose no threat; children were dismissed as simply looking up to older kids, and an older person thinks that everyone younger is good looking. Her belief system had boxed her into a corner so that she could never discover the truth. Only when this was pointed out to her, could she **consciously choose** to re-examine this belief. She did it by choosing to notice other's reactions to her. She said the next two days were so uncomfortable for her because everywhere she went people were looking at her. She made a bargain with God: she would believe she was pretty if He would make her unaware that people were always looking at her. To this day she still struggles emotionally to believe that she is pretty and although she knows it intellectually, she has to watch her mindset.

As with the barriers of Bad ATTITUDE and Candidate's FEAR, we usually find that self-esteem is well rooted in the candidate's belief system. Because her low self esteem is a long held belief she will be reluctant to give it up—even though it is hurting her. In order to begin seeing herself differently she must gain an accurate picture of where her strengths start and her weaknesses stop. She can not do this on her own. She must rely on someone she trusts to describe an entirely new reality, and then help her test it. Again we have found that when a candidate gains an understanding of her spiritual identity the transformation is easier. It is like a street person discovering that her long lost father is a millionaire and wants her to come home.

At the least, encourage the candidate not to limit her self-worth to her employment status. Praise the little accomplishments she experiences along the way. Be sure she is involved in her job search and feels ownership in choosing job titles and companies to approach. In all that you do, be sure the candidate is gaining tangible tools—good answers to difficult interview questions, a telephone script, a resumé, quantified selling points, business outfits for interviews and work, etc. These practical tools are what will build confidence—not mere words or a false sense of enthusiasm which will fade as soon as she is out the door.

TEACH A NEW SKILL

Sample
Solution

If the candidate's make-up is out-of-date or poorly applied, initiate a conversation like the following:

"Melissa, you are a very pretty woman. You have great skin and beautiful eyes. I think we could highlight them even more with a few small changes. May I show you what I mean? [wait for response] Great! First, I'd choose more subtle colors so your natural beauty shines through. The current style..."

Lack Of Confidence, Self-Esteem

Recognize that you alone cannot change the candidate's entire self-image, but your work with her can influence how others perceive her and how she views herself. Lack of confidence usually shows itself in poor eye contact, fidgeting, a timid voice, answering questions incompletely or negatively or the inability to use selling points effectively. On the other hand, the candidate who lacks confidence may overcompensate by talking too much, acting arrogantly or dominating conversations. Gently discuss how an employer might feel about these traits and provide the candidate with options for eliminating the negative perception. Do not be sarcastic or critical of the candidate who lacks confidence. If you are, her lack of self-esteem may send her into depression or force her to eliminate you from her circle of confidants. Rather, offer honest observations, tempered with positive solutions. Remind her of her strengths and teach her to encourage herself by reviewing her strengths and skills and setting short-term achievable goals. Be consistent, supportive and visibly concerned about her success and well being. Help her view you as a friend who cares enough to say the difficult things and will be there to help her through the job search process.

Although the practical tips given above are effective, the most dramatic changes in self-esteem that we have seen, occur when the candidate realizes that there is someone greater than she who has a wonderful plan for her life. Candidates who come into a personal relationship with God are the most open to throwing out their old beliefs in exchange for ones which give them a sense of purpose and meaning. Once the candidate realizes that her life has a purpose, her focus moves away from herself and toward fulfilling that purpose. She also gains a "partner"—God—in achieving that purpose, so she feels less isolated. This is why spiritually-based programs are often the most successful.

TEACH A NEW SKILL

Share with the candidate that you have noticed that in most conversations she talks more than 50% of the time. Explain that an employer might get the wrong perception about her—thinking that she is a "know-it-all," a "busy-body," or will often be talking and seldom working. Suggest that she become conscious of allowing others to talk as much as she does—even if that means allowing for periods of silence or that she does not get to tell all her stories. Teach her to ask a question and then to wait for the other person to end their answer before interjecting her comments. Teach her to become conscious of limiting herself to one story for each story the other person shares and to read the non-verbal signs which people use to end a conversation, such as looking away, moving away, or making placating comments, such as "that's nice."

Wow! That's Really Me!?

Linda dropped out of school at age 13 to have her first child. When she came to my office she was 34 with four children, 11 to 19 years of age. She had been clean and sober for a little over a year, had just completed her GED and was ready to get off welfare and begin building a future for her family.

As we talked about creating a resumé she announced that she did not have anything to put on a resumé because she had only had one job as a cashier at fast food restaurant more than 15 years earlier. She was convinced she had no skills, but agreed to humor me by talking about how she spends her time and the accomplishments of which she was most proud. During the interview I learned that she had volunteered with the Parks and Recreation Department for the past six years. She had run the summer recreation programs for children in her neighborhood park. She had done such an excellent job that she had been written up in the local newspaper and had rallied the support of city counsel officials at her annual events. She even had flyers, newspaper clippings and thank you letters from various events she had organized. Several days later I received a call from Lena. In an excited grateful voice told me she had just received the Skills Resumés I had created for her. She exclaimed, "I'm so proud to be me." I asked her to look over the resumé and asked her if everything I had written was true. "Yes," she said, "I'm so impressed with me. I never realized I was so talented."

Non-Supportive Environment, Self-Esteem

Often, low self-esteem is the result of a non-supportive or critical environment. The candidates who comes from a non-supportive environment will often display a fatalistic attitude and may deliberately sabotage a good situation to sub-consciously fulfill the low expectations placed on her.

First, assist the candidate to identify people in her life who "bring her down" or make her want to give up.

Second, encourage her to spend as little time as possible with them. We have found these first two steps to be very important, but often difficult. Although the candidate may become aware of the destructive results of her negative relationships, it is difficult to get her to move away from them, because she is comfortable with them. For greatest success, she should totally eliminate contact with these negative influences until she is well establish in her new self-image. One of the best ways to do this is to replace old relationships with new, more positive ones. Help her build a supportive network with positive friends from church, a recovery group, support group, volunteer activity, community college class, her employment program classmates, mentor and yourself. Then, challenge her to spend three times as much time with this group as she does with the negative group.

We have had only a few candidates who have been willing to totally eliminate contact with their negative influences, particularly when these influences are family. The people in the old, negative group usually resent the loss of control they experience when the candidate begins to change and often try to sabotage the new relationships. I constantly remind my candidates that, "you become like the people you hang around," and that they must choose how they want to live their lives.

A Basket of Crabs

A candidate once told me that life in the inner-city is like being in a basket of crabs—when one tries to crawl out, all the others pull him back down. That is why a basket of crabs does not need a lid.

The first candidate I ever assisted with Career Development was a young woman who had gone through the Job Corps and received training in welding. I assisted her with finding a job an apartment, enrolling in junior college, and buying a truck. Her life was going very well!

That Christmas I visited her extended family (her parents had passed away when she was young) in a government housing project four hours away. I was shocked to learn that rather than being proud of her accomplishments, they were openly hostile about them. Apparently, they saw her success as an accusation against them for living off the system. Within a few months, her grandmother had convinced her to put off returning to school, quit her job and move back to the projects. She called me less than four months later from a homeless shelter, telling me a disheartening story. Shortly after returning home, her uncle destroyed her truck by pouring sugar in the gas tank because she helped her aunt escape from him after he had been physically abusive. Between the loss of her truck and the California job recession, she was unable to find a work. So after three months, when her savings ran out and she had no means to bring money into the household, her family kicked her out. (She had no children so she could not receive Aid For Dependent Children as the other women in the house did.) Within a year she had come to stay with me, returned to school and was rebuilding her future.

Related Topics, Self-Esteem

◇ APPEARANCE: has poor appearance, a limited wardrobe or hygiene problems
◇ BUSINESS CULTURE: unfamiliar with or fearful of the business culture
◇ COMMUNICATION SKILLS: communicates poorly
◇ DISPLACED HOMEMAKER: is a displaced worker
◇ DOMESTIC VIOLENCE: has been a victim of domestic violence
◇ FEAR: fearful of success, failure, rejection or responsibility
◇ OVERWEIGHT: extremely overweight
◇ PUBLIC ASSISTANCE: is or has been dependent on public assistance
◇ REFERENCES: lacks references or feels that cannot get good references
◇ RESIDENTIAL STABILITY: is or has been homeless or in an unstable living situation
◇ WORK EXPERIENCE: has limited or no related work history
◇ WORK HISTORY: has a poor work history
◇ WORK RELATED SKILLS: does not know how to identify or present skills

TRANSPORTATION, Lack of Reliable

In this barrier the candidate is male and employer is female.

The employer's concern is that the candidate gets to work on time and, if required, has a reliable vehicle to conduct company business.

The candidate's concern is that he gets to work on time and, if required, has a reliable vehicle to conduct company business. If he is using public transportation, his concerns may include whether it operates in the area of his work during the hours he is required to work, how often it stops at his location, whether he will have to wait long and whether it is reliable, affordable and safe. If he has a car, his concerns may be whether his car is reliable, what to do if it breaks down, how to deal with the frustration of traffic and the expense (i.e., car payments, insurance, gas, repairs, parking and toll charges). If he is participating in a carpool program, his concerns may include who the other "carpoolers" are, whether they smoke, have poor hygiene or talk too much, whether it is reliable and how he will get to and from work if he is running late. A disabled candidate may be concerned whether the public transportation system is handicap accessible and if the equipment functions properly, whether there is a dependable dial-a-ride program in the community, if the company carpool is designed for handicapped riders or if he can afford a specially equipped vehicle.

In General, *Transportation*

Those of us who have reliable cars often forget what an important issue reliable transportation is, for both the employer and the candidate. Before accepting a position, the candidate must have a plan to ensure that he can get to and from work. His plan may include learning to use public transportation, buying or borrowing a reliable car, choosing a job close enough to walk or ride a bike, or choosing a company which has a carpool program or where a friend or family member with whom he can ride works. Another option is to get a live-in job so no commute is required. Several options for disabled candidates have been explored below.

Going The Extra Mile

Jason's car had broken down on the way to work. He knew his boss was a stickler for punctuality, so rather than be late, he left his car and caught a cab. When he arrived, he had to ask his employer for an "advance" to pay the cab driver. His employer happily paid the cab driver himself and commended Jason on his dedication to the company and his astuteness in realizing that his employer would prefer to pay for a cab ride than have his employees be late. However, he also told Jason to get a new car because he did not want to keep paying for cab rides.

Using Public Transportation, *Transportation*

Depending on the quality of your local public transportation system (PTS), this can be a inexpensive and effective means for the candidate to get to work. PTS systems may include buses, subways, commuter trains, trolleys and/or ferries. To assist the candidate, keep current PTS route maps, schedules and customer service numbers in your candidate resource room. When assisting a candidate making his transportation plan, ensure that the PTS runs near the company during the days and times when he will work and determine if his required commute time is reasonable, given transfers and indirect routing. For example, in Los Angeles, because of routing, a fifteen minute car trip between neighboring towns will take 90 minute on the bus, while a 30 minute car trip between the same neighboring town and downtown LA will take only 40 minutes on the bus. Once your candidate is confident in how to use the PTS to get to and from work on time, he can develop a good answer for the employer as to why he has selected this mode of

transportation. The answer may include issues such as convenience, comfort, cost and reliability.

DEVELOP A GOOD ANSWER

Sample Solution

Often, if the employer asks the candidate if he has a car, she is really asking about reliable transportation, not whether he has a car which can be used on the job. Find out why she is asking then address her concern, not just her question. For example, the candidate could respond, "Is a car required for this position? ... [if the answer is "no"] ... I prefer to use public transportation because it saves me the headache of fighting traffic and paying for parking. I know the bus system very well and enjoy reading the newspaper as I ride in. It allows me to arrive refreshed and ready to work."

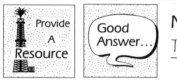

Not Using Public Transportation,
Transportation

Although public transportation is the most efficient and cost effective method of transportation in some cities, in others cities it is a nightmare. Below, we explore some other options, discuss the pros and cons of each and offer ideas for making them effective.

Having A Car: Having a reliable car is the most common means of addressing the employer's concern regarding transportation, because it gives the candidate flexibility, self-reliance and control over his dependability. If the candidate borrows a car, he should have a back up plan in case the person asks for the car back. He should also listen to the morning traffic report so he can allow enough time to get to work on time when there is congested traffic, accidents and bad weather. However, remind the candidate that employees with unreliable cars can be a nightmare for the employer. Teach him that his car problems are not the employer's responsibility and that he should not expect her to be tolerant of them. Most employers will be understanding the first time. Few will be understanding if it is recurring. A recurring problem will result in disciplinary action, being passed over for a promotion or could even result in termination. To resolve the problem, teach the candidate that if his car breaks down, his first priority is to call his employer and then get to work. The second time it happens, he needs to choose a more reliable means of transportation, whether buying a new car, joining the carpool or using the PTS.

Company Carpool: Joining the company carpool is another excellent means of getting to work. In addition to being reliable, the candidate can read or work during the commute, can regularly network with other employees in the company and avoid worrying about driving in traffic, running out of gas or breaking down on the way to work. Also, if the employer is required to assist with meeting clean-air standards, one means of doing that is to encourage employees to participate in the company carpool program. Often, employers will offer incentives to employees for participating in the program. Your candidate's willingness to participate will be seen as a plus by the employer. The candidate should call and ask about this option before attending the interview.

Working Close to Home: Another option is to approach companies close enough that the candidate can walk or ride a bike to work. To locate companies, use a local street map to section-off job search areas within an appropriate distance. Each day, have the candidate conduct his job search in one of the sections—on foot or on his bike. A few issues you may want to consider with these modes of transportation are the safety of the area, whether businesses even exist in that area (in many inner-city areas, businesses are few and far between) and if the required work attire lends itself to walking or riding a bike. If the candidate plans to ride his bike, be sure that the bike is reliable, that he has a tire patch kit and that he can do basic repairs.

Friends and Family: Getting a ride from friends or family members is another transportation option. For this to be a good option, the driver must be dependable and work at the same company and on the same shift as the candidate. If the driver does not work at the same company or on the same shift, this becomes the most unreliable means of getting to work because the candidate has little control over the situation.

Disability, Transportation

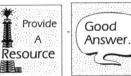

The most reliable means for a disabled candidate is to have a reliable friend or family member take him to work each day, because, unfortunately, in most cities, the PTS does not adequately service this population. If the candidate needs to use the PTS, help him research which routes accommodate disabled riders and during which days and hours the service is available. Other options include using the local Dial-A-Ride or working for a company whose carpool program has a handicapped accessible van. If the candidate is interested in finding out how to purchase his own specially equipped vehicle, which is a very expensive option, you may help him research national automobile manufacturers and organizations for the disabled that assist with this process.

Related Topics, Transportation

◇ DEPENDABILITY: lack of transportation makes him undependable.
◇ SELF-ESTEEM: transportation situation results in lack of self-confidence.

WORK EXPERIENCE, Lack of

For clarity's sake, in this barrier the candidate is male and the employer is female.

The employer's concern is that the candidate may lack the experience required to know how to do the job effectively or solve problems which arise on the job. She may also be concerned that he lacks an understanding of the American business culture and how to represent the company, interact comfortably with co-workers and promote the company's goals. Also, when hiring for positions for which experience results in a strong network, the employer may be concerned that the candidate has a useless, or worse, an illegal network, reducing his effectiveness.

The candidate's concern is that the employer will not recognize what little past experience he has as valid, no one will train him or that he will not be able to do the job. He may also fear that the expectations of the American business culture will be different from the culture he is leaving (whether another country, the illegal economy, school, home or another field) and he will not fit in.

In General, Work Experience

An employer will not hire a candidate she believes is not qualified to do the job. As employment experts, it is our job to assist the candidate in "proving" that he is qualified. Good work experience is a great means to do this. However, if the candidate's application has blanks under "Work Experience," but lists only experience from a different field or shows only employment outside the United States, he will need to find another way to prove that he is qualified. If he cannot prove that he is qualified, he will be screened out early in the hiring process.

Work experience is used to assess level of competency, level of understanding of American business protocol and the extent and quality of his professional network. If a candidate lacks work experience, he must prove that he meets the employer's needs in the areas mentioned above by incorporating qualifications gained outside the traditional arena of paid jobs and formal education. Pull your "proof" from the candidate's daily activities, hobbies, volunteer activities, participation at their childrens' school, church leadership, work assignments at a shelter or residential recovery program, prison work assignments and endorsements from mentors and business professionals. Use these to create a skills resumé, model application and the candidate's Quantified Selling Points the same way you would use paid work experience. Then, develop a good answer as to why this non-traditional experience qualifies him for the job. We have found that when hiring for positions for which competency is easily measured via testing, employers tend to be more lenient on work experience requirements because candidates' skills can be easily measured in only a couple of hours. In positions for which competency is more subjective, it is particularly important that during the interview the candidate justify his transferable skills, display knowledge of the business culture and share information about his professional network.

We have also found that due to the progressive nature of today's business culture, employers realize that they may have to hire based on basic aptitude, ability to learn and motivation—rather than on experience and job skills. There are several reasons why the employer is willing to train new employees: she cannot find anyone with the needed skills, she cannot afford someone with the needed skills, she wants to teach the candidate to do it the company's way or she is altruistic and wants to give back to "her" community by providing a training program. When assisting the candidate to secure a position which will "train" him, it is important that you determine whether the position is conducive to training. For example, ask about the quantity and quality of the supervision; if the supervisor is too busy to train properly or does not have the patience to train, it will likely prove a bad match for both the candidate and the employer and you could lose your credibility with both of them. This is equally true for entry-level or management-level positions.

First Legal Job, Work Experience

Good Answer...

There are hundreds of jobs which are traditionally held by young people entering the job market, such as a fast food server, cashier or cook, an inventory stocker, a grocery bagger, a sales clerk, a host or server at a restaurant, a movie theater ticket agent or concessionaire, etc. For the very best job matches, determine the candidate's field of interest and assist him in securing an entry-level job in that field. For example, if he loves music, help him find a stockroom clerk position at a music store; if he loves the movies, help him find a job at a movie theater; if he enjoys building things, help him find a job as a carpenter's helper; if he enjoys helping people, suggest a cashier position at a fast food restaurant. If he loves his work he will work harder, learn faster and gain excellent work experience to use in the future.

If the candidate is young (under the age of 18 and not attending college or under the age of 22 and has attended college) most employers will attribute a lack of work experience to being too young to work or having been focused on education. For most employers, this is acceptable. However, the presence of some work experience before graduation supports the claim that the candidate has a strong work ethic.

If the candidate offers very limited work experience or none at all, the employer looks for proof of his abilities by assessing whether the candidate:

Transferable Skills

Ray had been a very successful "numbers runner" (illegal lottery) and drug dealer for almost twenty years when he had a moment of clarity and realized he would end up dead or in prison if he did not get out. He left everything in Philadelphia and moved to Los Angeles for a fresh start. Following is the list of transferable skills we gathered from his illegal employment. Obviously, we cannot share this information with most employers, but it is useful in determining his skills and may help win the assistance of an altruistic employer:

STREET JOB	SKILLS	LEGITIMATE JOB
Numbers Runner	Excellent with numbers	Bookkeeping
Dealer	Loyal repeat customer Marketing w/out advertising	Customer Service Sales
Hustler	Recognizing and creating business opportunities	Entrepreneur, Job Developer
Hustler	Successfully building upon limited resources	Negotiator Business Developer
Illegitimate Business	Succeeding while staying out of trouble/jail	Politically Observant Upwardly-Mobile Manager

1. has a good work ethic
2. is dependable
3. is willing to learn
4. has a basic understanding of business protocol
5. has a basic aptitude for the needed skills
6. has a pleasant attitude
7. has an image which will attract her target customer market

To demonstrate these points, pull examples from the candidate's home life, school life, extra curricular activities, volunteer experience and comments from teachers, advisors, mentors, supervisors at the volunteer site or coaches. Assist him in developing good answers which show that he understands the importance of the seven areas listed above and how he meets each one. "Pleasant attitude" and "image" are best demonstrated by displaying them during the interview. Plan to spend some quality time conducting mock interviews since it will be a foreign experience for the candidate. Practice not only the good answers, but also how to enter the room, shake hands, sit, conduct small talk and close the sale. The more comfortable he is during the interview, the more mature he will seem and will thus be perceived to be more responsible. For more information, see *WNTS' Interviewing For Success Workshop, Teacher's Edition.*

DEVELOP A GOOD ANSWER

"This will be my first paid job, but I have always worked. At my house we have always had weekly work assignments, and of course, keeping my GPA above 3.0 while also playing basketball is work. You will find that I understand the importance of being on time, staying until a task is done and always following instructions. And I'm a great team player!"

A candidate who is older than 18 to 22 and has never worked will need to explain why he has not chosen to work. The employer's natural perception is that he does not like working and is lazy. The candidate needs to counter this belief. Help him do this by discussing with him what he has been doing since completing school. Look for additional learning experiences, such as travel, independent study or learning to use a computer. Also look for volunteer work, helping in a family business, taking care of siblings or a sick family member and getting married and setting up house. Then proceed with developing a good answer which articulates how much he has learned, how hard he has worked and what transferable skills he has gained. Mock interviews will again be helpful.

Develop A Good Answer

Sample Solution

"After graduating from school I decided to continue my education by seeing different parts of the United States. I spent one year in Texas with my uncle, six months in Ohio with my grandmother and a year in Boston before returning to Los Angeles. I used the time to get to know my family better, visit different colleges and explore various career options. I have decided I would like to go into animal husbandry which is why I want to work here at the Humane Society."

If the candidate was in prison, on-the-streets, "strung-out" on drugs, involved with the illegal economy or in some other negative condition, determine what change in his life has motivated him to enter the world of legitimate work. This "change" must persuade you that he is serious about starting over, because it will be the heart of his good answers and must also convince the employer that he is serious. Suggest that the candidate volunteer 20 hours a week and job search 20 hours a week to prove his willingness to work and to begin building a work history. The volunteer experience should also provide him with a good reference and verifiable work skills. Often, volunteer experience turns into paid work if the candidate proves he is a valued worker. Another option is for you to provide a direct referral to an employer who trusts your judgement and recommendation. Be sure to conduct extensive mock interviews before referring him to any employer. For more information on how to develop the good answer see *Developing A Good Answer* in Step 4 of The Ten Step Process.

New Field or Industry, Work Experience

Provide A Resource

If the candidate already has good work experience in one field but wants to change to another, suggest he conduct a dozen investigational interviews in which he talks to employees who presently hold the type of job he wants. By conducting these interviews, he can discover the skills, special knowledge and image he must have to meet the employer's needs. Once he has identified the needs, assist him in exploring what in his own work experience, daily activities, hobbies, volunteer activities and community participation he can use to prove that he can do the job. Create a skills resumé which clearly details these transferable skills. Two books we use to help teach our Career Developers how to write a skills resumé are *The Damn Good Resumé Guide* for professional positions and *Blue Collar & Beyond* for entry-level and skilled positions. Both are written by Yana Parker and are available at most bookstores. As the candidate conducts his investigational interviews, he can ask those with whom he talks whether they know of employees who transferred from another field. Then he can try to arrange investigational interviews with them also. Conducting investigational interviews with employees who were in another field then transferred will allow him to determine how he might enter the field. People often successfully transfer into a different field; your candidate can do the same. Endorsements or references from mentors, business associates and you make getting the job easier, particularly if these individuals will call and arrange the interview.

Starting Over

Robert had been a house husband and stay-at-home dad for nearly twelve years when he came to me for help in re-entering the job market. Although his work history was in construction and sales, he was not interested in returning to either of these fields. He convinced me that he had no skills but those in construction and sales, so we began to determine whether he could start by using these skills in a field which captured his interest. As we discussed his interests and how he spent his time, I learned that he loved to read. In fact, he read the paper everyday, read as many as four books a week, read to his children every night for years and knew the staff of several of the most successful bookstores in town. We immediately refocused his job search toward this industry. Using his extensive knowledge and natural network within the industry, he comfortably approached local book store owners. Within two weeks, he got two offers for positions which incorporated his skills and interests.

During the employment interview, be sure the candidate has a good answer for why he wants to leave his present field and move into the new field. The more passionate he is about the new field, the more persuasive he will be in the interview, the more time he will spend gaining the specialized knowledge required to do the job well and the more energy he will put into building a strong network.

No Work Experience in USA, Work Experience

Most employers want U.S.work experience so they can verify past employment, conduct reference checks and ensure that the candidate understands the American business culture. A candidate who does not have U.S.work experience should begin building a professional network here in the United States by joining an industry association or union, an ethnic association, a local service club, a church or volunteering where other people from his industry might volunteer. Most often, it is through networking that the candidate will get the interview. It will also be helpful for the candidate to secure letters of reference in English from past employers or business associates to include with his resumé. He should also learn the latest industry vocabulary. I recommend creating a skills resumé which highlights why he is qualified to do the job, rather than a chronological resumé which will highlight where he gained his experience.

Related Topics, Work Experience

- ◇ APPLICATION/RESUME: application does not show the needed experience.
- ◇ BUSINESS CULTURE: needs to learn about the U.S. business culture
- ◇ DISPLACED HOMEMAKER: displaced homemaker.
- ◇ EMPLOYER BIAS: fearful of the employer.
- ◇ FEAR: fearful of success, failure, rejection or responsibility.
- ◇ IMMIGRANT: has work experience from another country.
- ◇ OVERQUALIFIED: work experience makes him appear overqualified.
- ◇ PUBLIC ASSISTANCE: is or has been dependent on public assistance.
- ◇ REFERENCES: lack of experiences results in poor or no references.
- ◇ SELF-ESTEEM: lacks self-confidence.
- ◇ WORK HISTORY: has a poor work history.
- ◇ WORK RELATED SKILLS: lack of experience makes identifying transferable skills difficult.

WORK HISTORY, Poor

For clarity's sake, in this barrier the candidate is male and the employer is female.

The employer may fear that whatever the candidate has done in the past, he will do again. If on former jobs he behaved in ways which resulted in being fired or laid-off, if he quit, if he constantly relocated, or if he often resigned due to illness or personal problems, he will do the same to her. She will be concerned about whether he is stable enough to be dependable and stay with the company for a reasonable length of time, whether he possesses the attitude and work ethic needed to benefit the company and whether the issues which caused the poor work history have been resolved to her satisfaction.

The candidate's concern, if he is aware that his poor work history raises concern for the employer, is that no one will hire him if he is honest, so he may feel compelled to lie about his work history. He may also doubt his abilities, believe he has no selling points and be uncomfortable marketing himself to the employer.

In General, Work History

The employer uses a candidate's work history—seen plainly on an application and on a chronological resumé, and also disclosed in conversations with past employers and associates during the reference check and during interviews with the candidate—to evaluate whether she will consider him for the position. She quickly screens out candidates who have a poor work history or do not possess the necessary skills, then considers those who appear to be reasonably stable and qualified. Therefore, even if the candidate has the ability or knowledge to do a job, if he has a poor work history, he will usually not be considered. The following are ways by which the employer identifies poor work history:

◇ dates of employment: employment gaps, short blocks of employment, no recent work history, worked very few jobs since becoming of working age
◇ wages: reduction in starting and ending wage, reduction from one job to the next, minimal increase over a long period of time, no wage listed
◇ job titles: constantly changing titles with no direction, low-level positions with no progressive responsibility or upward movement, demotion, constantly starting over
◇ field: constantly changing fields with no focus
◇ negative reasons for leaving: quit, fired, laid-off, relocating often, recurring personal or medical problems, personnel conflicts or "bad boss"
◇ inconsistent reasons for leaving: "left for better opportunity" then did not work for a month or more, "career advancement" but next position was at the same, or a lower, level or wage, "returned to school" but no education listed, "relocated" but next position was in the same area
◇ suspicious employers: most or all of former employers are out of business, moved out of state or under new management

If the candidate's work history includes any of the preceding problems, you must eliminate the employer's concern before she will consider him for a position. Once you have determined specifically why the candidate has a poor work history and how the employer will become aware of it, you can begin to develop your solution(s).

In general, work history barriers can be addressed by the following process:

1) Thoroughly review the candidate's application, resumé, current interview answers and references to see where the barriers are apparent.

2) Honestly discuss each issue with the candidate so he can determine why he will not let it happen again. This usually requires a commitment made by the candidate (i.e., plans to stay in the area for at least 5 years, will not be having anymore children), a significant change (i.e., relationship with God, relationship with his children, recovery from addiction, recent discovery of what he will do as his "life's work") and a new understanding of how to be a

promotable employee due to recent Career Development classes. For more information, see the *WNTS' Career Development Workshop Series, Teacher's & Student Editions*.

3) Once the candidate is willing to take responsibility for his poor work history, use The Ten Step Process to help him develop good answers about why he has changed and why the problems will not recur.

4) Have him call the supervisor listed on his application for each company which may pose a problem. He should call his direct supervisor or a supervisor he got along well with and apologize for the actions which precipitated the firing. He should briefly tell her how he has changed and what he is doing now, remind her of a positive aspect of his employment with the company and let her know he is job searching. Afterward, you should call his past employers, as if you were a potential employer, so you can hear what they are saying, especially about why he left. For a more thorough explanation, see REFERENCES.

5) Help the candidate determine the type of work he wants to pursue by identifying skills he enjoys using and his areas of interest. Draw from his daily activities, natural abilities, hobbies, work experience, education, volunteer experience, shelter or recovery program work assignments, prison work assignments and career testing.

6) Once he has chosen a field and position to pursue, assist him in creating a strong skills resumé, six Quantified Selling Points (for more information, see Step 6 of The Ten Step Process), a phone script and good answers to difficult interview questions regarding work history, dependability and stability.

7) Considering his work history and other barriers, the field and position he is pursuing and his personality, decide whether he should approach employers in person, over the telephone or via introductions from friends and associates. Begin his job search accordingly. The following are suggested approaches for specific work history barriers:

Fired, Work History

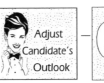

If the candidate has been fired more than once, the employer will be very leery of hiring him, assuming that he will conduct himself in a way that will compel her to fire him. To eliminate her concerns, she must understand that the factors which precipitated the firings are no longer a part of his life. Determine if he has changed and whether or not it could happen again. If you assess that the candidate has not changed, you need to assist him in changing his attitude by using Step 4 of The Ten Step Process or think twice about giving him direct referrals to your employers.

For candidates who have changed, begin by calling the former employer to see if she also says he was fired. Often, the employer does not have him listed as fired, but rather "resigned," "laid-off," "left by mutual consent," "project ended," or some other benign reason. The key is to ask whether he is eligible for rehire. If the answer is yes, simply adjust the information on the candidate's application and explain that he was not fired, so during the interview he treats it as if no incident happened. Remind the candidate that if the employer says he was not fired, that it is not a lie for him to say the same.

If the candidate is not eligible for rehire, distinguish whether the employer attributes it to a company policy about not rehiring former employees or to the candidate's actions. Note that even when it's "company policy" not to rehire former employees, savvy employers will realize that if your candidate was "such an excellent employee" the company would have adjusted its policy to get him back. So in these situations be extra careful how much you build up your candidate or search for positions with less experienced or smaller companies.

If the employer says he was fired, have him develop a good answer about how he has changed and have him call the employer to make amends. Often, this compels the employer to neutralize the "reason for leaving" in his file. You should conduct a reference check within 48 hours of the candidate's call. If the company has neutralized the reason, adjust the information on the candidate's application and in his mind. If the company has not changed their response, the candidate should choose an approach which allows him to market himself before completing the application, then explain in the interview how he has changed and that he has apologized to his former employer(s). When the candidate has to fill out an application, he should list that he was "terminated."

Gaps, Work History

All gaps in employment, whether due to negative or neutral reasons, must be addressed. To help explain a gap, consider why the candidate left the job and what he did while unemployed. Whether his intent in leaving the job was to return to school, change fields, get married, raise a family or relocate, he may now use these as valid reasons for the gap. It is important to reassure the employer that the time was spent doing something productive, or if not, that the candidate has learned from his mistakes.

To address neutral reasons for gaps, such as returning to school, getting married, relocating once, raising a family or changes in a former company resulting in a lay-off, have the candidate simply explain the situation and move on to how he can benefit the company. If possible, draw selling points from the experience, such as, "As a mother I have better understanding of how to market to other mothers," or "Now that I am married, I realize that it is very important that I build my career, I realize that I can build a good career in a stable company such as yours."

If the candidate plans to leave the company in the near future to have more children, return to school full-time or relocate, help him develop a good answer so that he will be prepared if the employer asks. The good answer may include how his short term commitment (at least one year) will benefit the company, that he would like to continue working part-time or that he would like to transfer within the company. If his plans are not "concrete," the candidate may choose not to mention them at all.

Addressing negative reasons for gaps, such as recurring medical or personal problems, inability to find a job, drug use, many pregnancies, prison sentence or welfare dependence will require special attention. First, assess whether you can neutralize the gap by attributing it to activity which occurred during the time, such as "raising my family" rather than being on welfare or "reassessing my career options" instead being unable to find a job. If so, help him develop answers to use during the interview. Good answers could include the neutralized reason for the gap, an explanation of what the candidate learned during the time or how the experience may benefit the employer. Do not forget to have the candidate end each "good answer" by refocusing on his selling points.

DEVELOP A GOOD ANSWER

Sample Solution

Create a skills resumé highlighting qualifications, not work history, with a brief chronology at the bottom. Here are a few tips to help minimize gaps on an application and/or resumé:

Replace the specific dates of employment with the years only

stock clerk 2/93 - 9/93		stock clerk 1993
stock clerk 3/94 - 2/95	becomes	stock clerk 1994 to 1995
driver 5/96 - 4/97		driver 1996 to 1997

Replace the dates of employment with the length of time at each job

Mgmt. Trainee 2/93 - 9/93		Mgmt. Trainee, 7 months
Assistant Mgr. 3/94 - 2/95	becomes	Assistant Mgr., 11 months
Sales Clerk 5/96 - 4/97		Sales Clerk, 9 months

Combine the amount of experience in each type of job

Cashier 9/91 - 2/93		Retail Sales, 24 months
Mgmt. Trainee 2/93 - 9/93	becomes	Retail Mgmt., 18 months
Assistant Manager 3/94 - 2/95		
Sales Clerk 5/96 - 4/97		

You Were Where?!

I worked with a man named Alfred who was sharp, articulate and a real go-getter. But at 28, he had an employment gap of nearly ten years! When I asked him about the gap, he said it was "no problem." When I pressed him further, he asked, "do you really want to know?" When I told him yes, he smiled and said simply, "I was a Moonie." I caught my breath and said, "Really! You mean, the guys at the airport... What was it like?" In response to my look of anticipation he said, "that's why it's 'no problem'." Apparently everyone, including potential employers, were eager to hear the story of how he had joined at a young age, then decided he didn't like it but they wouldn't let him out. He tried unsuccessfully for years to escape, but was always caught. He finally faked an asthma attack, was taken to the hospital and escaped. He spent the next 4 months hiding-out so he would not be caught, then fled to California to start over.

Occasionally, a candidate will have gaps due to curious and interesting situations, such as not needing to work because spouse supported him, having been born into money, having been involved with an intriguing, but benign, religious group or having gone to live among the indigenous people of a third world nation. These situations are easily dealt with because the employer is often curious to learn about them and because she will not fear that it will be a negative factor in the candidate's employment with her.

Lay-Offs, Work History

The employer may be concerned about the candidate having been laid-off because most Human Resources personnel and hiring managers have been involved in laying-off staff and realize that the process involves a decision about which individuals to let go. Therefore, the employer will immediately wonder why your candidate was laid-off while others were kept. It is better to attribute the lay-off to activity within the company and take the focus off the candidate. To do this, use alternate terms, such as "loss of company contract," "loss of business," "company downsizing," "elimination of department," "project complete," "company relocated." Do a reference check with the employer to see what she says and be sure your answer is consistent with the employer's statement. If possible, have the candidate contact his direct supervisor and request that the supervisor act as a reference to the quality of his work and to affirm that although they wanted to keep the candidate the company had to cut the department which ment losing some great workers.

The candidate who has been laid-off may feel very poorly about himself because he "lost his job" or may be angry and resentful because he "should not have been let go." In either case, you will need to do some self-esteem building and attitude adjustment with the candidate.

Quit, Work History

Good Answer... — Adjust Candidate's Outlook —

If the candidate has quit a job before, the employer may believe he is unstable, immature, has trouble taking instruction or has personality problems and that he may quit on her, too. Help the candidate to determine what caused him to quit in the past and assist him in gaining new skills to address those issues so he will not feel compelled to quit in the future. You may realize that he needs to learn to deal with anger or responsibility, that he is in the wrong field or position, that he prefers a specific kind of supervision or that he must learn to be promotable.

Because people quit for various reasons, you must determine why your candidate quit before you can help resolve the issue or redirect his job search. The following are common reasons candidates give for quitting along with some sample solutions. If he quit because:

◇ he got mad at his boss or co-workers: require him to attend an anger management class before you will give him direct referrals

◇ he keeps getting "bad bosses:" have him determine what he expects from a boss that he is not getting (i.e., structure, training, encouragement, recognition or a mentor) and teach him to accept only positions which will meets his expectations.

◇ he feels like his boss was always looking over his shoulder: ascertain whether it was because he did not meet the employer's expectations or because the position required close supervision. This can be done by asking other employers in the industry if the position requires close supervision and by observing the candidate's behavior and attitudes in your presence. Commonly, the same things you find irritating, (i.e., not completing assignments, interrupting you when you talk, promising more than he can deliver, blaming everything on someone else, dressing inappropriately, arguing, doing sloppy work, showing up late) will be unacceptable to the employer. Assist the candidate to adjust his attitude and behaviors so that a suitable position can be found or match him to a job in which these attitudes and behaviors are acceptable. For example, if he consistently arrives late, he may need to work from home at his own pace; if he does not dress appropriately, he can work for a company with no dress code; and if he blames everything on someone else, he should work in a position with little interaction with others. If the position traditionally requires close supervision, conduct career testing to identify positions which do not, such as a bus driver or long-haul driver, a consultant or gardener, and help him pursue one of these jobs.

◇ he did not get a promotion or raise: identify what about his work style would impede his advancement. Address this issue(s) and teach him to be a better employee using the information contained in the appropriate entry of this ENCYCLOPEDIA OF BARRIERS. For more information, see *WNTS' Career Path Strategies Workshop, Teacher's Edition.*

Sample Solution

ADJUST THE CANDIDATE'S OUTLOOK

Make an agreement with the candidate that if you help him get a new job, he is only allowed to quit if he has talked to you first. This should make him think twice before quitting. Often your words of reason will help him see the situation differently and make choices based on his long-term goals, rather than his immediate frustration. If, after talking with you, he decides to quit, respect his right to be responsible for his own life. Begin immediately to help him determine what must be done to prevent him from quitting his next job, then resumé his job search. If he quits without talking to you first, inform him that you will not assist him in finding work for a specified period of time (at WorkNet we use one year).

Relocated, Work History

If the candidate has relocated several times within the last five to ten years, the employer will assume that he is unstable. She will not want to invest money to hire train and supervise him, only to have him leave a few months later. To address this barrier, discuss with the candidate why he more stable now. If he is not stable, direct his job search toward temporary positions. For the more stable candidate, help him develop responses to questions about the relocations, including why he is dependable now and, possibly, how the relocations are a benefit to the employer. Carefully match him to fields which match his interests and to positions which he can do well, then assist him to job search in a manner that will allow him to avoid completing an application until the employer decides she likes him.

Sample Solution

DEVELOP A GOOD ANSWER

In an interview, the candidate must address the employer's concern that he might leave her too and he may even be able to turn the "lemons into lemonade." Observe how each move is legitimized by moving to be near a family member, wanting to see the country or being young, rather than merely to instability.

◇ As you see, I have lived in several cities across the country. I grew up in the Midwest but just had to see the East Coast and New

England. Then I went to live with my sister in California for two years but the culture out there is just too fast-paced for a country boy like me. I have been in Texas for six months and love it. I feel like I've lived here all of my life! I plan to stay here for many years.

***

◇ While I was growing up, we moved around quite a bit because of my father's work. I joined the Marines and continued to travel the world. When I finished my military service and began to work on my own, I was so used to moving around that I kept relocating every couple of years—I thought that's what I was supposed to do! But I'm tired of moving. I'm getting married in seven months and want to settle down and give my kids a place to call home. I chose Atlanta because I love the seasons and I know you have a growing economy and excellent universities. I also have an aunt in town. My hope is to begin as a driver for you, then return to get my degree in accounting so that I can continue to grow with the company. I know your company does national auditing, so if I get the urge to travel again, there will be an opportunity to do that.

DEVELOP A GOOD ANSWER

Sample Solution

When the candidate has to fill out an application, he should write that he relocated and the reason why, as well as that the issue is now resolved or that he plans to stay in the new area. For example:

Relocated to take care of sick family member - resolved
Relocated due to family emergency - resolved
Relocated due to personal issue - resolved
Relocated for a job offer - plan to stay
Relocated to attend school - plan to stay
Permanently relocated to live near family/girlfriend - plan to stay
Permanently relocated to east coast/California - plan to stay

Related Topics, Work History

◇ ADDICTION: poor work history is due to addiction to drugs or alcohol.
◇ APPLICATION/RESUME: application/resumé show a weak work history.
◇ CRIMINAL RECORD: has spent time in prison.
◇ DISABILITY: has a disability which has damaged work history.
◇ DISPLACED HOMEMAKER: displaced homemaker.
◇ DOMESTIC VIOLENCE: history has been affected by domestic violence.
◇ EMPLOYER BIAS: fearful of the employer.
◇ IMMIGRANT: work history occurred in another country.

❖ PUBLIC ASSISTANCE: poor history is due to welfare dependence.

❖ REFERENCES: lack of work history results in poor or no references.

❖ RESIDENTIAL STABILITY: poor work history is due to homelessness or residential instability.

❖ SELF-ESTEEM: lacks self-confidence.

❖ WORK EXPERIENCE: must prove qualifications without formal history.

❖ WORK RELATED SKILLS: lack of work history makes identifying transferable skills difficult.

WORK RELATED SKILLS, Lack of

For clarity's sake, in this barrier the candidate is male and the employer female.

The employer's concern is that the candidate will need additional training or extra supervision, will not be able to do the job, will not be able to learn fast enough to advance with the industry and remain a benefit to the company, will not maintain a current, cutting-edge knowledge of the industry, will pose a safety hazard by working unsafely or using tools improperly or that his work will need to be undone or redone because he did it wrong.

The candidate's concern is that he be able to get a job so he can make money, keep the job so he can continue to make money and advance so he can make more money. He may also be concerned about having to learn so much to perform well on the job or fear that someone will discover that he lacks important job skills or knowledge.

Adjust Candidate's Outlook

In General, Work Related Skills

Everyone has skills—even the homeless mother who helps at the shelter day care, the long-term AFDC recipient who knows the welfare and local social service systems well, or the young man who is intimately familiar with the city's public transportation system after using it for more than ten years. If you believe that your candidate has no skills, your first task is to challenge your own thinking and take a good look at his daily life, hobbies, interests and the hardships he has overcome, as well as volunteer activities, work experience, education and responsibilities. Here you will find his skills.

Lack of Basic Skills, *Work Related Skills*

Everyone has some basic skills. The key is to determine which industries and positions would benefit from the candidate's current skills and then pursue those positions. It is important to match him carefully. Fortunately, most fields offer entry-level positions in support departments. For example, the medical and entertainment fields offer positions in food service, housekeeping, building maintenance, customer service, clerical, etc. Once he is on the job teach him how to "work for advancement." For more information see, *Career Path Strategies Workshop, Teacher's Edition.*

Sample Solution

CHANGE THE CANDIDATE'S OUTLOOK

A candidate who had been on AFDC for the last twelve years and doubted she was employable, secured a great full-time position with her local public bus service as a Transportation Advisor. The aptitude testing we conducted with her showed that she was very detail-oriented and enjoyed working with information. She also had a pleasant personality, a good phone voice and first hand knowledge of the local bus service. These basic skills made her the perfect candidate for the Transportation Advisor position. Her high score on the company's aptitude test proved that it had been a good "match." Her Career Developer assisted her to develop answers which highlighted these skills as selling points and to present herself in a professional manner.

Transferable Skills

Randy had been homeless for over three years, when he decided to enter a one year recovery program to deal with his alcohol addiction. After completing the recovery program, he came to WorkNet because he was in need of a job. Since serving as an EMT in the army, his dream had been to become an Occupational Therapist (OT). However, his recent work history consisted only of small blocks of dishwashing positions, manual labor and a lot of unemployment. Rather than refer him to restaurants, hotels or a labor pool, we referred him to businesses within his field of interest where he could "work for advancement." Randy secured a dishwashing position at a local hospital where he began to network with OTs to begin the upward climb toward his dream. Six months after starting, Randy's hard work, positive attitude and dedication paid off. Randy's supervisors recommended him for the hospital's Education Reimbursement Program. Randy has a budding career—all starting from a dishwashing job in his dream field.

Lack of Specialized Skills, Work Related Skills

If a candidate lacks specialized skills needed to develop his career, help him research possible apprenticeships, internships, trade schools or volunteer opportunities which offer training in his area of interest. Once he secures his first position, the assistance of a professional mentor, continued education and on-the-job experience will help him advance. For more information see *WNTS'* Career Path Strategies Workshop, Teacher's Edition.

If the candidate cannot afford to return to school or cannot get into an appropriate paid training program, consider the following option which will allow you to help him start a career, rather than just get a job. First, determine his field of interest. If he is placed in a field he loves, he will work harder, learn faster and be more promotable. Second, determine his skills and brainstorm about where in his field of interest he could use those skills. Third, market him to companies within his field of interest for positions which match his present skills. Once he is working in the field, instruct him to be an excellent employee, begin building a professional network, explore career options and volunteer to learn or assist with the next job he wants. This option will allow him to receive paid on-the-job training, but requires him to take the initiative in his career development. For more information on matching, see the *WNTS'* Career Developer's Manual. For more information on teaching him to be an excellent employee, see *WNTS'* Career Path Strategies Workshop, Teacher's Edition.

No Transferable Skills, Work Related Skills

Finding A New Field

After two years as a junior-high teacher, Maggie realized that she did not want to be a teacher. Her only other paid experience had been waitressing—which she also did not want to do. We discussed what skills she had learned while in college. She had to handle multiple tasks, make sure deadlines were met, be sure her professor's priorities were met, conduct research, use a computer and use proper English. As a teacher, she also had to design daily schedules and implement them, motivate others, manage and resolve conflicts, evaluate performance, work well with other departments and participate in the staff meeting. She enjoyed using all the skills; she just did not like the kids. With these skills, along with her love of English and her professional presentation, we determined that she would pursue a secretarial position in the publishing industry while she explored the industry to see what other positions fascinated her.

If the candidate wants to enter a new field, but fears he lacks the skills to do so, help identify transferable skills. Transferable skills can be found in daily activities, hobbies, life experience, prison work experience, volunteer work, work assignments at shelters or recovery programs and natural abilities, as well as past work experience and educational course work or school activities. If after reviewing these areas, you want more information, there are many tools available to help you. A few of the tools we use are *Job-O,* Holland's *Self-Directed Search,* Richard Bolles' *The Party* and his field and title games. However, we have found that our interviews with the candidate and hearing their "stories of accomplishments" is where the best information is gathered. You can also gather information by asking dual case managers such as social workers, chaplains or sponsors about the skills they have seen the candidate use in various situations. Often they have observed skills such as caring for children at the shelter or a child care facility, public speaking, greeting or singing at church, showing natural leadership in 12-step meetings.

Once you have a list of the candidate's skills, identify his "killer skills" (those which he possesses but does not like using). Then determine what positions in his field of interest incorporate those skills, while requiring that he use his killer skills no more than 20% of the time. Create a skills resumé and begin the job search process. Be sure the candidate has strong answers for why he has chosen the new field, why he is qualified for the job and how his transferable skills are a benefit to the employer.

Out-of-Date, Work Related Skills

A sure fire way to tell that a candidate is out-of-date is if his resumé includes his height and weight, his marital status, names and ages of his children, his hobbies and a photograph. Other tip-offs are out-of-date vocabulary (the core vocabulary of most industries changes every 5 to 10 years), a network of business associates who are no longer in the field or retired, limited knowledge of current technology, and old-fashioned views of business protocol, such as expecting female peers to serve the coffee at a meeting. More subtly, the candidate fails to display a modern mindset, i.e., the entrepreneurial spirit, a willingness to take risks, an appropriate casualness, a sense of responsibility for the big picture, a social conscience and a sense of political correctness. To assist the candidate:

◇ update resumé information and style
◇ encourage him to read current industry publications to learn the current vocabulary
◇ set up informational interviews or encourage him to join industry-related associations to expand his network
◇ assist him to locate seminars or classes so he can update his technical skills
◇ discuss current business protocol and mindset, gain his permission to point out infractions as you become aware of them and encourage him to discuss any awkward situations he encounters during his job search and once working.

Related Topics, Work Related Skills

- ◇ APPLICATION/RESUME: application does not present work related skills.
- ◇ BUSINESS CULTURE: skills were gained outside the U.S. business culture
- ◇ EDUCATION: lacks work related education.
- ◇ EMPLOYER BIAS: fearful of the employer.
- ◇ IMMIGRANT: work related skills were gained and used in another country.
- ◇ OVERQUALIFIED: possesses excessive work related skills.
- ◇ REFERENCES: lacks good professional or personal references.
- ◇ SELF-ESTEEM: lacks self-confidence.
- ◇ WORK EXPERIENCE: does not have formal experience using specific work related skills.

WORKER'S COMPENSATION CLAIM

For clarity's sake, in this barrier the candidate is male and the employer female.

The employer's concern is an increase in an already expensive Worker's Compensation Insurance premiums caused by fraudulent claims or unsafe workers. Few employers mind paying for legitimate claims. However, most back, stress and head-related claims (those resulting in severe headaches, dizziness or back pain) are viewed with great suspicion. The employer does not want to pay for employees who are not working, nor does she want to pay lawyers to keep from paying the non-working employees.

The candidate's concern is that a past Worker's Compensation claim will keep him from being hired.

In General, Worker's Compensation Claim

In the worker's compensation system, it is the employer who must prove that the injury did not occur, rather than the employee who must prove that it did. Since the burden of proof is on the employer, fraudulent claims cost the insurance companies a lot of time and money to fight, which translates into higher premiums for the employer. Due to the high number of fraudulent claims and the significant increase in worker's compensation insurance premiums when a claim is filed, whether won or lost, the employer is hesitant to hire anyone she feels might add to this problem. As stated above, she is most suspicious of back, stress and head-related claims, since they are the most difficult to disprove.

Obvious injuries, such as a missing finger, broken leg or burned arm are seldom disputed. However, the employer is often as concerned that a past injury will recur or persist, as she is that the candidate will try to defraud her.

According to labor law, it is the employer's responsibility not to place an employee in a job he cannot do or subject him to work which is dangerous for him. Thus, if a candidate who says he is totally recuperated is hired, then experiences a "flare-up" of his injury due to his work, the new employer's insurance must pay the claim—which increases the new employer's premiums. Understanding all this will help you to understand why the employer is so cautious about this subject.

The best way to help the candidate secure an interview is to use an approach (see JOB SEARCHING FROM THE EMPLOYER'S PERSPECTIVE) which will allow him to avoid completing an application until after the interview. However, if he must fill out the application first, here are a few suggestions.

◇ For back, stress or head injuries, simply write, "Will discuss in interview." If his qualifications are better matched to the employer's need than other applicants, he will get an interview.

◇ For claims other than back, stress or head injury, minimize the injury by stating what it was in very few words and that it has not been a problem in many years (state the number if more than three years prior). This will make the employer less concerned and allow the candidate to deal with it in person during the interview.

◇ For the candidate who is unwilling to admit a previous claim, persuade him to leave the question blank rather than lie. Inform him that if the employer discovers that he lied on the application or in the interview, it is grounds for automatic termination.

During the interview, the candidate should only discuss his injury or claim if directly asked about it and say as little as possible about any extended absences and the financial settlement. If his claim was for an obvious injury, simply have him state what the injury was, how it happened (i.e., that it was a fluke accident, due to another's negligence or an unsafe work environment), that it will not affect his ability to do this job and why it will never happen again. If it was a stress, back or a head-related claim, work with him on developing a good answer which explains why it was an honest claim, what he is doing to ensure it will not "flare-up" again and why he believes this job will not aggravate the injury. Often, a change in position or field is part of a good answer about why the injury will not recur or lessen his ability to do the prospective job. To be hired, his answer must convince the employer that he is not a financial risk to the company. It has been my experience that employers who have been subject to these types of claims in the past are less willing to risk them in the future.

Several of my candidates believed that because it is not legal for the employer to discriminate against a candidate on the basis of having filed a Worker's

Compensation claim that it was also not legal for the employer to ask about previous claims or injuries. This is incorrect. The employer may ask about injuries or disabilities which she perceives might hinder the candidate's ability to do the job. This includes detailed information about all claims filed by the candidate and any compensation received. Because the burden of proof in labor discrimination cases lies with the candidate, not the employer, to protect herself the employer merely avoids disclosing that the reason she is not hiring the candidate is due to his past Worker's Compensation claim(s).

Sample
Solution

DEVELOP A GOOD ANSWER

"Eight years ago while working for a paper manufacturer, my shirt sleeve got caught by the machine I was operating. By the time another employee turned off the machine several of my fingers had been severed. As you can see, the doctors did a good job reconstructing most of my fingers. I have adapted well and experience no noticeable reduction in mobility. However, I have become more careful around machinery and I never use machines without the safety shield in place, if I have a choice."

***

"In a previous job I experienced a back injury when I fell from a conveyer belt which my supervisor told me to walk across to unclog some boxes. When I went to the company doctor, he said several vertebrae were damaged and I should stay away from lifting for a while. I returned to work for light duty as soon as the doctor released me. To ensure that I will not have future problems, I always wear a support brace when any lifting is required. However, working as an accounting clerk, I don't suppose, calls for heavy lifting on a regular basis."

Related Topics, Worker's Compensation Claim

◇ APPEARANCE: the incident associated with the claim affects appearance.
◇ APPLICATION/RESUME: unsure how to deal with the claim on application.
◇ CHRONIC ILLNESS: the incident associated with the claim resulted in a
   chronic condition.
◇ DISABILITY: the incident associated with the claim caused a disability.
◇ EMPLOYER BIAS: fearful of the employer.
◇ MEDICAL BENEFITS: the incident associated with the claim could increase
   an employer's medical insurance costs.
◇ REFERENCES: has poor reference from employer associated with claim.

There is no magic wand,
only great ideas, which,
when mixed with your
creativity and hard work,
can produce miracles.

OVERCOMING BARRIERS WORKSHEET

x	Step #1a: Barrier	Step #1b: Priority A B C D	Step #2: Candidate's Perception	Steps #3: Employer's Needs & Concerns	Step #4: Approach	Step #5: Solution	Step #8: Lemons into Lemonade	Step #10: Company or Position

Step #1a

List barriers identified

x each as it is resolved.

© WNTS 1996

Step #1b: Priority

When will the barrier be addressed?

A: resolve before even discussing job search
B: resolve while preparing to job search
C: resolve while job searching
D: resolve after employed

Step #2: Candidate Perception

1. unaware of the barrier
2. feels it cannot be solved
3. thinks it is employer's problem
4. needs your help solving it

Step #4: Approaches

1. develop a good answer
2. provide a resource
3. change where you look
4. adjust the candidate's outlook
5. teach a new skill

QUANTIFIED SELLING POINTS

Poistion Title and Field:

Employer's Needs	Candidate's Selling Point	PROVE IT!
1.		
2.		
3.		
4.		
5.		
6.		

Alphabetical Cross Referenced Index

Y

This book is a compilation of experiences, stories and successes of those in the employment field. As we have traveled the United States assisting job developers, employment counselors and career developers, we have discovered that sharing examples of how others have dealt with similar problems is often the best advice we can give. After all, if others can do it, so can you! It is for that reason that we wrote this book—initially for our own career developers, and later for all those who are helping others (or themselves) to overcome barriers to employment and secure a good job.

Your ideas, comments, stories and corrections are encouraged. Are there other barriers you would like to see included in the ENCYCLOPEDIA OF BARRIERS? Do you have stories, sample solutions or ideas which should be added to a second edition of this book? Did you find THE TEN STEP PROCESS helpful or do you have ideas to make it easier to use? Do you use approaches other than the five we described in Step 4? Did you find the information accurate, or has your experience been different? We would also love to get your comments on basic book design and usage. When you write to us, please include answers to the following questions.

Did you find the lay-out conducive to easy referencing?	☐ yes	☐ no
Do you regularly use this book?	☐ yes	☐ no
Did you read THE TEN STEP PROCESS before using the ENCYCLOPEDIA OF BARRIERS?	☐ yes	☐ no
Did you find *Job Searching from the Employer's Perspective* helpful?	☐ yes	☐ no
Did you review the ESSENTIAL VOCABULARY? If so, do you have suggestions on terms or format?	☐ yes	☐ no
Was any of the information revolutionary to you? If so, what?	☐ yes	☐ no
Do you use the WNTS worksheets?	☐ yes	☐ no
Would you like to be informed when an updated version is printed? If so, please send us your name and address.	☐ yes	☐ no

Thank you for your input and ideas. Correspondence can be sent to P.O. Box 5582, Hacienda Heights, CA 91745-0082, or worknetts@aol.com. We look forward to hearing from you.